BART

my life

J.B. Cummings

BART
my life

MACMILLAN
Pan Macmillan Australia

First published 2009 in Macmillan by Pan Macmillan Australia Pty Limited
1 Market Street, Sydney

National Library of Australia
Cataloguing-in-Publication data:

Cummings, Bart, 1927–

Bart : my life / J.B. Cummings.

9781405039659 (hbk.)
9781405040150 (pbk.)

Cummings, Bart, 1927–
Racehorse trainers–Australia–Biography.
Horse racing–Australia.

798.40092

Racing Victoria Limited
www.racingvictoria.net.au

Typeset in 12.5/17 Fairfield by Midland Typesetters, Australia
Printed in Australia by McPherson's Printing Group

Papers used by Pan Macmillan Australia Pty Ltd are natural, recyclable products
made from wood grown in sustainable forests. The manufacturing processes conform
to the environmental regulations of the country of origin.

Foreword

THERE'S A CAMEO THAT HAS BECOME PART OF THE FOLKLORE OF
Australian sport. The Melbourne Cup field is pulling up after
passing the post, a blur of bright silks and faded dreams. The
horses' nostrils flare and shrink and their legs go everywhere,
mainly because they can't feel them. The jockeys rise in the
stirrups, rest their hands on the horses' withers and grab for air.
Only one of them is grinning. The crowd bubbles and cheers
and groans. None of this is the cameo, which for our purposes
is defined as a character part played by a distinguished actor.

The cameo, the set piece that's been playing for decades, is unfolding in the grandstand. The television cameras are pointed up there, searching for one man, the trainer of the winner. Just about everyone in Australia knows what Bart Cummings looks like. Where is he? *There*. That's him. The bloke in the navy double-breaster who is trying to pretend that he has turned up only because he had nothing better to do. He has a mane of wavy grey hair, a generous mouth, brown eyes that can glint with mischief or glower with disapproval, and eyebrows that rear up as if searching for a trellis. He has just won the Melbourne Cup – again. And he looks sheepish, as he did last time, and the time before. No fist in the air, no hugs, no promises to shout the bar. Displays are for others and, besides, he's shy. Neither does his face convey relief or surprise. His way has always been to let the pressure get to everyone else while he gets on with doing what he does better than everyone else.

He descends the steps slowly. But then he never moves abruptly, not here or in the inky lights before dawn on the training tracks. Bustle frightens the horses and horses are everything. He allows himself a smile that comes and goes, as though the moment is at once joyous and awkward, which it is. He takes his work seriously; he refuses to take himself seriously. Most of him lives in a solitary world, always has, and outsiders are seldom offered more than a peep before the door closes again. He is popular, loved for his drollery and his naturalness, even by those who never go to the races. And he is at the same time unknowable. For him a speech is three complete sentences. In truth he is a contemplative man; he just doesn't want word of this to get about.

As he comes closer you see the rill of a tear on his cheek. That's because he always gets hay fever when he wins a Melbourne Cup. No one believes him but that's what he always says. The media is waiting and you can see him thinking up something arch to say. If what he says works well, his smile will briefly become lopsided, as though he's surprised himself. Humour is his defence, the moat around his secret world, and he is good at it, quick and dry and disarming. No one in Australian sport plays the wag better. He never talks American sports babble or takes on the airs of celebrity, never thanks 'the guys' or announces that he is focused. No one in Australian sport is as *Australian* as he is. His is the wit of the shearing sheds and stock camps. He has not changed in more than forty years of winning Melbourne Cups. And his way of winning them has hardly changed either, as he explains with characteristic light touches in this book, which is the first time he has opened the door to his private world and probably the last.

The horse comes first, he tells us. Be patient. Treat him kindly and coax the best out of him. Don't bully: outwit him. Think like a horse and get him 'thinking right'. Consider what your father might have done. Keep it simple. Keep cracking jokes, because racing isn't rational and a little tomfoolery helps you survive. Be competitive, ruthless if necessary, but don't be too obvious about this. Look ahead. Don't look back. Don't be distracted by fame and its baubles.

There is no one in Australian sport like him. He is the genuine exotic: an original. In a calling that is supposed to be cynical, here is a man who at eighty-one, and on a chilly morning, still thrills to the sight of a horse doing slow work with its neck arched. And when it comes to achievements, there is only one obvious point of reference, and that is Sir Donald Bradman.

BRADMAN RETIRED WITH A TEST AVERAGE OF 99.94 RUNS. ONE divides the cream of batsmen into two categories. There is Bradman, the freak, alone in a category of his own. And then, after a space as long as daylight, comes a rollcall of brilliant artists: Sobers, Hobbs, Hutton, Tendulkar, Ponting, Lara and others. Brilliant, yes, but none of them with an average much above 55. It is much the same with Australian horse trainers. The brilliant artists include Colin Hayes, who was racing's most polished ambassador, T.J. Smith, the ragamuffin from the Riverina who changed the way racehorses looked, Etienne de Mestre, who won five Melbourne Cups in the nineteenth century and Lee Freedman, who has won five during the last two centuries. What puts Cummings in a category of his own, makes him as freakish as Bradman, is that he has won more than twice as many Melbourne Cups as anyone else.

Now Cup wins alone are not the ultimate test of a trainer's worth. But to win a dozen times? The near-certainty is that we will never see this happen again. The Cup is the most testing staying event in the world. Twenty-four starters, a cavalry charge all the way (as one English trainer put it), jockeys riding tight, clanking bits and slapping whips, a raucous crowd that is not sure whether it has come for the sport or the party, a frisson of nerves on the track and off. Here is the ultimate test of a racehorse's heart and lungs – and also its temperament, its character, if you like. The wonder of Cummings is that since he had his first runner in 1958, he has on average won the race one year in four. One year in four over more than half a century, and the story is unfinished.

He has won it when it was a traditional handicap, when champion horses were asked to carry the equivalent of 10 stone. He has won it when, in recent times, it has been quietly turned into a quality handicap, with the scale of weights compressed to encourage the best horses from here and overseas to run. He has won it as a thirty-seven-year-old and as an eighty-year-old. He has won it when he was flush and when creditors were baying. He has won it by the keenness of his instincts rather than by the weight of stable money: the winners he bought as yearlings were all modest purchases. He has won it in the wet and in the dry. He has won it with lightly framed mares like Light Fingers and Amazons like Let's Elope. He has won it with quiet stallions like Viewed and nervy ones like Kingston Rule. He has won it with homely geldings like Red Handed, who poked out his kerosene-tin head at just the right moment. He has won it with horses he took over from other trainers (Hyperno, Kingston Rule, Let's Elope and Rogan Josh) and with a gelding he bred and raised himself. He has won it with horses with faulty engineering, like Galilee, and with horses that were still growing up, like Saintly, the aforementioned homebred.

What these facts eliminate is the charge of fluke. Bradman once told the English cricket writer Neville Cardus: 'Every ball for me is the first ball.' It is the same with Cummings. Nothing distracts him, least of all the false god called fame. The big one is the race coming up. If he wins a thirteenth Cup, he'll say his father told him thirteen was unlucky. If he wins a fourteenth, he'll say he needs fifteen because he has fifteen grandchildren. Then he'll offer a lopsided smile.

WHEN IT COMES TO SPORT, HOWEVER, STATISTICS ARE AS LIVELY as bleached bones. They don't tell you about the hot light in Light Fingers' eye as she reeled in Ziema. They don't tell you how Saintly used to flatten his ears when he sprinted, so that they became lost in his mane. My memories of Bart are not statistical.

There was the day in 1991 when he won the Cup with Let's Elope. She won easily, but she had blundered about, as she always did, in the home straight and the rider of the second horse, Shiva's Revenge, also trained by Cummings, lodged a protest.

The Cup was being decided in the stewards' room. Cummings stood outside the closed door. His expression was close to beatific. The pressure was getting to everyone else: this was fun. The media pressed in. Arc lights turned the air muggy. Sound booms trembled like dead rabbits on sticks. Pens hovered over notebooks. But nothing was happening – not out here anyway.

Eventually a reporter asked: 'What does it feel like to be protesting against yourself, Bart?'

'Can't lose,' he said, deadpan. Now he did look beatific.

One morning, after track work at Flemington three years later, I walked into the café near the stripping sheds with Lee Freedman, who was having a rich spring. Bart wasn't. He sat alone, reading the morning paper and, one rather fancied, plotting.

Freedman tried a conversation-opener. 'Spring goes fast, Bart.'

Bart didn't lift his head from the paper. 'Does when you're winning.'

Laughter broke out all over the café. Cummings still didn't look up or change his expression.

'He got me again,' said Freedman, who does a nice line of humour himself. His mistake was to try to match it with W.C. Fields.

Two years later Cummings won the Melbourne Cup again with Saintly. Darren Beadman, a born-again Christian, rode him. He stood on the dais to accept his trophy. 'I'd just like to thank the Lord Jesus ...' he began in his light voice.

Good-natured catcalls rang out. This was no hotbed of unbelievers. The crowd merely felt that this time Beadman had alighted on the wrong messiah. The faithful around the mounting yard gave Cummings three cheers and other trainers asked him to sign their race books.

In the weeks before, we'd seen a lot of the Cummings way of training. The foreign horses entered for the Cup were stabled at Sandown racecourse in Melbourne's southeast. We'd watch them gallop, after which they would be followed around by trainers, travelling head lads, veterinarians, farriers, speech therapists, butlers, dieticians, astrologers, motivational experts and sundry flunkies carrying buckets. One thought of the rock star and his entourage leaving the hotel. Next day we'd go to Flemington to watch Saintly gallop. Afterwards he would pick grass in the infield and watch birds while being held by a lone strapper. Bart would be close by, leaning his elbows on the running rail, staring at the horse and telling jokes. If he felt beneficent, he would hand out the boiled lollies in cellophane wrappers that had been left on his bedside table back at the hotel.

One day he explained what was going on. Horses liked listening to his jokes, he said. He also said horses didn't like too many flunkies fussing around them. He was right about the second point.

Many wondered at this time whether Saintly could run 2 miles. Cummings had no doubts. One morning a journalist asked him why he was so sure. 'Instinct,' said Bart, without taking his binoculars down.

One word, and it nearly summed up his career.

On the day that Saintly won the Cup, Bob Charley, then the chairman of the Australian Jockey Club, said this of Cummings: 'He doesn't command horses; he psyches them.' With that one sentence, Charley had captured, better than anyone has before or since, the spirit of Cummings' life with horses.

And I was reminded of an incident at Caulfield five years earlier. Cummings had just won the Caulfield Cup with Let's Elope. The sun was hot and the mare had made a long run around the field. Even so, she had come back with only a few soapy flecks on her coat. It is the wont of race sponsors, most of whom wouldn't know which end of a horse to feed, to adorn the winning horse with a satin rug bearing their logo, even when the sun is blazing. Let's Elope was soon dripping sweat from brisket to tail. As soon as he could escape from the presentation, Cummings ordered the rug taken off.

He was angry. 'No one ever thinks of the horse,' he said softly.

Bart does. That's why he's Bart.

Les Carlyon
Melbourne, 2009

Contents

Acknowledgments

WHEN YOU HAVE LIVED AS LONG AS I HAVE, AND BEEN ASSISTED BY so many people, your memory cannot be good enough to name them all. Our stable has succeeded due to the tireless efforts of very many workers, several of whom I have named in these pages. To those I have not named, I give my sincere thanks.

My special thanks go to Malcolm Knox, whose guidance, patience and skill helped me write my life story.

Personally I owe the greatest debt of gratitude to the owners who have supported the stable and of course to my family. I thank my children and grandchildren, my brother and sister, my mother and father, and above all my wife, Valmae.

Prologue

A LONG TIME AGO, I STARTED SPENDING THE LATE WEEKS OF January in New Zealand. I would fly to Auckland, hire a car – nothing special, just whatever comfortable Holden or Ford they had – and drive off into the countryside.

New Zealand's North Island is beautiful in every season, but I can vividly remember those midsummer days, warm but tingly, as I escaped into the lush farmland. A lot has changed in New Zealand but not that sense of freedom on peaceful two-lane roads as you motor out into the fields.

Racing is a noisy, sociable, chaotic, twenty-four-hour-a-day sport, but I have always liked spending time on my own. Even amid the colour and excitement of race days, I sometimes feel that I am in my solitary world. As I drove around the North Island with only my thoughts for company I couldn't have been happier. In the back of my car I had my notebooks and stud books, a catalogue for the upcoming yearling sales, a suitcase full of clothes and that's about all.

Thanks to the high year-round rainfall, the grass was thick and green and the air had a healthy farm-fresh smell to it. I drove south from Auckland, past spectacular sights, such as the enormous freshwater Lake Taupo and, further south, in the distance, mounts Tongariro and Egmont. Even in mid-summer their peaks were capped with snow. Later in life, when I travelled to Switzerland, I would immediately be reminded of this part of New Zealand. I started going there in January 1958 and haven't missed a year since.

That first January, my future was all up in the air and success was by no means assured. I was still a young man, thirty years old, unproven and hungry. I was a newly licensed horse trainer who had gone to New Zealand to follow a hunch. I had left my wife, Valmae, at home in Adelaide with our two infant children, Margaret and Anthony. (A third, Sharon, was on the way, and another two, John and Anne-Marie, would soon follow.) It was hard to leave them, of course, but I was driven by an irresistible idea. In retrospect I suppose I was a pioneer – setting off into the unknown, armed with little aside from the hope that I was about to stumble across something special.

Everything I knew about training horses I had learnt from my father, Jim. Although he had never been to New Zealand, he had instilled in me the idea that its grass and the soil and the climate nurtured the best staying thoroughbreds in the Southern Hemisphere. With good sunlight and rich grass, the stallions there grew three-quarters of an inch thicker around the knee than anywhere else in the world. The area south of Auckland, surrounding the towns of Hamilton, Matamata and Cambridge, was made for the thoroughbred. New Zealand-bred horses didn't figure quite as prominently among Melbourne Cup winners then as they do now, but there was Phar Lap, of course, the greatest of all, and a string of others; also Tulloch, the name on everyone's lips in 1958. If you studied breeding as intensively as I did, you knew that two-thirds of the horses who won Group, or major, races in Australia owed some of their breeding to New Zealand. Dad had guided me towards this idea, and I listened to him in all matters to do with training. Having trained a Melbourne Cup winner himself, he knew a thing or two.

But in 1958, when I first drove off around the North Island, Dad was happily retired and I was out on my own. A handful of other young Australian horse trainers, including Colin Hayes and Tommy Smith, were also there, driving around in their own cars, thinking their thoughts just as I was thinking mine. We knew there had to be potential champions in these fields, future Melbourne Cup winners, and we were in a race of our own to be the first to spot them.

January was crucial, because at the end of that month several hundred yearlings would be offered up at the National Yearling Sales at Trentham. Like all sales, it had issued catalogues in advance. I had studied the breeding of the yearlings, but the catalogues only went so far. Because the catalogues were sales documents, they only showed you all the winners that the parents of each yearling, the sire and the dam, had produced. I wanted to know the losers as well. You might be attracted to a yearling because its dam had produced a stakes winner – but she might also have produced five or six failures, and the catalogue wasn't going to tell you that! Racing is a game of probabilities, and the buyer of a yearling is taking the biggest gamble of all, so I wanted to arm myself with as much knowledge as possible so as best to calculate my chances. I would interleave the sale catalogues with other information I'd glean from stud books and form books and every other source I could get my hands on.

So my books sat on the car seat, heavily marked and dog-eared with that extra information. I had to know absolutely everything about the families and predecessors of the year-lings I was going to look at. I was obsessed and thorough. I kept a hardback Premier Sale book, with the horses listed on one side and my comments on the other. I wrote down the sale price of every earlier yearling thrown by a mare I was interested in. I believe I was the first trainer to go around with this degree of cross-referencing.

The breeders knew I was coming, even if they didn't know exactly what I wanted. In my diary I would have a list of appointments I'd already made to visit a certain number of horse studs. In that lovely green countryside, all of it prime land, the horse studs and dairy farms predominated. This was a long, long way from the dry lands of South Australia, where I had grown up and where my father had bred and trained his horses. By comparison, New Zealand was horse heaven.

Each day for a week, I tried to visit at least six or seven horse studs. I drove in with a particular list of yearlings I would want to see before they went to the sale ring. If I waited until the sales, it would be too late. They'd be groomed and tizzed up for the buyers, and if there were good ones the word would have got around. I wanted to see them for myself, in their natural environment, see how they were treated and what they were eating, see if they were happy, make my own assessment about breeders and yearlings alike, and get the jump on my competitors.

As well as making appointments, sometimes I would just show up. It didn't matter, as things were quite informal. The stud farms were mostly small family operations, owned by a husband and wife or a pair of brothers or a father and son. By today's standards, the money involved was small and the corporatisation of horse breeding was in its earliest days.

Even though I was an unknown young Australian trainer, the stud owners welcomed me with great warmth. Of course they would – I was there to buy their stock! But I also learnt over the years that New Zealanders were very happy to see you because they got depressed when you *didn't* show up. They had a natural pessimism which they must have inherited from Britain, often expecting the worst, but very open-hearted and enthusiastic when they saw a glimmer of hope.

They would stroll through the yards, and I'd follow them with my books and my pen. The yearlings would be groomed and walked in the mornings and the afternoons – having been broken in to stable routines, they were now being prepared to look beautiful and be on their best behaviour in the sale ring. I would study the ones I had come to see, furiously make notes, and also keep an eye open for a surprise, for the one that

I didn't know about. There was something covert about my operation, too – I didn't want the owners to know if a yearling particularly interested me, because they would immediately bump up the reserve. So while our exchanges were friendly, I had to play my cards close to my chest.

On my first trip, in 1958, I bought a couple of yearlings. While they weren't race winners, they taught me a lot. In 1959, I bought three more yearlings and they all turned into winners. At that time there was a sire who fascinated me. Le Filou had been foaled in France in 1946, and was sent to New Zealand because he wasn't thought to be on the top shelf as a European sire. He was, however, a direct descendant of St Simon, one of the greatest stallions of all. Le Filou stood at Pirongia Stud at Te Awamutu, owned by a very good horseman called Jack Macky. As it turned out, Le Filou's Europe-based offspring had had a pretty slow start in the late 1950s, but I thought he had a lot of unfulfilled promise and I liked his bloodlines well enough to buy a son of his, out of the mare Cuddlesome, on my third visit, in 1960.

That colt I named The Dip, and he was one of the first offspring of Le Filou to race in Australia. The Dip would win the Metropolitan Handicap at Randwick, the top Sydney staying race of the spring, over 2600 metres. 'Le Filou' means 'thief' in French, and I liked the idea of giving his son the sobriquet of a pickpocket. The Dip was certainly an honest performer, however, and made an honest living.

Trainers like me weren't in New Zealand to buy horses on our own account. We simply didn't have the money to own all the horses we bought and wanted to train. So the plan was to buy a horse on behalf of an owner, or buy one with a view to on-selling a whole or part share, or splitting it up among a group of owners. In the case of The Dip, that owner was Wally Broderick, a Victorian businessman who did very well buying grain from the brewer Foster's and selling it as feed to dairy farmers. Wally would later be on the Victoria Racing Club committee, and was just the sort of owner a young trainer liked to have: he trusted you and backed your judgment and let you select and train the horses. I've been asked countless times how much I charge to train a horse, and I say to owners, 'I'll train it for fifty bucks a day, but if you want to give me a hand, I'll charge you seventy-five.' A lot of trainers have copied that saying, because it's so true. The best owners are the ones who enjoy the wins and put up with the losses and leave the training to the trainer.

During those visits in the late 1950s and early 1960s, I was enjoying New Zealand more and more. It wasn't all horses. I got into the routine of taking a fishing trip on Lake Taupo, hauling in some trout if I was lucky, then having them smoked so I could take them back to Valmae and the children in Adelaide. Later, I would indulge my love of deep-sea fishing, and go on the hunt for marlin and shark in the Bay of Islands. But fishing was only a brief diversion from my main interest, which was getting good young thoroughbreds at a good price.

Two years after I bought The Dip, I visited Fred and Molly Dawson on their property at Te Awamutu, where they bred horses as a sideline to their normal work. Molly was Jack Macky's sister, and Fred worked as a stud hand. They were fine, humble people, and you would never have known from their quiet demeanour that they'd bred one of the greatest stayers to have come from New Zealand, Redcraze, who had won the Caulfield Cup under a record 63 kilograms in 1956 and run second in the Melbourne Cup carrying an incredible 65 kilograms.

During my 1962 visit, I saw a number of yearlings and foals. Wally Broderick, having shared some success with me and The Dip, asked me to look at a certain filly for him. The Dawsons had recently bred a full sister to The Dip and a horse agent, Jim Shannon, had told Mr Broderick that the filly was worth keeping an eye on. She was only a foal in 1962, a chestnut filly, and she didn't impress me much. She was light as a cork and all skin and bones.

When I returned to Australia I told Mr Broderick that she was 'pretty darn small'. But he wanted me to keep an eye on her the next year, when she would be a yearling.

In 1962, circumstances were difficult for me. I went to New Zealand in January under a twelve-month suspension from training (the circumstances of which I will get to later). It was not the last time I would be suspended, but my response then was the same as it would be with later suspensions; I had disagreed with the suspension and fought it tooth and nail. I did not believe I had done anything wrong. But once I was punished, I was not one to sit around wallowing in self-pity, wondering if I'd lose my livelihood forever. Instead, there were many jobs I could get on with in preparation for my return to training. I always looked to the future, not the past, more than ever when I was under a suspension. It was necessary for my sanity and a part of my nature.

One of the jobs I could go on with while suspended was to travel to New Zealand and buy more yearlings. There was no better tonic.

When I returned to New Zealand in January 1963, The

Dip's unimpressive-looking little sister wasn't on my secret list of prospective yearlings, but Mr Broderick was still keen and I was ready to get back into the action. Mr Broderick had written to the Dawsons and they'd sent him a colour photograph of the filly. He was persistent – during my suspension, Dad had taken over training The Dip and he'd won the Metropolitan in September 1961. Mr Broderick said he wanted to buy the little sister, who was named Close Embrace. The Dawsons, however, had responded that she wasn't for sale. They intended to keep her as a broodmare, as a way of carrying on the stout Cuddlesome line. Cuddlesome's sire was Red Mars, a son of Hyperion, one of the most influential and formidable sires of the era, so it was clear that Close Embrace, even if she looked light and weak, had some breeding potential.

As Fred and Molly showed me around, we watched a group of three yearlings. Something alarmed them, and two of the three set off at a wild gallop across the paddock. I couldn't take my eyes off one of them. It was a light-framed filly with hardly any muscle on its hindquarters, but I wasn't looking at that: I was looking at the way she ran. The length of her stride, and the way she kept her head and tail in a straight line even when she was extended in a full, frightened gallop, was something you didn't normally see in a yearling.

When I took a closer look, I saw that this was the chestnut filly Wally Broderick wanted me to inspect, The Dip's little sister. My senses went on the alert. There wasn't a great deal more to her than when I'd seen her the previous summer, and she was one of the shortest yearlings I'd ever seen. But I liked her head and the slope of her shoulder, and for such a small filly she had an enormous girth. As my father had always told me, the girth was all-important, because if a horse has some size in the girth it means there's plenty of room for a large heart and a good set of lungs.

The next thing to look at was the bones in her front legs, particularly the cannon, between the knee and fetlock joint, or ankle. My father said that the shorter the cannon, and the closer the knee was to the ground, the longer the stride. It made perfect sense. And this filly had nice low knees.

Finally, the length of the rein was something to look for. A horse's centre of gravity is its wither, the ridge, or hump, over the shoulderblades where the neck runs into the back. The longer the rein, or how far the horse's head and neck extend, the better balanced it is when its hind legs, the engine room, stretch out to the rear. And in racing, balance is everything.

All this, together with the length of her stride, which really was extraordinary for such a flimsily built yearling, sent me into my notebooks and catalogue to make some more secretive jottings.

The Dawsons still refused to sell her, but they said they would be willing to lease her out to race for a few years before she went back to the stud. I told Mr Broderick that even though we could only lease her, we had to have her. I'd come around to his view; the moment I'd seen her take off in that gallop, I knew I had to train her.

You had to be an optimist to be doing what I was. But as much as I liked that filly, I couldn't get carried away with myself. I'd only trained a handful of stakes winners, which had come after years of hard work and near misses. And at the time, I was under suspension. So as hopeful as I was, I could never have guessed that I had just seen my first Melbourne Cup winner.

1

Out of the desert he came

MY NAME IS JAMES BARTHOLOMEW CUMMINGS. I MIGHT HAVE been called Jim, but that was my father's name and everyone called me Bart from the beginning.

It was a good thing that I was distinguished in this way from my father, because I grew up as his shadow: his helper, his apprentice, his companion, his employee and his protégé. Even our birthdays were in the same week in November. If my mother was calling to the stable to fetch 'Jim' at any time of the day, she might have brought both of us running. So Dad was Jim and I was Bart.

As I have said, I learnt everything I know about horses from my father, and in more than half a century of training, I have always seen myself as simply continuing to apply the lessons he taught me. If you have come to this book to discover the magic key to training Melbourne Cup winners, I'm going to disappoint you. There is no magic. There is relentless work, discipline, adherence to your methods and plans, taking a genuine interest in the horse's welfare and, above all, plain commonsense. Luck? If you've got all those things covered, you make your own luck.

Dad had likewise inherited his horse-training blood from a James Cummings, but in this case it was not the father but the uncle. I don't remember discussing our family history much; it's a Cummings trait to look forward rather than backward, and even in my eighties it's something I can't and won't change. I don't sit around dwelling on the past: I'm too busy plotting to win the next race. So what follows is just what I've heard from others.

My known forebears arrived in Adelaide from Ireland on the ship *Epaminondas* on Christmas Eve 1853. Thomas Cummins was a ploughman keen to start a new life in South Australia. He and his wife Anne had six sons – Patrick, Jim, George, Michael, Tom and Jack – and a daughter, Flo, who died as a child. They changed their name to Cummings (the reasons have been lost in the mists of time – maybe people couldn't spell!) and moved to Eurelia, a rural town of about 500 people, 300 kilometres north of Adelaide in the southern Flinders Ranges.

South Australia had been founded by some Church of

England zealots who were not always charitable towards other religious groups. My family were Irish Roman Catholics, and they were shunted off with other Catholics to this barren area. It was desperately tough and dry land. Eurelia could only sustain one sheep per 16 acres! You couldn't grow wheat or any grain in an area with so little rainfall, right on the edge of the Flinders Ranges, and it was skin-of-the-teeth stuff for those 500-odd Irish.

But when the Cummingses first arrived, the Lord must have intervened, because they had record rains for fifteen years. They were able to farm profitably and raise a large family. Of the boys, Patrick (my grandfather) and Jack were blacksmiths, Michael was a wheelwright, and Tom, James and George were farmers. George had an interest in horses, and became a steward and handicapper for the Eurelia Racing Club.

Unfortunately, those good years were the worst possible preparation for what was to follow – one of the deepest droughts and depressions in Australian history. In retrospect, those first years of good harvests were an anomaly, and the drought was just a reversion to normality. Years later, my father would take me on drives through the Eurelia area, and for mile after mile all we could see were limestone chimneys out in the scrubby land. It was a ghost civilisation. Those chimneys were all that remained of the houses that had been abandoned during the 1890s depression.

When it became too hard to earn a living from the land, the Cummings boys dispersed into the outback to look for work. My grandfather Patrick went to Broken Hill, to work in the newly sunk mines, and his brother James went to farm on a property at Ellery Creek, thousands of kilometres north near Alice Springs.

Patrick and his wife Eliza already had five children, the eldest of whom was James Martin Cummings, my father, born in Eurelia on 10 November 1885. (Later in life, Dad apparently rubbed out the year on his birth certificate and replaced it with 1892 – his one and only vanity!) Eliza and the children stayed in Eurelia while Patrick travelled the country working in mines. Dad first became interested in horse racing through his Uncle George, who was buying and selling thoroughbreds around Eurelia. Dad started to ride his uncle's horses. He didn't like school much, and left in his early teens; his one ambition as a boy was to work to save up money to buy a horse of his own. He was determined. His first horse, Sir Thomas, cost him £20 and he swiftly made his money back, riding it to three wins at picnic race meetings.

Dad made a living riding horses and doing general farm labour, but when he was eighteen, tragedy hit the family: he received news that his father, Patrick, had died at a mining site at Black Range, in Western Australia. A Kalgoorlie newspaper report the following week noted:

A man named Patrick Cummings died suddenly on Saturday morning last. On Friday night he appeared to be in the best of health, and played cards with his mates from about 8 o'clock until 10, and shortly afterwards went to bed. Some time later groans were heard and on going to his camp his mates found him seriously ill. As his condition did not improve, Constable Williams was sent for and everything possible was done for Cummings, but without success, and he died at 1.30 on Saturday morning.

It is horrible to think about the pain my grandfather was in when he was suffering from what may have been serious food poisoning. (The exact cause of his death remained unknown.) The consequences were felt on the other side of the desert, where Dad suddenly had to become the family's breadwinner. He tried his hand as a wheat buyer for the Adelaide Milling Company at Belalie North, but it was a hard business to be in. Such companies were a legacy from the years of plenty, and there were many competitors in a small area striving for a share of a fast-shrinking market with dropping prices.

Dad told me that he had been hoping things would turn around, but when he went in a bicycle race in the Eurelia area, the scales of hope finally fell from his eyes. It was a 25-mile race, and for 3 miles of it the road was covered by desert sand and he had to carry his bike. He still won the race, but he decided while he was trudging along with his bike in his arms that there was no future for agriculture in this area. Nor would he ever race bikes again. At the presentation, first prize was a bike pump – which Dad reckoned was the most useless thing he'd ever been given.

Dad was stood down from the struggling wheat company, and went off to work for his Uncle James at Ellery Creek in the Northern Territory, a few hours west of Alice Springs on the edge of the Hermannsburg Mission, which produced the great Aboriginal artist Albert Namatjira. If you have seen Namatjira's landscapes, you will have a good idea of the kind of country Dad was in. A gorge ran through the Ellery Creek property, with springs bubbling up from under the ground, so even though this was deep in the Australian interior there was always water, a welcome sight after Eurelia.

Dad had heard that there was money to be made shooting dingoes for bounty or kangaroos for their skins. But when he arrived, Uncle James had just broken his collarbone in a bad fall from his horse. He asked Dad to stay on the property and work as its manager. When James recovered, Dad stayed on, droving cattle through the stony outcrops and sandhills of the desert. It was in this wild country that he continued his education in horsemanship.

Dad's Uncle James was another of the Cummings horsemen. He belonged to a group of men organising match races in Alice Springs, which must have been a real frontier town in the early 1900s. Dad's Uncle James rode horses himself in the matches, but mainly he bought and sold them. He mentored Dad both in looking after horses and as a rider.

Apparently Uncle James was a bit of a skinflint, so Dad had to scrape together some extra income as a relief driver on the Birdsville mail coach between Bloods Creek and Alice Springs, and by riding his uncle's horses in the match races. He also did work rounding up wild horses on the huge Central Australian properties. Although it must have felt like the end of the earth, some of these horses were very well bred. The British Army was using huge stations such as Loves Creek and Undoolya to breed and raise the horses that their cavalry and officers would use in the Raj in India. Thousands of horses were raised there, thoroughbreds as well as the draught horses who would haul artillery and stores for the army. Sometimes the thoroughbreds escaped, and Dad would ride off looking for them among the brumbies.

It was unpredictable work; one day he'd come across a mob of eighty horses, the next day 180. But he soon developed an eye for a thoroughbred – he could distinguish one by its action, even in a huge mob of brumbies stirring up tornadoes of dust and thundering in at 40 miles an hour.

If he spotted a thoroughbred, he'd have to lasso it, wrestle it to the ground, take it in to the station, and put shoes on it. Doing so was no easy task, and he spoke of the frustrations of losing the horses in the mob and nearly getting trampled. He watched how the stockmen broke the horses in, and some- times it was wild stuff – they'd sling a rope around a horse's leg and throw a saddle onto its back, then the moment they untied the rope it would take off again. Once it was exhausted from bucking, they'd take it into the paddock and walk it around, break it in. 'Breaking' in was an apt way of putting it. The stockmen treated the horses roughly, imposing their will and extinguishing the horse's wilder ways.

Dad observed – and would later tell me – that this confron- tational way was not the best manner of breaking in a thoroughbred horse. If you challenged it, tried to break its spirit, it would spend its whole life at war with men. No matter how old it was, it would always want to buck you and run off. Dad learnt that to break horses in successfully, you had to do it gradually, gently and with empathy. It shouldn't be a war between man and horse; the horse should want to work with you. Nowadays they have invented a term for this: 'horse whispering'. My father was a horse whisperer decades before someone dreamt up the word.

Once Dad and his Uncle James caught these wild thorough- breds, they had the opportunity to sell them to the British as remounts. The horses would be walked down to Port Augusta, 1000 miles south, and sent off on boats to India for a life in the cavalry of the Raj. Or Dad and Uncle James could buy the horses and race them in the picnic meetings.

Dad quickly got a feel for what made a horse run fast, and what slowed it down. The picnic meetings were large affairs, drawing in settlers from hundreds of miles around, for the raucous festivities as much as for the races. Dad lived and breathed horses, and learnt that when racehorse owners thought their horses had been unlucky in the picnic races, they were keen to put up their money for private match races on the trails and dirt roads linking the outback hotels. These match races, involving stakes of up to thousands of pounds, could be considerably more lucrative than the race meetings. Someone would wander into a hotel and talk about a challenge, and Dad would come up with one of his horses and find a jockey. The two owners would put up some money, and whichever horse got to the next hotel first would win the wager.

Dad told me an interesting theory he developed from one of these horses. It had been broken in by an Aboriginal man, who told Dad it was faster than anything around the town. Dad put it into one of these pub-to-pub match races, and to protect his money he put on it a well-tried rider, who happened to be a white man: himself. The horse flopped. He'd seen the horse run, and it went like the wind, but with him in the saddle it wouldn't go a yard. Three days later, Dad organised a rematch. This time, he put the Aboriginal horse-breaker on it. Dad said that even though the Aboriginal man wasn't a very good jockey, the horse bolted in. It's rarely discussed now, but Dad believed that a horse can sense the difference between an Aboriginal and a white rider, and this horse, after the Aboriginal man had broken it in and ridden it everywhere, just wouldn't try with anyone else on its back. Dad felt that if a horse had been treated well, whoever had broken it in and educated it would always be the best rider for that horse, because it loved the breaker and would give all its heart racing for him. The key to the lesson wasn't so much about black jockeys and white jockeys; it was that horses have a great intelligence and a long, long memory, and if you want to get the best out of them, you have to respect the fact that they are remembering things that you might have forgotten or never have known.

Dad's Uncle James owned an aged mare called Myrtle. Knowing how desperate Dad was to own and race horses, James told Dad that if he won the 1910 Alice Springs Cup on Myrtle, then he could have her as his prize.

Dad told me he wasn't much of a race jockey, but he duly won that Cup, and Myrtle was his. But he wasn't going to hang around working for his uncle. He told me that by now, after all his time in the sun chasing horses, he looked older than Uncle James, and if he stayed much longer, he'd look like he was eighty years old before he turned forty.

Dad must have looked after Myrtle very well, because a few months after that Alice Springs Cup, when she must have been seven or eight years old, he set off with her on the 900-mile trek south to Adelaide. He'd resolved to leave the hard life in the Northern Territory and try his luck down in the city. James wanted him to stay, and promised that when he passed on Dad could have the property. Dad decided that Uncle James was looking much too healthy and wouldn't be going anywhere for a while.

Needless to say, there was no rail connection yet between Alice Springs and Adelaide. On that long walk south, as well as Myrtle, Dad was also taking a thoroughbred gelding called Radamantos, and a stockhorse. They were his wages from working for Uncle James. He was accompanied by an Aboriginal policeman as a guide. They walked down the line of what is now the Stuart Highway, before cutting eastwards along the Oodnadatta Track past Lake Eyre.

Along the way, Dad's guide had to turn back. A telegram summoned him to return to Alice Springs to pick up a prisoner to take to Adelaide. Fearlessly, Dad and his horses kept walking south. Dad was only 24 but he had enough experience in the outback to feel confident that he could make the long journey safely on his own. He walked by day and camped under the mulga trees by night, boiling his billy and dreaming about the new life he would make in Adelaide as a horse trainer. It was a solitary journey, but as long as he was with the horses, Dad wasn't lonely. It's another characteristic I've inherited from him.

He passed through Eurelia, which was just a shadow of his childhood memories, even more drought-ravaged than when he had left. He stayed with his family for about two weeks, showing off Myrtle's galloping speed and keeping his ear to the ground for news of any upcoming race meetings.

Family legend has it that at one point, in a town called Peterborough, not too far south of Eurelia, Dad and the horses came across a Lutheran pastor in a black hat riding a penny-farthing bicycle; the horses took fright and Dad was thrown. He had to chase them 20 miles back along the track before he could bring them under control again. When he came back, he skirted around Peterborough until the horses got used to people and wheeled traffic. It was easy to forget that for horses who came from the red centre, a black-hatted clergyman on a bicycle must have looked as frightening as an invader from outer space.

For a lot of the walk down from Alice Springs, it rained. Dad would tell me about the great thunderstorms dropping 4 or 5 inches of rain in half an hour. Immediately, the Mitchell grass would spring out of the dust and grow 4 feet high. Mitchell grass is wonderful feed for horses, containing more protein than oats or maize. By the time Dad and the horses arrived in Jamestown, just north of Adelaide, where there was a race meeting on, Myrtle was both rock-hard from the walk and well fed, with dapples all over her coat. Dad noticed that there hadn't been the same rain in Jamestown itself. The local horses were 'tucked up', or dehydrated, with their ribs showing. He scented a coup.

The Jamestown race meeting would take place over three days, spread over a week in March 1910. These days Jamestown is too drought-ridden to support regular race meetings, but at that time the town had a growing population and a profitable racecourse. On the first day, Dad entered Myrtle in a 6-furlong race (a furlong is 200 metres), the Belalie Stakes, and backed her – not with the bookmakers, but with what was an experimental form of the totalisator.

Totalisator betting would revolutionise racing. It would also be one of the best things to happen to the sport, because of the money it pumped back into the clubs to support meetings and prize money. Unlike a bookmaker, a tote machine won't complain about returning money to the sport or blow all of its profits on high living or bad bets.

Instead of pitting his wits against a bookmaker to take the odds on a horse at the moment the bet is laid, a punter on the 'tote' would not know what odds the horse would pay at the time he placed his bet. The 'tote' has no brain, no judgment, no gambling instinct; it simply measures how much money is wagered on the race, and then allocates odds as a measurement of how much is put on each horse. So if, for instance, $1000 is bet, and $500 of it is put on one horse, that horse will pay back $2 if it wins. If only one person places a $1 bet on an outsider, then if that horse wins it will pay $1000. And so on.

The tote at Jamestown was a rudimentary mechanical gadget with levers and buttons, but it did what today's TAB does: produced a ticket when the punter laid his bet. Dad bet 2 shillings and sixpence on Myrtle in her first start at Jamestown, and when she won she paid something in the order of £60 or £70. Judging by those odds, he must have been just about the only punter who backed this unknown mare from the desert.

As the meeting progressed, other punters and trainers wised up to Jim Cummings and Myrtle. There was a horse she'd only just nosed out on the first day. That horse's owner wanted to avoid Myrtle on the following days, but as soon as he entered his horse in a race, Dad would enter Myrtle – and she kept beating it.

The other owner must have been pleased at the end of the meeting when Dad offered to buy his horse for £20. It was little more than a bag of bones when it finished second to Myrtle, but Dad would take it to Adelaide, care for it and feed it up, and under the name Trentham's Hope it would win a handful of races for him in the city.

My father settled back in Eurelia for a while and became a horse trainer licensed by the South Australian Racing Club in 1911. Sadly for him, in May of that same year his Uncle James died after falling off a horse on his station. The horse tripped on the mulga plains, threw Uncle James like a javelin out of his saddle, and when he hit the ground he broke his neck and died instantly. So perhaps, if Dad had stayed at Ellery Creek, he would have been a Central Australian property owner all his life and I would have followed him down that path. You never know where the accidents of fate are going to take you.

Uncle James had become an institution of the new horse-racing scene in Alice Springs, and his memory has been preserved in a plaque at the Central Australian Racing Club's headquarters. Like Dad, and like me, Uncle James thought of little else but thoroughbreds. In about twenty years living at Ellery Creek he'd only left the area once: to go to Darwin to race a horse.

2

'We've done our dough'

MOVING FROM ELLERY CREEK BACK TO EURELIA WAS A GAMBLE, but Dad trusted his instincts and the move south would be a turning point in his life. He took his horses around the country circuit of race meetings north of Adelaide – towns such as Burra, Quorn, Port Pirie and Jamestown. In 1911 he took Myrtle down to the Cheltenham course in Port Adelaide, and she ran twice in one day, finishing sixth and then second – earning him his first prize money cheque from a city meeting.

He continued riding in match races, and trained gallopers both on the flat course and over hurdles, his jumper Vanardo finishing third in the Adelaide Grand National in 1913.

Soon after the 1914–18 War he met my mother, Annie Whelton, who came from Rosscarbery in County Cork, Ireland, and beguiled him with her demure manner and rich Irish accent. In the early 1920s they had two children, Patrick and Teresa.

Dad bought some acreage at St Leonards, near Adelaide Airport, west of the city, which he used as an agistment and breeding property. His home base was not far from there, a house on an acre and a half on the bank of Sturt Creek, near Glenelg. They were close to Morphettville Racecourse, which was one of three big metropolitan tracks in Adelaide, along with Victoria Park in the centre of town and Cheltenham in the northern suburbs.

Mum, who was petite, quiet, a loving mother and a very supportive wife for Dad, called the house Rosscarbery. Dad built ten looseboxes, or stabling for ten horses, at Rosscarbery and expanded his training operations for the races not only at Morphettville and the city tracks but for meetings outside Adelaide. He was also doing some horse dealing and riding, but mainly he was committing himself to a career as a trainer and a breeder. His first big city winner, in 1918, was Opera Bouffe, a brown filly by the English-bred stallion Comedy King, who had become the first Northern Hemisphere-bred horse to win the Melbourne Cup in 1910. Opera Bouffe didn't win in her first eleven starts, but then she won three races in two weeks at Balaklava, north of Adelaide, and Cheltenham. Dad backed her – and rode her! – and the winnings helped him pay off his two properties.

In 1921 Dad brought all his experience in spotting thorough-breds to the Adelaide Yearling Sales, and made the purchase that would pay the ultimate dividend nearly thirty years later. He saw a colt with a suspect knee, but he liked the breeding so much that he overlooked that minor irregularity and got him at a bargain price. It was a lesson I would learn to my great good fortune: many buyers in the sale ring are looking for the perfect horse and will be put off by any deformity, no matter how small. What Dad knew, and what I learnt, was that there is no such thing as the perfect horse, and you can use other buyers' caution to your advantage.

As Anton King, that horse with the suspect knee won £4400 in stakes for Dad and his first city feature races: the 1923 South Australian Stakes, in which Dad rode him, and the Port Adelaide Guineas. Dad took him to Melbourne for the spring carnival, but they didn't get off to a good start. Horses were transported by train in those days. The rail gauge changed at the South Australia–Victoria border, and when the horses were coming out of their carriages Anton King's hoof got caught in the tracks. He panicked and twisted his leg trying to pull it free.

He couldn't move for ten days, but ran fourth, only half-fit, in the Caulfield Guineas over a mile. When he was fully recovered, Anton King flashed home for third behind Whittier in the Victoria Derby and also came third in the Williamstown Cup, now known as the Sandown Cup, before finishing his campaign with a win over 10 furlongs at Flemington, ridden by the great Bobbie Lewis. Dad was very impressed by the spring racing in Melbourne, which was on a much bigger scale in every way than Adelaide, and his success planted the seed of an ambition to eventually go over to Melbourne and race regularly in the big time.

Dad was as interested in breeding as in training, and when Anton King broke a bone in his leg during training the next year, Dad stood him as a stallion, for a fee of 20 guineas. He was a great looker, even with the dodgy knee, and Dad felt that his pedigree would make him a successful sire. Since training Opera Bouffe, Dad had an affinity with the Comedy King stock, and late in the 1920s he sent another Comedy King mare, Miss Comedy, to Anton King. The offspring was a filly called Witty Maid, who, years later, would change all of our lives.

DAD'S TRAINING CAREER PROGRESSED SUCCESSFULLY THROUGH THE 1920s, mainly in Adelaide but also in Melbourne and Perth. By the time I was born, on 14 November 1927, his horses had won an Adelaide Cup and a South Australian Derby among other feature races, and he was well known on the racing scene in Adelaide and interstate. He was a softly-spoken, gentle sort of man who didn't like to talk about his horses' prospects with the press, putting them off with a few modest comments and a friendly smile. If he was ever asked for a tip, he would always say the same thing: 'Have a little each way.' He became so famous for the phrase that a friend sent him a card one Christmas with a poem that read: 'Good luck to Jim Cummings, great trainer of today. No great saint, no great sinner – just a little bit each way!'

I was born close to Rosscarbery, at Waringa Nursing Home in Farrell Street, Glenelg. I probably didn't make much noise – I never have.

Our house was usually quiet and low-key. Dad and Mum both had the black Irish looks – very dark hair and pale skin – and were a harmonious couple. I don't remember one being dominant over the other, or any real conflict. They enjoyed singalongs at home, with Dad playing the piano or the accordion while everyone joined in, mostly singing Irish tunes. Dad was even-tempered and a devout Catholic. His hair was thinning out as I was growing up, which supports the theory that the hair gene is passed down the mother's side. Dad had all his horses blessed by a priest, a tradition I'd later maintain. The priest would also say a Mass at the stables at Easter. Dad was sure it worked. But he didn't just observe religion to influence his luck. He said his prayers every night before bed, and the only thing that lit up his temper in the stables was people swearing or taking the Lord's name in vain. He only got cranky at me when I'd done something wrong and he couldn't catch me. Mum was very calm and placid, and when any mischief happened she'd say in her thick Irish accent, 'It's done now and may the Devil mend you.'

My first love was animals and I always had pets, including a magpie which sat at the top of my bed every night. I'd found Maggie sick in the yard and taken him in. Mum said he'd pick my eyes out, and my brother Patrick, who slept across from me in the house's sleep-out, wasn't keen on him at all. But I said, 'This one's all right,' and I fed Maggie and kept him for years.

My earliest memories are of the house and the stables. I must have been sniffing around the horses, shadowing Dad, almost before I could walk. I have a clear memory of our neighbour, Mrs McManus, who had three sons about my age and made the world's best rice puddings, with a dusting of nutmeg on top. I can still taste them. The house Mrs McManus raised her boys in (I never knew if there had been a Mr McManus) was across the road from us on Macfarlane Street and on the bank of Sturt Creek. She had 3 or 4 acres, while we had a much smaller block. The bricks underfoot at the threshold of Mrs McManus's house were so worn down with age that they had a dip in them – I remember being amazed at the idea that so many people could walk on bricks, over time, that the accumulation of their footsteps could actually wear down bricks.

Mrs McManus had a concrete slab laid down and a small school built on her property, which she ran. There were gum trees along the line of the creek, including one that was so tall and broad it stood out from miles away.

Just after Christmas, when I was about nine, I noticed a lot of people milling around the McManuses' fence, all dressed in their best picnic clothes, looking like they wanted to get in. I wandered up and asked them what they were doing. They said they wanted to see the gum tree. I asked why. The visitors said it was because they wanted to have their photos taken standing under it.

I followed up with the young child's favourite question, but one which I've found is pretty useful no matter how old you are: 'Why?'

It turned out that it was under the biggest of these trees that the colony of South Australia had been proclaimed.

Back in the midsummer of 1836, Sir John Hindmarsh, the first governor of South Australia, had led a maritime expedition from Victoria to the site of what is now Adelaide. They had disembarked from their tender on Sturt Creek and sought shade under an enormous gum tree. It was there that Hindmarsh proclaimed his governorship of the colony.

The land on which the gum tree stood was now Mrs McManus's backyard, and these people wanted to take each other's photographs standing or sitting under that tree on the centenary of the founding date.

It wasn't easy to get into Mrs McManus's yard, so I went into the house and pulled some strings. I asked if I could borrow her key to let the tourists in. She gave it to me, and I opened the gate – but I must have inherited some of my father's financial nous straight off, because I charged them a small fee for going through the gate. By the end of the day I considered myself a very rich man, having netted fully ten shillings. For a nine-year-old in the aftermath of the Great Depression, I was doing all right. But I didn't keep it to myself; I took it home and gave it to Dad, who was grateful, as it helped him pay the wages of his small stables staff.

THE DEPRESSION BORE DOWN ON EVERYBODY, BUT I DON'T remember us ever going hungry or being desperate. There was the rabbitoh coming up the street on Tuesdays and Thursdays with his horse and cart, selling rabbits for sixpence a pair, and fishermen up from the wharves offering their best. Although money was scarce, for us it wasn't nonexistent; we were able to buy enough to fill our stomachs and Dad provided us with a nice house and education due to his success with horses. These were boom years for racing – Phar Lap was obviously the greatest horse of the era, but the sport was popular throughout the nation. During such hard times people enjoyed the diversion and entertainment and colour of the racetrack, and of course were drawn in by the chance of eking out some kind of income, and perhaps making a fortune.

Dad sent Opera Bouffe to Anton King at the property near the airport, and the coupling produced St Opera, Opera King, Opera Queen and Sweet Opera, who between them won numerous stakes races, including the Victorian Oaks and South Australian Derby. Races are classified and ranked according to their quality. Top races like the Melbourne Cup and Victoria Derby are 'Group One', and there are around sixty such races each year. Below them are Group Two, Group Three and, finally, 'Listed' races. Some weeks in advance, stables enter numerous horses in the biggest of these races; in the Melbourne Cup, for instance, the initial entrants may number in the hundreds, with dozens coming from each of the top stables. As the races get closer, the numbers are whittled down. But as a trainer, you will err on the side of caution because you don't want to miss out on one of the big ones. All these races together are called 'black type' races, and are the most important thing to pick up from a breeding point of view. When you look at a pedigree and see a lot of bold black type, you know you have high-quality horses.

When Anton King retired, Dad replaced him with Powerscourt, a stallion with blood from the champion European sire Chaleyer on both sides of his pedigree. Powerscourt was underrated, Dad believed – so underrated that when he'd first been put up for sale as a sire after a short and fractious racing career, nobody had even wanted to take him for free. So Dad snapped him up and stood him in the years leading up to the Second World War.

Mᴜᴍ ᴅɪᴅɴ'ᴛ ɢᴏ ᴛᴏ ᴛʜᴇ ʀᴀᴄᴇs ᴍᴜᴄʜ ʜᴇʀsᴇʟꜰ, ʙᴜᴛ ᴀs ᴡᴇ ɢʀᴇᴡ older she let Patrick, Teresa and me go along with Dad. I also loved working in the stables, doing whatever he wanted me to do. I got to ride around the paddocks on Cushla, a lovely mare who won two guineas races, but she must have wondered what she'd done to deserve a young boy larking about on her when she could have been resting in her stall.

Much as I loved the stables, often I came out of them wheezy and coughing, my eyes streaming as heavily as if I'd been cutting onions. When I was six, I started to have attacks of breathlessness, turning purple as I gasped for air. I was taken to a Dr Stoddart, who gave me the worst possible news: I had asthma, and I got it from the stables! Whether it was from the hay, or the horse hair, or the dust, we didn't know.

I can't remember if he ordered me to stay away from the horses, or if Mum discouraged me. Somebody did, but it was useless; there was no way I was going to let a mere attack of coughing and runny eyes keep me from the place I loved most. If I couldn't follow Dad around the stables, life wouldn't be worth living. I decided I'd just put up with the breathless attacks when they happened, and battle my way through them. To steer clear of the horses was absolutely out of the question.

Later, when I was sixteen, Dad took me to see a specialist named Barlow in North Terrace, in the centre of Adelaide. Dr Barlow ran a lot of newfangled tests on me: scratching my arm and exposing me to toxins from chaff and hay. If my skin went red, it meant I was allergic. Of course I went red at just about everything: hay, horse hair, feeds. So Dr Barlow said I had to stay away from horses and stables if I wanted to avoid chronic asthma and allergies for the rest of my life.

As we walked off up North Terrace, I turned to Dad and said: 'We've done our dough.'

Dad agreed. If the only medical advice they could give me was to stay away from horses, then we'd all been wasting our time.

A BIGGER THREAT TO MY LIFE AS A BOY WAS, ON ONE OCCASION, the water. I loved diving off the jetty at Glenelg Beach, even though I wasn't much of a swimmer. It seemed safe enough: you'd jump off and climb back up. One day I was doing that with some friends, but hadn't taken account of the change in tides. We'd gone out at low tide, but by the end of the day it had come up about 3 metres. I jumped in for the last time and began to swim back to the shore, but the water was far deeper than I'd expected, and I was struggling against the current. I fought against it but only succeeded in wearing myself out. I was starting to panic, but luckily a schoolmate, a much stronger swimmer, saw me and dived in.

'What are you doing?' he said as he got near me.

I only had enough breath to gasp: 'I'm going down.'

He pulled me out and saved my life. His name was O'Grady – he was the son of the barber at Glenelg – and he got a commendation from the Royal Humane Society of Australia. If he's still out there somewhere, I can only hope that he's had a few good bets on the Melbourne Cup.

When it came to asthma and stables, I could bustle my way through any obstacle. I just put up with it. But sometimes, as with the sea, there are forces greater than a boy's determination. The scare at the jetty prompted me to learn how to swim, and I have swum for exercise ever since. It also shook me around a little, inside myself. Having looked death in the eye at such a young age, I became a little more introspective and reflected on the need, always, to keep on fighting and never give in.

ONE AREA IN WHICH I DIDN'T APPLY MUCH DETERMINATION WAS MY schooling. I went to Marist Brothers Sacred Heart College in Adelaide, and to say I was an 'average' student is probably an insult to those who tried hard and did keep up with the required average standard. I just wasn't interested. My whole life was now in the stables, with Dad, and I couldn't see the point of school. I was no good at all, and the Brothers held me back a great deal. They gave me a hard time, getting upset with me when I didn't know the answers to their questions. I thought the teachers were all mad. I understood basic commonsense, and I wasn't bad at maths, but for the most part what they wrote on the blackboard and what they had in the textbooks just wouldn't go into my head.

I was more interested in the outdoors. I couldn't see any reason why I should continue studying subjects I was never going to use. I just wanted to get back to what I liked best. I had friends, but even then I had little time to devote to running around in a pack making mischief. Outside school hours, I only liked working. I'd always felt sorry for my parents, because they had to work so hard. I enjoyed the odd game of cricket or football, but soon I would feel guilty about the jobs that needed doing at home so I'd wander off to help Mum or, more likely, Dad. Then, as now, it was all about the horses. What else in life was important? So when I was fourteen, I went home one day and told my parents I'd had enough. I must've been *really* bad at school, because they didn't argue. Dad said it suited him to have me working at home, and Mum said she would back me up as long as I was happy. Dad and I shook hands on it, and that was the end of school.

MY SCHOOL EDUCATION MIGHT HAVE COME TO AN END, BUT MY real education was only just beginning. Dad wasn't a joyless man, but he was less interested in making you laugh than in making you think. He always encouraged me to ask questions. I've been asking questions ever since.

Here's an example of where asking questions led me. As a boy I would sit for hours watching Dad mix the horses' feeds, a job he did himself. This became a tenet of the Cummings training method: always mix our own feeds, never ever buy pre-mixes. I'd sit on a hay bale and watch him sifting, sifting, sifting the feed endlessly through a big sieve. Eventually I asked him why he sifted it so many times.

'There are thirty-two teeth in a horse's mouth,' he said, 'and you've got to sieve the dust out thirty-two times to make it cleaner for them to eat. If you look after the horses, they'll look after you.'

Especially when the times were so lean, concern for the horse had to be paramount. You couldn't take them for granted. Many trainers saw it the other way around, and when their resources were stretched they would scrimp on the horses, feeding them less and racing them harder. Dad taught me first and foremost that horses are not machines, they're personalities. They are highly intelligent creatures and they understand affection and love.

Many years later, I trained a very popular grey horse called Ming Dynasty. He won two Caulfield Cups in his long career, and Valmae and I part-owned him as well as me training him. After Ming Dynasty retired, we gave him to the Australian Jockey Club (AJC) as a clerk of the course mount, a job for which greys were favoured.

Well, Ming Dynasty wouldn't behave. I heard stories of him throwing his rider and wreaking all sorts of havoc. Then, about two years after he retired, I was sitting in my office at our Randwick stables when one of the staff came in and said, 'Boss, there's this strange grey horse here standing in a stall – I don't know whose it is.'

I walked out and took a look. The horse had walked into a box, turned around and stood there waiting for somebody to close the door. I thought, 'Hang on, he's standing in Ming Dynasty's old box . . . Hang on, he looks like Ming Dynasty, but it can't be; he's a clerk of the course horse now . . . Hang on . . .'

And then the phone rang. It was someone from the AJC, saying Ming Dynasty had wandered off. Had I seen him?

Yes, my old friend had returned. Ming Dynasty appreciated a good home, and preferred to be here with the experts rather than with those roughnecks on the course.

There are many stories that tell us the same thing: horses do think. When they're looked after well, they appreciate it. They never forget you. And if you are a good trainer, you will never forget a thing about them. Soon I realised that this was the reason why Dad was so quiet: every scrap of information, every insight and observation about every one of his horses, he was retaining in his mind. Horses are often riddles waiting to be worked out, and Dad would be circulating all of that information like a human computer, asking questions and figuring out answers. When people talk of a 'passion' for training, this is what they mean. Dad would be thinking about little else. And while I was still a boy, I was fast becoming the same. No wonder I couldn't take in what my school teachers had been saying: with all the horses running around in my head, I had no room for anything else.

3

Life without horses

BEFORE I WENT TO WORK FULL TIME IN THE STABLES, I REALISED
I had something to prove to myself. I couldn't just quit school
and work for Dad. If I did that, I'd never know if I could do
anything out in the world on my own. And during this period,
around 1942, Dad had to stop training. With the Second
World War in full swing, Sir Thomas Playford, the premier of
South Australia, banned horse racing and directed the sport's
resources towards the munitions industry. All South Australian

manufacturing had to be restructured for the war effort, and for fifteen months Dad had to give up training and work in a factory making armaments.

Meanwhile, I ventured out into the big wide world. I went to do some grape-picking out east of Adelaide in the land irrigated by the Murray. I'd been up there on holidays with Kevin Murphy, a schoolmate, and knew there would be opportunities for work. Soon after I arrived in Renmark, the town at the centre of the industry, I spotted an opportunity. There were dozens of men in their forties and fifties sitting around in the pubs and on the streets, more interested in drinking than working. I found out that the pay was quite good for picking fruit for the fruit-based beers the companies were brewing. I'd go up to these men and offer them a bottle of wine if they'd come and help me.

They were easily persuaded, and we'd pick 4 or 5 tonnes of fruit a day, filling up trucks by four thirty in the afternoon. I'd get paid, distribute wages and wine, and be able to pocket a little for myself. It was a good lesson in commonsense: anyone could have rounded up work gangs as I did, but nobody else had the initiative. These men were much older than I was, but if you got them moving, they would work for you. Probably they should have been doing it for themselves, but they weren't.

When I came back to Adelaide I worked for eighteen months at John Martin's menswear store in Rundle Street for eighteen shillings a week. As it cost six shillings a week to get there and back in the bus, I felt I had to work that much harder to make it worthwhile.

Working in menswear put some polish on me – I learnt how to talk to strangers and respect them. I also learnt how to pull a swiftie. There was a code system that would show which salesman had made which sales, and you'd get an extra commission from that. There were a lot of city spivs coming in buying nice suits and shirts, and I figured out how to decode the system. Before we knew it, I was recording more 'sales' than some of my colleagues who'd been there for twenty years! I liked the challenge of that, but when they worked out what I was doing I thought it was time to leave quietly.

My next job was back where I loved to be – in the outdoors. Harry McDowell was a navy veteran from the 1914–18 War who had a fishing ketch down at Anna Harbour. He had crayfish pots and a big well in the middle of his boat.

When he took me out, I realised what the well was for. We were out for four or five weeks, and when Harry would catch snapper he had to keep them fresh. No refrigeration or ice on that boat! So he'd bring them in, take out the hooks, squeeze the air out of them, and throw them into the well where they could happily swim around and stay fresh for weeks until we got back to shore.

I'd enjoyed fishing in Sturt Creek as a kid, but my time with Harry really imbued me with a love for going out on a boat into the deep blue sea. We had some amazing experiences. Our lines were thick cord with two hooks on them, and at times we'd pull in a 30-pound snapper on one hook, with a 20-pound one on the other hook. Without gloves, I was cutting my hands to shreds on those coarse lines.

One day we caught 3 tonnes of whiting in about four hours, but all we were pulling in on the ends of our lines were the heads – sharks were waiting around the boat having a great old feed, biting off the whiting from our hooks as we brought them in. Harry was furious.

As well as sharks, there were storms and fearsome reefs and rocks to avoid. One night, we came into an area where the sea was alive with porpoises – 20 acres of porpoises; I've never seen anything like it. Harry wanted to catch one for bait. His idea was to cut it up into pieces and let its oil leak out from the stern of the boat, which would bring the sharks in, and he could then catch them or shoot them. So this night, he climbed up on the bowsprit with a rope and a crowbar with a spear tip attached, and tried spearing a porpoise. The boat was going 18 or 20 knots and I couldn't believe how brave and skilful he was.

He liked to go after the sharks, which had enormous power. At six o'clock one morning, I was woken by the crashing of kettles and pots falling off the cabin walls. I asked Harry what was going on, and he said a baby shark was hammering the boat with its tail. A baby!

On a recent trip that I hadn't been on, Harry had seen a shark that he reckoned would have weighed 3000 pounds – a world record. He usually took his .303 rifle with him to shoot sharks if they got close, but on that occasion he didn't have his gun and the massive shark began to push the boat around. Harry said he was so scared he just lay in the bottom of the boat until it was over. The shark pushed him 8 or 10 miles offshore, then left him. When he got back to port late that night, he discovered some of the shark's teeth were still in the hull of the boat from where it had taken hold and tried to shake him out.

I sat agog listening to Harry. The experiences were great, but the stories were even greater. All I could say was that I was glad I wasn't on that trip.

THESE JOBS OUTSIDE RACING WERE VALUABLE EXPERIENCES FOR ME, building up my self-confidence and my sense that I could do anything, not just work for Dad. But the period was always an intermission, a kind of preparation for what I knew I was going to do with my life.

During the year or so when racing was banned in South Australia, from 1942 to 1943, Dad had had to sell his most prized possessions. Witty Maid, who had won several races in the late 1930s and was now a broodmare, went to the Bowyer brothers at their Bowe Neire stud at Normanville, south of Adelaide towards Kangaroo Island. Her stakes-winning daughter Witty Lass was also sold, while Powerscourt, the stallion Dad had bought as a replacement for Anton King, was sold to new owners in Victoria. Money was so short that the Bowyers offered 110 guineas for Witty Lass and Witty Maid, well under the going rate pre-war, and could only pony up 20 guineas as a deposit. Having to sell the horses at all, let alone on such terms, was a severe blow for Dad, but given that it was brought on by a war, he took it with good grace.

But we went mad if we were kept away from horses for too long. After his fifteen or so months working in the arms factories, Dad had had enough. In 1943 he got some racehorses together, put them onto a boat and took them to Tasmania. The trains were too rough, and the motorised horse floats were too dangerous for such long trips. The horse float of the day was powered by coke or coal, lit by a bunsen burner. You couldn't look out the back window because of the flames leaping up. It's a wonder they didn't blow up. So instead, Dad took the horses interstate by boat and enjoyed the fresh air. When they got to Tasmania his horses won a few races in Launceston, then they boarded another boat, this time going to Melbourne.

Dad was fully into rebuilding mode now, and while in Melbourne he made enquiries about his old stallion Powerscourt. He found out that the horse was for sale again, but at a price too steep for Dad's reduced means. Here providence intervened. During his walks on Glenelg Beach he had met an old gentleman named M.B. Wilson, a retired businessman from Victoria who had a beach shack at Glenelg. When he returned home in late 1943, Dad managed to pique Mr Wilson's interest in Powerscourt. Dad was very clever at this: enthusing people about racing, and convincing them that to bring their dreams to fruition they need only finance the purchase of a certain horse. M.B. Wilson did agree to buy Powerscourt, and the stallion came back from Victoria and stood at Bowe Neire, where Witty Maid was sent to him and, as sometimes happens, the dream Dad had sold to Mr Wilson was to come true. In 1945, while I was working for John Martin's menswear store, Witty Maid foaled a colt to Powerscourt. He would be named Comic Court.

4

The listener

I WORKED IN DAD'S STABLES IN THE LATE 1940s, BUT NOT IN THE senior role as the main strapper. That job belonged to Freddy McIntosh, a long-term employee of Dad's. Like many of the horses, I was being brought along patiently.

I had no further ambitions: to work under my father was all I wanted. It didn't matter how menial the job was, or how lowly paid – I earned £2 a week, plus my bed and board – I relished it all. Even walking his broodmares from Glenelg to the airport property, for 3 or 4 miles along West Beach and Henley Beach, thinking my own thoughts, talking to the horses, I was as content as a young man could be. It sure beat working.

Horses were always teaching me something new. It was in that period that we had a very cranky racehorse that tried to kick me every time I was within range. I couldn't figure out why. We fed him well, and looked after him humanely. We could only suspect that he had been mistreated by an earlier owner, before he came to us.

Then one day, just by chance, I picked up a stockwhip when I was going to the horse's stall. We didn't use stockwhips, so it must have been there as a souvenir or for ornamentation. But the moment I walked into that stall with the whip, the horse looked at me, came around and laid his head on my chest. I gave him a pat and left him.

When he'd seen me with that stockwhip, he decided I was the boss. That was all it took. Possibly someone had whipped him when he was young? We would never know but whatever the reason, my possession of that whip made the horse respect me, and he was never another moment's trouble. Who says horses don't think? They think just like humans.

Three weeks later, that horse won the Moonee Valley Cup.

THINGS HAD STARTED HOTTING UP FOR THE PROGENY OF POWERS-court and Witty Maid. Comic Court's elder brother Comedy Prince, foaled in 1944, won his first race for the Bowyers and

Dad persuaded the Lee family to buy him for 2100 guineas. The Lees – father Arthur, a hotelier, and his sons Bob, Bert and Jack – had met Dad through Dan Moriarty, the clocker at Morphettville racetrack and a fine gentleman. Two of the sons, Bert and Jack, fought in the Second World War and were decorated for their courage, while Bob looked after the business at home. Moriarty convinced the Lees that Jim Cummings was one of the best judges and trainers of a horse. They also took out an option on the next Powerscourt–Witty Maid youngster, Comic Court. Dad would train both.

Comedy Prince won twenty races, but soon Comic Court was stealing the limelight. He won four races as a juvenile, then the 1948 Victoria Derby and St Leger as a three-year-old. In the 1920s, Dad had been friendly with Jim Scobie, the veteran trainer who had prepared four Melbourne Cup winners early in the twentieth century. According to Dad, Scobie imparted many secrets to him regarding the Melbourne Cup, principal among them that you select the horse for the race and you aim everything at getting it to peak on that day for that distance. (It's been said about me that if the Melbourne Cup was run a minute before schedule, my horses would still be sixty seconds away from peaking. That's a flattering assessment, but if it's true, I owe it to Dad and, through Dad, to Jim Scobie.)

The race Comic Court was set for was the 1948 Derby, which he won. It must have been an enormous thrill for Dad, though he wasn't one to come home and brag about it. Back in Adelaide, Mum was quietly overjoyed at the news. Next Comic Court would run in the Melbourne Cup – not because he'd been trained for it, but because he was going so well it was worth taking the chance. The Victoria Derby, over 2500 metres, is run on the Saturday, three days before the Melbourne Cup over 3200 metres. It is rare for a spring three-year-old to take on the Cup, and seldom are they mature enough to win. Comic Court ran a creditable fourth behind the 80/1 outsider Rimfire.

The next year, he again won some top-flight races before failing in the Melbourne Cup. By winning the Memsie, Craiglee and Turnbull stakes in the spring, he established himself as the top weight-for-age horse in the country. Weight-for-age races allocate set weights depending on a horse's age, not its achievements – so horses aren't penalised by a handicapper for their wins. For that reason, the best horses usually run at weight-for-age, and sometimes they avoid handicap races altogether because they will be weighted out of contention.

Because they will play such a prominent role in the careers of the horses in this book, I will outline the sequence of these weight-for-age races here. In the spring and autumn, a series of weight-for-age races over increasing distances takes place, leading up to the climactic staying races of the season. In Melbourne in the spring, these are:

Freeway Stakes (1200 m, Moonee Valley)
Memsie Stakes (1400 m, Caulfield)
Feehan Stakes (1600 m, Moonee Valley)
Craiglee Stakes (1600 m, Flemington)
Underwood Stakes (1800 m, Caulfield)
Turnbull Stakes (2000 m, Flemington)
Caulfield Stakes (2000 m, Caulfield)

(The names of these races have changed over the years, with sponsorship, but these are the names they are originally registered under.)

Well-credentialled Melbourne Cup horses are usually pro-grammed to run in these races. (Up-and-coming horses, without the threat of big weights, might instead run in handicaps.) A week after the Caulfield Stakes is the first big cup of the season: the Caulfield Cup, a handicap race over 2400 metres. The following week the spotlight is back on weight-for-age, with the W.S. Cox Plate at Moonee Valley over 2040 metres. The week after that, the L.K.S. Mackinnon Stakes, over 2000 metres at Flemington, is the last weight-for-age lead-up to the Melbourne Cup.

There are also weight-for-age spring races in Sydney leading up to the Metropolitan, a handicap run over 2600 metres. And amid all this are the sprint races, mile races, and races for two- and three-year-olds. The prestigious three-year-old races culminate in the semi-classics, the guineas races over a mile, and the classics, the derby for colts and fillies, and the oaks just for fillies. Both are run over the 'classic distance' of a mile and a half, 2400 or 2500 metres.

In the autumn, the program is similar. In Melbourne it starts with the William Reid Stakes over 1200 metres at Moonee Valley, then goes through the C.F. Orr Stakes (1400 m, Caulfield), Futurity Stakes (1400 m, Caulfield), the Blamey Stakes (1600 m, Flemington), Carlyon Cup (2000 m, Caulfield) and the Australian Cup (2000 m, Flemington). The bigger carnival in autumn is Sydney, which climaxes around Easter with the Golden Slipper at Rosehill (over 1200 metres for two-year-olds), the AJC Derby (2400 m, three-year-olds, Randwick), the Doncaster Handicap (1600 m, Randwick) and the Sydney Cup (3200 m, Randwick). The major weight-for-age races culminate with the Rawson Stakes, over 2000 metres, and the H.E. Tancred Stakes, over 2400 metres, both at Rosehill.

In winter there is a carnival in Brisbane and another in Adelaide, and in summer it's all on in Perth. But the year's biggest carnivals are autumn in Sydney and spring in Melbourne.

Comic Court justified his reputation in the big spring races of 1949, finishing third in the Caulfield Cup, second in the W.S. Cox Plate (the weight-for-age 'championship' of Australia) and first in the L.K.S. Mackinnon Stakes, the weight-for-age 10-furlong race on the Saturday before the Melbourne Cup. But running as second favourite in the Cup, he came twentieth behind Foxzami.

DAD OFTEN TOLD ME, FROM HIS EXPERIENCE OUT IN CENTRAL Australia, that you learnt more about horses on outback stations than you ever did in a racing stable. When you worked in these places, he said, you could learn thirty years' worth in thirty days. I certainly found this at my next job, in Little Topar, where I went for a few months in the middle of 1950.

There was a man named Harris who lived near us in Glenelg. He was always raving about this property he owned between Broken Hill and Menindee, several hours' driving north-east of Adelaide. I thought I'd like to take a look at it, maybe stay for a month or two. Mr Harris said his son was up there running it and he'd be happy if I went up and offered my services.

Little Topar was the true Wild West. There were constant dust storms and the pub didn't have or need any doors because it was open twenty-four hours a day. When it rained, the trucks would stop and the hotelkeeper made all his money. He wouldn't feed the men anything, because he made more on the beer he sold. So they'd be drinking nonstop on empty stomachs. Men would fall out of the pub and jump on motorcycles together to go off shooting kangaroos. The fellow on the front would be riding, the one behind standing up with his gun poised. They'd hit a buried tree stump and in the jolt the shooter would shoot the rider in the head. It happened every week! You've never seen anything like it.

I'd leave the pub and cross the road to the gate to Little Topar station. From there it was several hours' walking to the farmhouse on my own, often in the dark or the pouring rain, but I'd do it just to get away from that pub and the madness going on there.

Harris's son was an enormous lump, about 6 foot 4 and 18 stone. The first thing I learnt about him was that he didn't work too hard. When I arrived there were eleven working wells and windmills. Within weeks there was only one. They'd once had 3000 sheep, but now they only had about 200.

One of my fondest memories of the place was the meat we ate. They killed their own livestock and butchered them in their cool room. There was a vestibule where you entered, between two wire doors. You had to stop there and kill the blow flies before they followed you through the second door into the cool room. Inside, the meat was hanging up.

The men sliced the outside meat off, in case it had fly eggs, and gave it to the dogs. Then, as the meat got older in the cool room, it got better. It was delicious beef and lamb – that was one reason why Harris's son was so big and heavy. He didn't work much, but he ate well. He also enjoyed spending time at the pub.

I learnt to crutch sheep – I couldn't shear them, but I could crutch 112 a day – and I also learnt more about horses. The muster on Little Topar took ten or twelve days, and the mulga hills were too rough to do the mustering on motorbikes. So they had a fellow come to break in some colts for the muster. He was a South African, very experienced, and went out to round up whatever wild horses were roaming the property. Two days later I could hear the drumming of their hooves from miles away. The dust whipped up and a great herd of wild horses came charging in.

I sprang up to help, and jumped onto one of the colts. It bucked about 10 feet in the air and took off, running 150 metres. And that was only a small one! Eventually they told me that the bigger, older ones were more manageable, and I found an eight-year-old that I could deal with. We went out for ten days, got all the sheep we could find in the mulga hills, and brought them in.

By this stage, though, the place was about to dry up. I thought I'd better get out of there before the last windmill broke down – plus, there was a Melbourne Cup coming up and I had a feeling Dad might take me on the big trip over.

BY THE SPRING OF 1950, THE GENERAL WISDOM ABOUT COMIC Court was that he was at his best up to 10 or 12 furlongs (2000 to 2400 metres), but not the 2 miles, or 16 furlongs, of the Melbourne Cup. He'd missed the placings in the Cup twice as one of the favourites, and when that happens everyone seeks an explanation. His breeding was held against him; Powerscourt and Witty Maid were both sprinters, and weren't seen as a pairing that could produce horses that handled the gruelling distance of a Melbourne Cup. Their other progeny, St Comedy and Comedy Prince, performed well over shorter distances, which only served to entrench the scepticism about Comic Court running 2 miles.

But Dad had never given up on anything, and he wasn't going to let this horse, the best he'd ever trained, finish his career without throwing everything he had at the Melbourne Cup.

I believed in the horse too. As Dad's strapper now, I got to ride Comic Court between his workouts and he was a beautiful, easy, long-striding horse with a rich brown coat, the first horse of that quality I'd ever sat on.

Comic Court's lead-up in the spring of 1950 wasn't ideal. He tore a muscle in his chest at the start of his campaign. But once he was right, he was the old Comic Court: he won the Memsie, Turnbull and Caulfield stakes, was unplaced in the Caulfield Cup but won the Mackinnon again.

This time, however, he wasn't going to be a Melbourne Cup favourite. The punters had overreacted the other way: to our astonishment, Comic Court was at 33/1 for the Melbourne Cup, firming only to 25/1 as the race approached. He was carrying 9½ stone, or 59.5 kilos, and apparently his 1948 and

1949 unplaced runs had told the punters all they needed to know.

The day before the Melbourne Cup, the most crucial sequence of events played out. Comic Court's usual rider was Jack Purtell, one of the champion jockeys of the day. Purtell liked to assert himself over horses. Comic Court was a bold strider and Purtell fought against him to settle him down. However, instead of relaxing him, the battle between horse and rider only sapped the horse. Comic Court was good enough to overcome this in shorter races, but the effects of the battle told in the latter stages of a Melbourne Cup.

After one of Comic Court's races, Purtell came back and I noticed that his hands were bleeding. I said, 'What happened?'

'The horse pulled so hard it cut my hands,' Purtell said.

From that moment we had our doubts about matching Purtell with such a free-running horse as Comic Court.

In a twist of fate, the matter was taken out of our hands. The best three-year-old of that spring was Alister, who won the Cox Plate and the Victoria Derby under Purtell. When its owners decided to run Alister in the Melbourne Cup, Purtell asked the Lees if they would release him to ride the glamour horse rather than Comic Court.

We only had two days to come up with an alternative rider. Pat Glennon, one of the more underrated jockeys, was without a mount. Glennon was the opposite to Purtell. Once, when Glennon was riding track work for us at Morphettville, we instructed him to take the horse easily over 2 furlongs, then put it on the bit for another 3. As it turned out, the horse flew, and ran a tick over 1 minute for the 5 furlongs – as fast as a race.

When Glennon came back in, I said, 'What did you go so hard for?'

He said, 'Well, son, it's no good us both fighting, so I let him go.'

Glennon was that sort of fellow – happy-go-lucky with fine, sensitive hands. Later he went to Europe and won the Prix de l'Arc de Triomphe and English Derby, among many feature races, though – possibly because of his laidback manner – he never got the credit he deserved.

Dad recommended Glennon to the Lees, and on the first Monday of November, Melbourne Cup eve, they agreed to engage him for Comic Court.

I had many responsibilities as the great horse's strapper, and was enjoying the big-city atmosphere of Melbourne. But I was probably underqualified for my main job the night before the Melbourne Cup, which was to look after Glennon.

Dad said, 'Keep an eye on him, he can be a bit of a night owl.'

Talk about understatements. The night before the Cup, Glennon was out until two-thirty, going to some wild joints in St Kilda the likes of which I didn't even know existed. Talk about trouble – I'd have needed a lasso to get him out of these places. I ended up loading him onto a milk cart heading up St Kilda Road.

I was so excited about the Cup that the late night didn't bother me, and I was up at dawn to take Comic Court through his usual routine at Flemington. The stables were just behind the racecourse, and I got on the horse to ride him to the track where he had a light run, then took him out the Hill Stand gate to the stripping sheds, where I hosed him down and fed him. He cleaned up his tucker, and I came back and gave him two more dippers of oats. Then, as the afternoon race time approached, I put on his saddlecloth, bridle and saddle – always leaving the girth strap only three-quarters tight until the last moment when the jockey got on – then walked him to the 'birdcage' and waited for Glennon. Dad checked the horse out and gave Glennon his instructions, which were probably to let him run and not fight him.

Walking Comic Court around the ring, I felt the buzz of the 80,000 crowd but wasn't nervous about the horse's prospects. I just felt, 'What will be will be.' This is my temperament, but I would find that it also helped. My approach, if I can call it that, is to let the pressure get to everyone else. The calmer the handlers are, the calmer the horse. Just as a dog is a reflection of its master, a horse is a reflection of its trainer – and its strapper!

I tightened the girth strap and helped Glennon onto the horse, then went up into the stand overlooking the long Flemington straight, taking up a position three-quarters of a furlong from the winning post. With such a long straight, wide open spaces and sweeping turns, I think Flemington is one of the best-designed racetracks in the world. I stood with my young friend Tommy Hughes, who was working for a trainer named Theo Lewis at a stable opposite ours. Tommy and I knocked around together when I was in Melbourne, and had some good times. He lived in a boarding house beside the stables owned by a well-known trotting driver and trainer called Shinn. One day, Mr Shinn had asked me if I'd ever driven a trotter. I said, 'No, but I'll give anything a go.' On the Sunday afternoon during the Melbourne Show, Mr Shinn put me on a trotter and I did two or three laps of the track – an interesting experience, but one that I was never to repeat. Mr Shinn, by the way, was a member of a family who would reappear in my story nearly sixty years later, through the jockey Blake Shinn, who at the age of twenty-one would ride my twelfth Melbourne Cup winner. The racing world can seem like a small one.

So there I was with Tommy Hughes, watching Comic Court in the Cup. (Twenty-nine years later, Tommy and I would be facing off in another Melbourne Cup under very different circumstances, as trainers of the horses fighting out the closest-ever finish. But we'll get to that in due course.) I'd be lying if I said I wasn't tingling a little, but nor was I overcome with nerves. I just trusted in luck, Glennon and the horse.

Comic Court sat in the front half of the pack for the first mile, but then, 1400 metres from the end, Glennon did as he was told and let him go. Along the back of the course, Comic Court surged to the front. Rounding the turn, he bowled along ahead of the pack. Glennon certainly didn't cut his hands fighting him. The other jockeys were all maintaining position, watching each other. They would have been expecting Comic Court to fall back – he wasn't the main danger.

But he was. He just kept going away from them, and in the end he won by three lengths from the top mare, Chicquita. Although he was an outsider at 25/1, he was such a popular horse that the crowd stood and cheered him all the way in.

I was in a bit of a dream until Tommy gave me a nudge and said, 'Go on, you've got to lead him in.'

I hurtled down the steps, three or four at a time, and led Comic Court and Glennon back to the birdcage where the Lees and my father took over for the presentation. It all began to sink in. Comic Court had run the race in 3 minutes 19.5 seconds, a second and a half faster than the race record set by Rimfire in 1948. More astonishingly, Comic Court's last 6 furlongs, run in 1 minute 12.5 seconds, were faster than a sprinter, Commentator, ran to win the feature straight-six race the same day. It was not only Dad's proudest moment as a trainer, but one of the greatest Melbourne Cup performances before or since, especially considering the heavy weight Comic Court was carrying. Not that I'm biased or anything, but he was a truly wonderful horse.

The Lees won the first prize of £9050, of which Dad would have got his trainer's commission of 10 percent. To put that into perspective, £150 would have bought a standard three-bedroom house in Adelaide in those days. Unfortunately there was no sling for a strapper, though I had placed about £10 on Comic Court with the bookies, so at 25/1 or 33/1 – I can't remember the exact odds when I'd laid my bet – I'd done all right.

Alister, meanwhile, had finished sixth. As the horses eased up, Jack Purtell was asking the other riders who had won. Apparently he nearly fell out of his saddle when told it was Comic Court.

Glennon, Dad and the Lees had a fine night out at Wirth's Circus in Melbourne, where the Cup winner's connections were traditionally given a big dinner. With all the excitement, I must have been in a bit of a tizz by then, because I remember being unable to find the entrance to the circus tent and running around like a crazed man outside. I was pulled up by a large tent peg outside the big top that went up my trouser leg and tore it down the side. I've never been to a circus since, and soon after they moved the post-Melbourne Cup dinner to a much safer venue, a hotel in the city centre. In any case, it would be fifteen years before I was invited to one again.

5
Out of the shadows

SPURRED BY HIS SUCCESS, DAD BEGAN TO SPEND MORE TIME IN
Melbourne, where the racing scene was more lucrative than in
Adelaide. This gave me the opportunity to take more responsibility for the day-to-day running of the stables back at home.
There were twelve boxes and four or five staff, and I had to
learn quick. Mum was there in the background, keeping an
eye on things but, as always, giving me as much independence
as possible.

One of the great privileges of my job was looking after Comic Court. I rode the horses in their slow work down at the beach. The track jockeys rode them on the track at Morphettville, and then I'd ride them home again.

In April 1948 there had been a commemorative event when the entire Australian naval fleet anchored off Glenelg Beach. They were hit by a category 2 cyclone, 120-mile-per-hour winds, which developed very quickly and blew the roof off the Glenelg Town Hall. At the time, most of the navy sailors were having a party on shore. One of the boats, a frigate called HMAS *Barcoo*, finished up on West Beach. It was stuck there for weeks before a channel was dug and it was tugged back out. I clearly remember having to trot Comic Court up into the sandhills to get around the frigate's beached hull. The sailors would sing out to me from the boat, wanting to know who the horse was and if I had a tip for them. I imagine how surprised they'd be to know that the horse they watched trot by every morning went on to win the Melbourne Cup.

Dad always stressed the virtues of training horses on the beach on slow work mornings, something that has gradually gone out of the racing game, to its detriment in my opinion. Dad told me the story of Bitalli, a horse the great Jim Scobie had trained back in the 1920s. Bitalli had finished in the placings in the Adelaide Cup, and Scobie took him to Melbourne to put him into training for the Melbourne Cup. In a break with all orthodoxy, he didn't race the horse at all. He only galloped it on the sand track at Flemington, which was made up of coarse river sand from the Maribyrnong River. If it was properly rolled and maintained, a river sand track was second to none for exercising horses. With a few inches of rain, when the turf tracks became too heavy to use, the sand expanded and formed a firm training track with a bit of 'give' in it that worked the horse's muscles, joints and ligaments hard without threatening to injure them. Bitalli, purely by dint of non-race galloping on the river sand track, was fit enough to be backed into favouritism for the Melbourne Cup. Sure enough, he won at odds of 5/2.

They had more commonsense a hundred years ago than they have today. I used river sand tracks extensively when I was first training, but gradually they were phased out. The sand track at Flemington has been replaced by a car park. I believe this was done for two different commercial reasons. One is that river sand is not a money-maker for the big concerns. Unlike artificial surfaces, there's no rort with river sand. It's just a natural product. It may be the best product aside from grass, but the racing clubs aren't interested in it because nobody's pushing it as a profit-making venture.

The other reason they replaced it at Flemington was that during the spring carnival, the 'nursery' area became more and more popular with a certain type of racegoer. These are the people who come to the carnival in their Rolls-Royces to have a great day and set up their picnic tables. They enjoy themselves to the hilt without knowing much at all about what's happening on the race track. Yes, sometimes they will wander off and have a bet, but really they're coming to enjoy their day out. There's even been a tote set up for them so they don't have to roam too far from their picnics. I have nothing against that, except that the area set aside for them was expanded over the years into the area where we'd had the sand track, which was subsequently removed.

Yet again, the sport and the horses suffered at the expense of competing interests. I complained when they tore up the sand track, but I was only a small-fry trainer back then and the VRC didn't listen. In fact, when I became a bigger-fry trainer they didn't listen much either!

Comic Court developed his strength and speed throughout his career by training on sand, whether on the course or at the beach. It enhanced his versatility to the point where, when he came back from his post-Cup spell, he put on one of the greatest performances I've ever seen. It was in the William Reid Stakes, a 6-furlong dash at Moonee Valley. You couldn't imagine a less suitable race for a hardened stayer like him. The track is tight-turning and the straight is very short, a little less than a furlong. At the home turn he was last, and the leader, Dornoch, had dashed two lengths clear. Comic Court got out of the ruck, and in the length of that straight he overtook the whole field and ran a race record. It was only over time, when I realised how rare was the feat of coming back from a Melbourne Cup to beat sprinters, that I came to appreciate how good he was.

He raced for another two seasons, staging a great ongoing rivalry with the mare Chicquita. In all, they ran against each other eight times. Six times Comic Court won the race with Chicquita finishing second. The other two times they were both unplaced. There must have been a special chemistry between them, because when Comic Court went to stud Chicquita was sent to him, and they produced Comicquita, a handsome black colt who went on to finish second in the 1962 Melbourne Cup.

Comic Court retired with more than £41,000 in stakes

winnings, fifth on the all-time list behind Shannon, Phar Lap, Amounis and Gloaming. He was that good. He was one of nine foals Witty Maid produced to Powerscourt, and between them they won seventy-one races in Australia. Dad must have looked back to those despairing years during the war, when he couldn't train and had to slog away in the armaments factory, and figured he'd got something totally right.

DAD AND MUM HAD NEVER – AND I MEAN *NEVER* – TAKEN A DECENT holiday. In 1953, with Comic Court retired, Dad was sixty-seven years old and must have reckoned if he didn't take a break then, he never would. He and Mum went to Ireland for a planned six-week holiday, and stayed for six months.

He'd left me to look after the Adelaide and Melbourne stables, in my capacity as his assistant. But as the weeks turned into months, the South Australian stewards told us that I would soon exceed the time limit as a stand-in trainer, and had to apply for a licence in my own right or let the horses go to a licensed trainer. Mum and Dad were travelling in Europe as well as Ireland, and were clearly having too good a time to rush back. So this was how I became a licensed trainer on 29 May 1953 – more or less by accident. It certainly wasn't by design. As I've said, my ambitions were fully satisfied by working for Dad. And when I got my licence, all I did was continue the methods Dad had taught me. When you're on a good thing, stick to it. So I did as Dad did: bought all our own feed and mixed it myself, cared for the horses as if they were humans, kept a close eye on their track work, and programmed their racing campaigns sensibly. As a trainer, I wanted to make the transition for our owners as seamless as possible so they wouldn't take any of our horses away from such an inexperienced young man. We had no phone, so I couldn't call Dad for advice whenever I was in doubt. I'd always been a close observer and listener, so I just tried to do what Dad would have done. It turned out that by the time he came back we even had a few more horses than when he'd left.

THAT SAME YEAR, 1953, I WAS GOING TO CHURCH SOCIALS ON Saturday nights. This was pretty much the full extent of my social life, and I enjoyed the break from my responsibilities. The dances were mostly progressive ones, such as the Canadian barn dance, where you moved around the room from one partner to another.

There was one young lady I took a shine to, but I must have been a little hay-feverish because I kept forgetting her name. Whenever I came back to her in the Canadian barn dance, I'd say, 'Who are you?'

And she'd say, smart as a whip: 'You asked that last time.'

I found out her name was Valmae Baker. Her father was Jack 'Doughie' Baker, a well-known Australian Rules footballer in the district. He wasn't actually a baker; he drove a truck. But they called him Doughie because, well, that was the fate of every Baker.

Valmae worked for a stockbroker in Adelaide, and I took to dropping in on her from time to time. She even had some dealings with Sir Donald Bradman, who was said to be a better cricketer than he was a stockbroker. I remember meeting Valmae once at the gas company office, where she was paying her boss's bills. I think we were both playing hard to get, and a lot of our conversation was good-humoured wise-cracking. Eventually I started asking her out. I'd never been out with another girl, and I figured I'd struck it lucky the first time. When I asked her to marry me, to my great surprise she agreed, and we tied the knot at the Holy Cross Catholic Church in Goodwood, a low-key affair with my brother Patrick as best man.

DAD AND MUM HAD RETURNED FROM IRELAND BEFORE THE wedding, of course, and in recognition of my status as a full-fledged trainer Dad gave me the bottom set of his Glenelg stables and a couple of horses, including his Port Adelaide Cup winner, Welloch.

He built eight more boxes up the top end, I built a further six, with yards and roofs, and before long our twelve-box facility had turned into thirty-five boxes with two trainers, a big complex by Adelaide standards. Later, we expanded it still further by buying neighbouring stables from Matt and Bill Raven, and then leasing Harry Butler's establishment in Alison Street.

But that was still ahead of us. In 1954 and 1955, I was just desperate to train a winner. Those two years passed without me training one single race winner. I have never forgotten how hard that was, and what a test of my persistence. With a new wife to look after, I also had to build us a nest. We rented some rooms in a house in Brighton Road, Glenelg, within walking distance of the stables. Dad also had a house which he'd put in my name, and I was able to sell it and then buy a quarter-acre block of land over the road from the stables, on Russell Street. In 1955 we built a stone-and-tile bungalow. At first it had only three bedrooms, but in the ensuing years, as our family grew (and grew and grew), we kept adding on bedrooms and a billiard room and widening the house until it was big enough to hold our family of seven. We would live there until 1976.

My first city winner was a horse called Wells, in the 6-furlong Devon Transition Handicap at Morphettville on 12 February 1955. Finally! It had been a while coming, and I don't remember feeling any great joy or exhilaration, just relief. It was then, as with every race win since, mainly relief.

Dad was continuing to win big races, including the 1953 Goodwood Handicap, South Australia's top sprint race, with First Scout, the 1955 Adelaide Cup with Storm Glow, and the 1956 South Australian Derby with Auteuil, whom he had named after visiting the Auteuil racetrack in France in 1953. I was still learning to crawl before I could walk, and it's just as well I was born patient, because I went through those years with a small team and no feature-race winners. It was a long struggle with little success. But I kept my horses in the weakest company and myself in the best company, a good formula for life, and continued to hope for better times.

IN MANY WAYS, 1958 WOULD PROVE A WATERSHED YEAR FOR ME. Valmae and I had three babies now, Margaret, Anthony and

Sharon, and life was extremely busy, with Valmae pitching in to wash the racing silks and help out with other stable-related jobs – such as the nominations for races and much of the other paperwork – in between running around after the kids. My mother, as well as Valmae's, would come in quite often to lend their support. In our office we were a two-person operation, just myself and Valmae, as it was some years before we could afford to take on anybody other than the most essential stable staff.

I needed to start training some significant winners. In 1958 I made my first Tasman crossing to visit the New Zealand studs to spot some yearlings. Dad had always said that the ultimate achievement in racing would be to start with a very young horse, say a yearling, or even breed it yourself, and take it through the several years of preparation needed to ready it for a Melbourne Cup, and then win one. That was certainly my dream, and having touched the Melbourne Cup with Comic Court I was quietly determined to do it myself. Going to New Zealand was a first step in that grand scheme.

In 1958 I finally won my first feature race, with Stormy Passage in the South Australian Derby. He knocked off the odds-on favourite in the race, the top staying classic for three-year-olds in the state, and the significance of the win didn't escape me. Over thirty-one years, Dad had trained three Derby winners: Ethelon in 1925, Opera King in 1931 and Auteuil in 1956. I didn't want to compare my achievements to Dad's, but other people would, and I certainly didn't want to appear to let the family name down.

Also in 1958, I trained my first runner in the Melbourne Cup. His name was Asian Court, and he was owned by the

Lee brothers. After winning the Werribee Cup he finished twelfth behind Baystone in the Melbourne Cup. He simply didn't stay the 2 miles, but he is probably a pretty good answer to a trivia question somewhere.

I WASN'T ONLY APPLYING DAD'S METHODS NOW; I WAS EXTENDING them and trying to keep up with the latest technology. I studied pedigrees, diets and pathology. It was a new thing at the time to focus on the horse's blood to give you clues on when to work it and when not to, how to feed it, and what was wrong with it. I met the veterinarian Percy Sykes, a recent arrival from England, when he went down to Melbourne with Tommy Smith, and we discussed high-protein feeds and pathology. Soon I was taking my own blood samples from the horses and sending them up to Percy in Sydney. I'd get up at five o'clock in the morning, take the samples to the airport myself, put them on a plane and wait eagerly for Percy to phone through the results. If you knew what was happening in a horse's blood, you could correct deficiencies through diet, medication and training. If horses had worms, which was a common ailment, blood tests would tell you early on and you could put the horse through a worming routine.

Another vet, Sykes Geschmey, was a great help in this line. During the 1914–18 War, he had controlled 1000 cavalry horses for the Austro-Hungarian army. But when the war went badly for his side, he escaped with his wife on a motorbike and sidecar, riding across the lines all the way to the west, and ended up in Australia as a migrant. He bought a property in

Hutt Street, Adelaide, and did very well financially as a small-animal vet before coming to offer us his expertise.

I remember him saving the life of one of Dad's horses who had worms. This horse, who was expensively insured, was nearly dead. Worms can paralyse a horse by blocking the blood flow from the spinal cord to the hind legs. There was a medication called phenothiazine, and while it killed the worms it also affected the horse's performance. Mr Geschmey had his own treatment, managing the worm-affected horse much more gradually with diet and limited medication, and over two months he got the blood flowing and nursed that particular horse to health, not only saving its life but bringing it back to racing.

Pathology, better diets, and careful study of pedigree were some of the methods I was refining. I believe I was ahead of the pack in South Australia. Another new tool of the trade was blinkers, which had been used in the United States for some time. Blinkers are a kind of mask that is fitted over the horse's head, with little half-cups on the sides of the eyeholes. I read books about what was happening in America, and there had been some very successful gallopers wearing one-eyed blinkers. A horse won't go where it can't see, so if a horse has a habit of hanging out to one side, you put the blinker on that side of its face. Or, if the horse is wayward on both sides, you put the blinkers on both eyes to cut down its peripheral vision. Blinkers were made legal in Australia in 1961. But sometimes, as I would soon find out, you can be too far ahead of the pack.

THE 1950S AND 1960S WERE A GOOD TIME TO GET INVOLVED IN horse racing. Prize money was beginning to boom, thanks in large part to the vision of the head of the Victoria Racing Club (VRC), Sir Chester Manifold. A successful agricultural businessman, he encouraged the formation of off-course totalisator betting. One by one, the states established their own Totalisator Agency Boards (TABs), which brought the excitement of racing to millions of people who couldn't get to the track. In one fell swoop, he put the illegal off-course bookmaking industry on the ropes. He took on the politicians who had been bribed by bookies' money, and won.

Bookmakers don't give enough back. Bookmakers buy fur coats for their wives and take them on holidays. And that is just the legally licensed ones. A TAB is a machine that returns a percentage of its turnover to the racing clubs, who were represented on the TAB boards. The TAB system was a clever symbiotic relationship, where the sport and the gamblers supported each other. The state benefited, too, through regulated taxation. I believe they should erect a statue to Sir Chester Manifold. His legacy stood for forty years, until short-sighted governments decided to privatise TABs and legalise corporate bookmakers, setting off a chain reaction that could, in our time, damage the sport beyond repair.

I was beginning to rack up some winners of important races. In 1959 Trellios won the Underwood Stakes at Caulfield, a big weight-for-age lead-up to the spring cups. It gives a trainer extra cachet to train a weight-for-age winner, because you're not getting any help from the handicapper. You've simply trained the best horse on the day, and Trellios upset Lord, regarded as one of the classiest weight-for-age gallopers in the country.

New Zealand kept drawing me in each January with its magnetism of hope, and when I saw the Le Filou–Cuddlesome colt on my 1960 visit I snapped him up for Wally Broderick. The nicest-looking yearling colt at the sales was by the top stallion Summertime out of Nereid, and I bought him as well, for 2300 guineas, for the Lee brothers.

The first colt would race as The Dip, and the second as Sometime. I brought both of them along patiently, feeling they had great potential. For the first time I was really excited about the quality of what I'd bought. Sometime started racing in April 1961, and won three races in a row that winter as a two-year-old. He was a gross feeder and needed plenty of work and racing to keep his weight down, and I was looking forward to bringing him and The Dip up for the big three-year-old classics in 1961–62.

Sometime seemed set to fulfil my hopes that spring. He won some minor races and then finished second in the Caulfield Guineas, fourth in the Caulfield Cup, third in the Victoria Derby and sixth in the Melbourne Cup. He went agonisingly close to winning at least one of those big races, but I was sure he would be even better the next year.

I never got the chance to find out, though.

On 25 November 1961, I had a two-year-old colt running at Morphettville. Cilldara had failed badly on his previous start at Gawler, only a few days before. Then, at Morphettville, he won running away.

Also in the field was a horse trained by Colin Hayes and owned by one of the richest men in the game, Wyndham 'Windy' Hill Smith, the head of Yalumba Wines. He was chairman of the Port Adelaide Racing Club, and had the Governor of

South Australia as one of the guests in his box that day. Colin Hayes had become the trainer of choice for the old-school Adelaide establishment, and would develop over time as one of my biggest rivals in the state and across Australia. Their horse was the 6/4 favourite, and Cilldara, which had opened in the betting at 33/1, had closed in to 7/2. When Cilldara won, Hill Smith's pride was wounded in front of his important friends. He ran down the steps, collared the head steward, and said, 'If you don't have that horse [Cilldara] disqualified, I'll have you replaced!'

The stewards called me in for an inquiry. It was true that Cilldara had improved suddenly, but I had a perfectly above-board answer: blinkers. Cilldara was 'field-shy', or uncomfortable racing in a pack of thoroughbreds. I put blinkers on him to limit his awareness of the other horses and focus him on running. This was his first start with the new gear, and it worked!

The problem was, blinkers had only been made legal a month before, and few people were convinced that they had the power to improve certain horses' performances so suddenly. In hindsight I should have listened to Dan Moriarty, the clocker, who'd told me that even if what I was doing with Cilldara was legal, I should wait another week before racing him, allowing more time to pass since the Gawler race, because then if he won the stewards wouldn't necessarily hold an inquiry – his improvement wouldn't seem so instantaneous.

I said, 'Why would I do that? I'm not doing anything wrong.'

So I ran him. What I didn't take account of was the politics of powerful men and the impact of the betting plunge on their egos.

The stewards simply wouldn't accept my explanation. They wouldn't even take Percy Sykes's word for it, when he flew down for my appeal hearing. In retrospect, as we all know now, this was a crazy and incorrect decision. Blinkers quickly became an accepted method for focusing field-shy gallopers and have often had an immediate effect. But not in November 1961. I was hit with a devastating twelve-month ban from training.

It was a bitter pill. The Lee brothers took Sometime out of my stable and gave him to Les Patterson to train. Two years later he would win the Caulfield Cup.

I couldn't let my whole establishment disintegrate, and was blessed by good fortune when Dad came out of retirement at the age of seventy-six to train the horses. He didn't mind – in fact he seemed quite chuffed to be involved again. The next spring he trained The Dip to win the Metropolitan at Randwick and the Turnbull Stakes at Flemington, as well as a close-up fifth behind Even Stevens in the Melbourne Cup. Not bad going for a retiree.

But I wasn't allowed to have any input into training or attend any race meetings. I busied myself with general work in the Adelaide stables. I painted and repaired the boxes, planted trees, weeded the garden beds, and brought the facility up to as high a standard as I could make it. I helped Valmae as far as I could with the children, and didn't let myself fall into bad habits or impatience. With Dad doing such a good job, I didn't need to panic about all our owners taking the horses away.

And there was nothing in my suspension saying I couldn't go to New Zealand.

6

'Mother'

As a sire, Le Filou would turn into what Zabeel is today: the progenitor of champions over all distances from 5 furlongs to 2 miles. When I first inspected his offspring, few buyers had heard of him. But by 1962, on my fifth visit to New Zealand, the world was waking up to Le Filou's potential thanks to the performance of The Dip and others, a fact the breeders Molly and Fred Dawson were fully aware of.

When I went over there in January 1963, there was no

chance the Dawsons were going to sell The Dip's sister, the
skinny chestnut filly by Cuddlesome. But whether you own
or lease a horse, if she can run you will still want to race her;
Wally Broderick was very keen, and when I brought her back
to Adelaide I set about planning her career. Her name, Close
Embrace, was deemed a little too saucy by Australian racing
authorities, so we had to think of something new. As 'Le Filou'
means 'pickpocket' in French, and we'd named her big brother
The Dip, it was natural to follow the theme. We called her
Light Fingers.

Because she was small, I couldn't see any point in rushing
her. Her flanks felt so slight, I imagined that if I cupped my
two hands around them my fingers would meet. The only two-
year-olds worth setting for the big juvenile races are the early
developers, and Light Fingers certainly wasn't that.

After The Dip's fifth in the 1962 Melbourne Cup, I was
training again. The stewards clipped a month off my twelve-
month suspension due to 'good behaviour', a term full of irony
seeing I had never behaved badly in the first place. But if I was
a horse I'd have been champing at the bit for Dad to hand the
operation back to me, and soon I had The Dip in training for
an autumn campaign in which he won four races, culminating
in the AJC St Leger Stakes over 2800 metres at Randwick.

Meanwhile, in Adelaide, his little sister was filling out
nicely. When you bring a young horse into the stable, you only
have a few months when they're still growing and you can
watch their improvement. It's a time of great anticipation: how
will the horse fill out? As we fed her and trained her during
those six months, she went on improving, improving, improving. She wasn't growing much taller but she had that huge

heart and athletic action that I'd admired so much when I saw her galloping in the paddock at Te Awamutu.

When she came into the stables, I followed our typical program for a young horse. I started galloping her in pace work – just light gallops – then giving her 3 furlongs, or 600 metres, in 'even time', which is 15 seconds per furlong. She coped with that well, so I upped it to 4 furlongs in even time. She would work like this for eight weeks before her first barrier trial, a 'practice' race against other horses, most likely youngsters learning to race or more experienced horses returning from a spell. As the name suggests, these trials are also designed to help horses get used to standing in a barrier and waiting for the gates to spring. Some horses behave terribly in barriers and ruin their chances of winning, so the more schooling you can give them the better. Within four weeks of her first barrier trial, she would have a couple more trials before she was ready for the real thing.

I set her for the Lipson Handicap, a maiden race for fillies over 5 furlongs at Cheltenham, on Boxing Day 1963. I thought she was ready to win first up, and told Wally Broderick. He was already very excited about her prospects after our success with her big brother, and wanted Pat Glennon to ride her. But Glennon was on another horse, La Mariese, so we engaged Bob Cox. She looked like she was going to win until Bob hit her with the whip, maybe the first time this had ever happened to her. She dived in sharply with the shock and Pat Glennon's horse came home to beat her by a short half-head, the smallest margin in racing. (In decreasing order of narrowness, the smallest winning margins are a neck, a head, a half-head and a short half-head.)

With light-framed horses, you can't push them too hard. Dad had taught me that when you have a light horse and it's had a tough first-up race, you should rest it for at least three weeks before its next start. Go particularly easy with such horses, and don't give them close-spaced races until they're fully fit later in their preparation.

It was a month before Light Fingers' second start, again over 5 furlongs. We had Glennon on her this time, and she won. He told us she needed more distance. He said she would stay all day and had tried as hard as any horse he'd ever ridden, but that she needed a longer race to give her time to get settled. Two-year-old sprints are hurly-burly affairs, and Light Fingers was clearly a racehorse who needed patience.

Bob Cox rode her well, without using the whip, to a win over 7 furlongs at Cheltenham at her next start, and we took her to Melbourne for the autumn carnival. When she beat a strong field over 6 furlongs at Flemington, I'd seen enough. She was a horse who would be ideal for the fillies' three-year-old classics, the oaks races in the next spring. If I kept racing her against two-year-olds in the autumn I risked burning her out. So off she went for a rest.

In the spring of 1964, she raced seven times, won five and came second twice. Patience always pays, I've found. She won her first start, in Adelaide, then went over to Melbourne. Pat Glennon had gone to Europe for his successful riding career there, and we engaged a young fellow named Roy Higgins to ride her.

Higgins came from Deniliquin, over the border in New South Wales, and in the early part of his career he hadn't wanted to leave the Riverina. He rode for a trainer named Jim

Watters and had a prodigious record. He also liked the quiet lifestyle there. But he was too good to stay in the small-time, and by about 1962 the pull of Melbourne, and the chance of earning the respect of other jockeys and top trainers, was too strong. Also, there was the chance to ride better horses. If you are a good driver and someone is asking you to race their Ferrari, why would you stay in your old bomb?

I had engaged Higgins once before, to ride a horse of mine called Native Statesman. He was beaten as a favourite, and Higgins, by his own admission, didn't ride at his best. I appreciated his honesty, but sacked him nonetheless.

He kept riding winners for other trainers, however, and Wally Broderick asked Higgins if he'd like to join our team as a regular rider. After that earlier hiccup, he and I got on well. I've always kept my distance from jockeys, as it is an employer–contractor relationship and you don't want to muddy the waters by getting too friendly. But I got on as well with Roy as I have with any jockey. He listened to what I said and did what I told him – the first rule of success, in my book – but he also had what few jockeys have: intuition and awareness. By that I mean he didn't just put his head down and ride like he had blinkers on. He was aware of the way the whole field was racing, the way it took shape as a race went on, and because of that he seemed to sense something was going to happen just before it did. Due to his powers of perception, he was usually in the right place at the right time. The value of that is obvious. If the rider feels that a horse up ahead is starting to tire, it's going to have a domino effect on the field. Even if the tiring one is three or four horses ahead of him, when it drops back it might affect him most of all. So if he knows what's going on, he can steer his way out of trouble before it actually happens. That was what Higgins had, more than other jockeys: that extra split-second in which to avoid any building mess. Some jockeys can't see further than their own nose. Higgins had a clear head and wide peripheral vision. Perception is a rarer quality than balance or power or any of the other talents a jockey may have. They can all ride, but very few of them can think. In that regard, Higgins was at the top of his profession.

Just as with horses, you can tell a lot about a jockey by looking into his eyes. This is something Dad taught me and it's a lesson I've always applied. You need to look deep into their eyes until you see their spirit. If they have that will to win and the brains to achieve it, they're the ones you want to work with.

Higgins rode Light Fingers in track work in Melbourne for a week, and told me she felt more like a six-year-old mare than a three-year-old filly. She was level-headed and intelligent, never fussed or nervous about things going on around her. Higgins nicknamed her 'Mother' because she was so mature she would mother some of the other young horses in the stables, and she was so tractable he used her as a lead pony for older horses who were meant to be wiser.

She only had one quirk: for her own reasons, she hated grey horses. She even went out of her way to bite a clerk of the course's pony, who was the traditional grey, when she was leading the field out. It just shows that every horse, from the friskiest to the most placid, has its own personality and its own passions.

Roy Higgins' first ride on Light Fingers was over 6 furlongs at Moonee Valley in September 1964. She started a very short-priced favourite . . . and lost. It turned out not to be Higgins' fault, or the horse's. Her saddle had slipped as she came out of the gate and he'd been riding her from back on her hindquarters, with a reasonably heavy weight, for the entire race. Although she lost by a neck, Higgins said she should have won by a hundred yards and told us that whenever she raced in future, he wanted to be on her – as long as the saddle was properly fixed. Apparently, out of all the horses he would ride in his four-decade career, Light Fingers remained his favourite. He rode 108 Group One winners, including two Melbourne Cups and champions like Gunsynd, Century and Manikato – but he loved none of them the way he loved Light Fingers.

Success helped! He rode her in the program I set of top three-year-old fillies' races that spring. She won the Edward Manifold Stakes at Flemington, came second in the One Thousand Guineas at Caulfield, won the Wakeful Stakes and then the big one, the VRC Oaks. At the end of her campaign we ran her against the colts in the Sandown Guineas and she won that too.

After a summer spell she ran third, third and fourth in three autumn sprints, then won the two big fillies' races of the Sydney carnival, the Princess Stakes and the AJC Oaks. I knew I had a good horse and possibly a great one, so I put her away for a nice solid spell in the winter. Fifteen years after Comic Court, I had a warm feeling about the Melbourne Cup again.

BUT JUST AS I WAS THINKING ABOUT THE POSSIBILITY OF EMULATING my father's achievement, we lost him. He was at home in

Adelaide in March 1965 when he suffered an attack of shortness of breath. There's nothing positive about the death of your father, but we could console ourselves that he didn't have to suffer through a long illness. He died quickly, in his own home, with his family around him. He was seventy-nine. At his funeral, which was well attended by people from within and outside the racing world, we were comforted to see how highly thought of he was.

One of his fellow Adelaide trainers, Tom Jenner (who prepared Pago Pago and Manihi among others), recalled how just a year before he had suffered a stroke in Melbourne and had been rushed to hospital. He said that as his family was in Adelaide, he didn't have any close relatives or friends in Melbourne, but the first person through his hospital room door was Jim Cummings, aged seventy-eight but still involved with racing. 'Jim and I weren't close friends,' he said. 'We had a chat on race days but that was all. You might say that we had a nodding acquaintance. But Jim knew I was in trouble. He was there to help. That's the sort of man he was. I never knew anyone who had a bad word to say about Jim Cummings. You just don't meet finer people.'

Nobody thought higher of him than I did – so highly that I modelled my entire life and career around his. To this day, even in my eighties, I see myself as a son applying his father's lessons and carrying on his father's work.

IN THE STABLES, LIGHT FINGERS WASN'T THE ONLY HORSE GIVING us a sense of anticipation about the spring. In January 1963

I'd bought a colt by Summertime, the sire of Sometime, at the New Zealand sales. This one was a big, handsome black colt and I sold him to Max Bailey, an Adelaide builder, and his wife Venice. They called him Ziema, and he began winning races as a three-year-old in the same year as Light Fingers. Different kind of horse, though! Where Light Fingers was as calm as a thoroughbred could be, Ziema was gross and muscular and a bit wild. He would carry on and buck and throw his rider at track work. Funnily enough, he would often only settle down when Light Fingers was brought along to lead him to the track.

Light Fingers spelled well, and won her first race as a four-year-old, a 5-furlong dash at Victoria Park. Of all the sprints, that is the most suitable for a staying horse, because the 1000 metres at Victoria Park is a straight race. Since there is no turn, the staying horse has room to wind up and come home as the others slow towards the end. So it happened with Light Fingers.

We took her over to Melbourne and she won the weight-for-age Craiglee Stakes over a mile, ahead of a top-class field including the champion Winfreux.

Then, a wobble. She caught a virus from somewhere, and when I saw that she was off her feed and running a temperature I could do nothing but rest her. I'm not one to 'crash through or crash', especially with a horse as genuine as Light Fingers. She never played mind games; when she was sick, she was sick. In the next three weeks we nursed her back to readiness for the Turnbull Stakes at weight-for-age at Flemington, and she came second, half-fit, to the top-liner Craftsman.

The run did her good, and she seemed to be over the sickness. In her next start, the Caulfield Stakes, she went out as favourite, but 800 metres from home she clipped Winfreux's heels and nearly fell. She was nothing if not a trier, though, and she kept hitting the line and finished third.

Sometimes a horse can try too hard for its own good, and the Caulfield Stakes effort had taken a lot out of Light Fingers. She pulled up sore with a ricked muscle in her neck and shoulder. Even trotting she threw her head about and whinnied in pain, so there was no question of running her in the Caulfield Cup a week later. Not only did this dash our hopes of winning that race – she was certainly good enough – but it threw her preparation for the Melbourne Cup into disarray. Could I get her fit enough to make the race? And even if I could, would she have enough hard galloping under her belt to give her the necessary stamina for the 2 miles? Good questions, but I had no way of forcing the issue. Her health came first. I couldn't gallop her until she was fit again. All I could do was walk her, let her swim in the Maribyrnong River behind the Flemington track, feed her well, and hope for the best. We'd walk her down the ramp into the river and row along beside her in our dinghy. Racing her wasn't a priority; we had to get her over her pain. You have to be fatalistic in racing. What would be, would be.

Fortunately for the stable, we had plenty to focus on. In Light Fingers' absence, Ziema should have won the Caulfield Cup, but he hit some heavy interference and came second to Bore Head. The next week he was unlucky again, running second in the Moonee Valley Cup. But he was rock-hard and ready for the Melbourne Cup. The Dip was running well too, so at least I had that pair in the big race. But I couldn't help feeling a little anxious; the little mare was, I believed, the best horse I'd ever trained, and it was looking like she wouldn't make the starting gate.

Seven days before the Melbourne Cup she was well enough to have a track gallop at Flemington. It was only a look-and-see, but Higgins reported that she had run easily and without pain. Still, we were cautious. One thing in her favour was that, as a lightly framed horse, she didn't need the kind of constant galloping and hard work that a heavier thoroughbred like Ziema required to keep him fit and trim. But still, her preparation was light-on at best.

Higgins was offered the ride on Matloch, the Cup favourite. He knocked it back because he couldn't bear the thought of Light Fingers running and someone else on her. At that point Matloch's trainer, George Hanlon, believed Light Fingers couldn't make the start. But Higgins loved Light Fingers so much, he was prepared to stick with her even if she might not run. He was taking a big risk, but it can be an admirable quality in a jockey if he has a bit of a gambler's spirit – up to a point!

By the Friday, four days before the Cup, we knew that track gallops alone weren't going to tell us if Light Fingers was capable of running in the big race. So on the Saturday she ran in the Mackinnon Stakes, over 10 furlongs, and finished a game third, three lengths behind Yangtze. This was good news and bad. Good, because she pulled up without showing any pain; bad, because although she'd tried hard she had finished well behind horses we regarded as her inferior. At the course, I was preoccupied with doubt – so preoccupied that I didn't notice the great hullabaloo on Derby day surrounding the English model Jean Shrimpton, who caused a stir wearing a very short minidress. I only had eyes for one female that day, and she wasn't a two-legged one.

So a Cup start was still up in the air. By the Monday morning, we still hadn't decided. I let Higgins canter her for a furlong or so, and she seemed all right. But Percy Sykes had run some blood tests and he said, 'Bart, you can't run her.' Her red blood cell count was down and Percy suspected that she was still feeling uncomfortable. He believed she had pain coming from her sacroiliac joint, possibly as a result of sciatica. Pain from the sciatic nerve is a common lurking danger with racehorses, and very often it explains why they run badly when you didn't think there was anything wrong with them. We decided to give ourselves until the last moment to make up our minds. In my view, I only had to listen to the horse: she would give me her answer.

At dawn on Cup morning, we gave her another jog over a furlong. Higgins said she was improving each day and would be at her best in two or three days. But we didn't have that long. We had to decide right then and there. Wally Broderick wasn't sure, but Higgins was adamant: Light Fingers was well enough, and fit enough, to run in the Cup. She wasn't at her best, no, but she deserved the opportunity. And – what he didn't need to say – Higgins deserved his opportunity too! Having given up the ride on Matloch, for Higgins it was either Light Fingers starting or him watching from the stands.

Finally, I gave her the nod – almost reluctantly and with nagging doubts. I said, 'Okay, she's running,' but even as I said it I didn't know for sure. She was such a mighty little mare, I didn't want the marathon of a Melbourne Cup to knock her about too much. There was always next year.

Reflecting our uncertainty, the punters shunned Light Fingers. Not only had she been hampered by the virus and the pulled muscle, but the handicapper was asking her to carry a massive 8 stone 4 pounds, or 52.5 kilograms. She did have a fine record, but I thought (not for the last time) that the VRC handicapper had gone too hard on our stable. In 104 years only eight female horses had won the Cup, and the heaviest weight a winning mare had carried was the 8 stone, or 51 kilos, Evening Peal had on her back in 1956 when she beat Redcraze. The handicapper was asking Light Fingers to prove she was the greatest mare ever to run in the Melbourne Cup. The punters and bookmakers didn't think she was, not on her limited preparation anyway, and she started at 15/1. Ziema, at 10/1, was one of seven horses above Light Fingers in the betting. It was a strong Melbourne Cup year, the field including Craftsman, the favourites Sail Away and Matloch, and the rising new weight-for-age star, Tobin Bronze.

Percy Sykes gave Light Fingers a cortisone injection in her sacroiliac, an admission that she was not fully fit. But with a Melbourne Cup, you never really know if a horse is fit until it runs. The Cup is its own ultimate fitness test.

That Cup was 2 miles of incessant jostling and bumping. Higgins had Light Fingers in the front half of the field, with the plan of following Ziema, who was ridden by the Perth jockey John Miller. As we knew how fit Ziema was, it seemed a good idea to trail him. He was the form horse in our stable, so Higgins wanted to stay in touch with him and have the last crack. Of course, for Miller the idea was to go ahead and wear Light Fingers out. They were both good plans. The Dip was running in the back half of the field, and it emerged over the first mile that he was no longer at his best.

About 1000 metres from home, Matloch clipped another runner's heels and went straight to the turf, bringing down Caulfield Cup winner Bore Head and River Seine, winner of the Sydney Cup earlier in the year, who were racing behind him. Unfortunately The Dip was held up by the melee and his already receding chances of being in the finish were spoilt.

But Higgins had Light Fingers ahead of the ruck, and he took her into the home turn in fifth place. Flemington has a very long and open straight, just over 2 furlongs, and often the key for a Melbourne Cup jockey is patience. Everything in his body – not to mention everyone in the stands – is screaming at him when he enters the straight to go full-tilt for home. But many a Melbourne Cup has been lost by a rider accelerating too soon. At the end of 2 miles, that straight feels like an eternity for a tiring horse.

Yangtze, Ziema and Tobin Bronze were the leading three. At 300 metres out, Miller took Ziema past Yangtze. Tobin Bronze faded. Yangtze faded. The only horse coming out to challenge Ziema was Light Fingers. I leapt to my feet as I saw Wally Broderick's silks, white with blue spots, emerge to take on the bigger horse.

It really was one of the most exciting Cup duels. Ziema, with Miller in the Baileys' red and gold hoops with black sleeves, held onto his lead. He dwarfed Light Fingers, but she was gaining on him with each stride . . . only a few inches at a time. The last 100 metres seemed to go in slow motion. I was on my feet in the stand as they went past us, three-quarters of a furlong from home. I can't say that because I had the only horses in contention I was calm, knowing I'd win either way. This is what horse racing is all about – great finishes at the end of a lung-bursting race – and I was sucked in by the excitement. Between two horses he's preparing, a trainer can't play favourites any more than if they were his own children. Ziema and Light Fingers were both horses I'd found as yearlings in New Zealand and trained all the way through to this moment. I respected both owners and both jockeys. But I suppose I did have a soft spot for the mare.

Half a furlong out, Ziema was still leading Light Fingers by three-quarters of a length. Higgins, knowing both horses so well, said he felt that Light Fingers had a psychological edge over Ziema, due to her greater maturity around the stable and on the track. Ziema was like a boisterous football-playing boy, while Light Fingers calmed him down with her natural, low-key authority. Higgins sensed that once Ziema felt Light Fingers by his side, the male horse might weaken. I don't know about that. As far as I could see, both horses were trying their hearts out. They both had an exceptional will to win, and now we were going to see whose was stronger. Light Fingers moved up to Ziema's girth, then his neck, but the winning post would be too close. All those interruptions, all the pain she had suffered, and she was just going to miss out.

And then we all witnessed why Light Fingers was Higgins' favourite horse. He was flogging her with the whip all the way down the straight, and it hurt him more than it hurt her. But as he hit her, she just went lower and lower with that gorgeous grass-cutting gallop. Her body went lower and her neck stretched further. Four, three, two strides from home, she stuck her neck out as far as it would go. Ziema stuck his out too. But Light Fingers had that fraction more momentum . . .

The judges called for a photo, and the horses and jockeys waited out on the track. Neither Miller nor Higgins – let alone the trainer – knew who had won. I wouldn't have minded a dead heat. But then the developed print came up, and the course announcer said Light Fingers had won by a half-head. Higgins came in and I helped him off the horse. He grinned. 'Sorry I pipped you, Bart.'

I didn't quite know how to react. Of course I was thrilled for Wally Broderick, but I was also sorry for the Baileys. I'd backed Ziema, and had really thought he was the fitter horse on the day. But when I gave Light Fingers a pat, I couldn't hold back my admiration for the horse. I haven't been at all of them since 1861, but I doubt there can ever have been a more courageous Melbourne Cup winner.

Our stable made history with her win. Only twice had a trainer scored a quinella – first and second place – in the Melbourne Cup, and never in the twentieth century. I was following William Forrester in 1897 and Dad's friend Jim Scobie in 1900 in achieving the feat. It would give me special satisfaction to match the exploit of a man who had played an important mentoring role for Dad.

But at the time, I have to confess that those historic facts impressed me about as much as they impressed the horses. In the midst of a Melbourne Cup celebration, I don't like to dwell on my own thoughts or feelings. It was the pleasure of the owners and the jockey that gave me most satisfaction. Of course I thought of Mum, watching the race from Rosscarbery in Adelaide. And of course I thought of Dad.

I was always thinking about Dad, by which I mean asking myself, 'What would Dad do in this situation?' This time I was wishing he could have been there with me at Flemington. He would have been so pleased to see Light Fingers win. But it wasn't to be.

7

The cripple

DAD'S LEGACY WOULD CONTINUE TO PERCOLATE THROUGH OUR LIVES, and bestow us with good luck in ways we could not have anticipated.

Right to the end, he had never given up his involvement with horses completely – it was as impossible for him as it is for me – and right to the end he was still breeding thoroughbreds on his property near Adelaide Airport. His partner in the breeding operation was my elder brother, Patrick.

As always, the family was fully involved. My sister, Teresa, worked for Dad for many years as his secretary and confidante. She often travelled with him interstate, and owned some good racehorses and broodmares of her own. Glendaloch, who won twelve races, was probably her best-performing galloper, but she also part-owned the mare Sojourner. Dad had Sojourner jumping hurdles as an aged mare, but I thought she was better than that. He'd lost faith in the horse so I bought her from him and Teresa. I knew a man named Clive Waterman, who owned a picture theatre and wanted to do some horse breeding, and sold a share in Sojourner to him. He didn't know much about the business, because when he bought her he said to me, 'What am I going to do with her? I don't have a farm.'

I advised him to agist her in the Adelaide Hills with a friend of mine called Malcolm Wuttke. I'd known the Wuttke family for some years, since the 1950s when I first drove up there looking for a property on which I could spell my racehorses. I couldn't find any, and was motoring around one day when I saw a place that interested me because of its open pastures and gently sloping terrain.

I thought, 'Nothing ventured, nothing gained,' and drove straight in and introduced myself. I asked the owner, a Mr Wuttke, what he did with the land and he said he was growing potatoes.

I said, 'You must be an Irishman!'

And he said, 'No, I'm German.'

I said, 'You can't be. No German knows how to grow spuds as well as the Irish.'

We had a bit of a laugh, and I said, 'You can do a lot better with this land.'

'How?' he asked.

I said, 'You can convert it to an agistment property to spell racehorses. Turn it into acre-and-a-half paddocks, put in windbreaks, and trainers like me will happily pay you money for it.'

He said, 'Come back in two or three weeks.'

In that time Mr Wuttke thought about it, realised it was a good idea, and got to work. It would certainly be an easier way to make a living than growing and harvesting potatoes, and before long we had forty or fifty thoroughbreds spelling there. He had another farm up the road and grew some potatoes on it, but the spelling property became the main thing.

Mr Wuttke had a son about my age, Malcolm, who took over the property when old Mr Wuttke passed away. Malcolm and I became firm friends and even took a tour to Britain together to watch the English Derby. We've been good friends ever since. Malcolm later sold part of the property to the winemakers Shaw and Smith. This shows how much agriculture and land use was changing in the Adelaide Hills in those decades: first potatoes, then spelling horses, then grapevines. It tells a whole history of the region on its own. But the characteristics of the land itself didn't change. After buying the property from Malcolm, Shaw and Smith were trying to fix up the grass and some big operation was threatening to charge them something like $12,000. Malcolm came in and did the job for about $50, and Shaw and Smith begged him to move back onto the property to look after it. They gave him a house on the property's highest point and everything he needed, so before long he was back as the winery's head gardener. He's there to this day, enjoying a very good life.

All that was way off in the future when, in the mid-1960s, I became interested in Sojourner. Having sent her to the Adelaide Hills for eighteen months, paying service fees and so on, Clive Waterman lost patience. He was a businessman, and started asking, 'Where's the return on my investment?'

I tried to explain that aged broodmares didn't give an immediate return, but Clive wasn't listening by now. So Malcolm Wuttke and I bought her back from Clive. I took over the breeding and sent her to the top sire Better Boy; she produced a filly whom we put up at the South Australian yearling sales. David Hains, an astute businessman and breeder from the Mornington Peninsula in Victoria, bought the filly for $16,000. He would name her Kingston Rose, and one of her daughters would be the champion Oaks and Derby winner Rose Of Kingston, the Australian horse of the year in 1981. Another daughter of Kingston Rose was Spirit Of Kingston, who also won multiple Group Ones.

Rose Of Kingston's son, in turn, would come back to me a quarter of a century later for the most unlikely Melbourne Cup success. This is the way racing goes: you plant a seed, and it can take many many years to grow and bear fruit. If you are lucky, the circle can be completed decades later, when a mare owned by your sister and jumping hurdles for your father can end up, by a long and circuitous route, being partly responsible for the fastest runner of the 2 miles at Flemington in history, under your hand as a trainer. Somebody up there likes me.

My brother Patrick worked closely with Dad. Patrick was a much more academic boy than I was, and he graduated from school and university, where he studied accountancy, and worked for the taxation department in Adelaide. After that, he worked in and around our stables and also did quite well as a professional punter.

Patrick and Dad had a mare called Storm Gleam, whom they had bought in the mid-1950s from George Richards, a chemist in Albury. She was by Sun Storm out of Crown Appeal, and I had also bought her full brother at the Adelaide yearling sales. As Stormy Passage, he had been my first Group One winner in 1958.

My brother and father sent Storm Gleam to the sire Coronation Boy, a son of the mighty Nasrullah. Storm Gleam threw a filly foal in 1963, and my father and brother sent her, as a two-year-old, to me to train.

She was an out-and-out champion by the name of Storm Queen. She lost her first start but then won eight straight races. We had no hesitation in sending her to Sydney for the 1966 Golden Slipper Stakes at Rosehill over 6 furlongs, the biggest and richest race for two-year-olds in Australia (and, later, the world).

I didn't go with her. I had a horse running in the Birthday Cup at Victoria Park in Adelaide, and the Queen Mother was presenting the prize, so the Adelaide Racing Club suggested to me that it was a good idea to be there, just in case.

In the lead-up to the Slipper, the betting involved a titanic battle. The bookmaker Bill Waterhouse took a set against Storm Queen, in spite of her record. He had her at 3/1 second favourite behind Academy Star. The other bookies, who rated Storm Queen more highly, had her at a shorter price of 5/2. Waterhouse just didn't think she could win. My brother Patrick went all-out on his filly. I can't remember how much he wagered on her, but it was a lot. By the end of the race, either Patrick or Waterhouse would be having a very, very bad day.

In the helter-skelter race that the Slipper always is, Storm Queen had no luck at all. I'd instructed Roy Higgins to be patient on her. I'd observed that the straight at Rosehill was precisely 5 feet longer than the straight at Randwick, which was contrary to popular belief among interstaters.

Higgins said, 'No, the Randwick straight's longer, isn't it?'

I said, 'The Rosehill straight is 5 feet longer. So all you have to do is stay patient, get her around the turns, which are tricky on that track, don't go too early, get her balanced at the top of the straight, and there's enough distance, 2 furlongs of straight, for her to wind up and go after the leaders. Even if you let her fall right back to stay out of trouble, she's good enough to win from the rear of the field.'

In the early running she got trapped wide, almost a certain death sentence in the Golden Slipper. Waterhouse was in the habit of following big punters onto the steps while they were watching a race, and even laying bets while the race was being run! As they rounded the home turn, he offered 2/1 against Storm Queen and Patrick backed her yet again. To his delight she came home with a withering burst to nose out Academy Star. Bill Waterhouse was filthy, and Patrick Cummings was transformed from a modest gambler into a big-time punter.

I know I have a reputation as a trainer of older stayers, but I've also trained four winners of the Slipper. Storm Queen was the first and possibly the best. As a three-year-old she went on to win the Caulfield Guineas, the George Adams Stakes and the Lightning Stakes, for a career record of thirteen wins from twenty starts. Her Golden Slipper win came almost a year to the day after Dad's death.

But it was the one Slipper win that I missed. I was doing my duty in Adelaide. As it turned out my horse did win the Birthday Cup, which I accepted from the Queen Mother. During the presentation, the dignitaries and Queen Mother were speaking, but I was a little distracted – I was listening to the call of the Golden Slipper over the loudspeaker. I think all I said during the presentation was to blurt out excitedly, 'Yeah! We won!', meaning the Golden Slipper. The Queen Mother must have thought I was an unusual type.

The Birthday Cup-winning horse was an unusual type, too. His name was Galilee.

SUCCESS BREEDS SUCCESS, AS ANY TRAINER KNOWS. YOU WIN A FEW races, and all of a sudden the owners with the best horses are falling over themselves to have you as their trainer. Before Light Fingers and Storm Queen, I had been struggling along for the best part of ten years. Now that I'd won the major Group One races of the spring and autumn, the pace of my operations picked up. You can't make a silk purse out of a sow's ear, and there's no more valuable asset for a trainer than a reputation for winning that attracts the best horses to your stable.

But the best horse of that era, and the one that I think could be the best horse I've ever trained, was one I had selected myself as a yearling in New Zealand. While new owners were showering me with horses to train, my old method was still working.

On my trip to New Zealand in January 1964, I had noticed a yearling colt with good breeding but an ungainly walk at Trelawney Stud. This was one of the most famous New Zealand studs, near Cambridge, the birthplace of Tulloch and of two Melbourne Cup winners, Macdougal and Foxzami (and later a third, Silver Knight).

The awkward colt's father was Alcimedes, a champion New Zealand stallion, and his mother was Galston, whose dam was Nereid, the dam of Sometime – the one that got away from me. And it was that year that Sometime won the Caulfield Cup for Les Patterson, the trainer to whom the Lee brothers had taken the horse during my 1961–62 suspension.

In spite of his good breeding, this bay yearling colt was likely to come at a bargain price. He threw his offside foreleg out at an angle, and was distinctly pigeon-toed. People said he walked like Charlie Chaplin. But that didn't discourage me, because it didn't contradict any of the principles of spotting yearlings that my father had taught me. First among those principles was to look at the dam's side, and see what proportion of winners she had produced. A good mare will usually produce a useful horse no matter what the sire. When a good mare goes to a champion sire, the chances are increased that she will produce top-line offspring. Then you want to see the yearling in its natural environment before it's presented in the sale ring. You need to know how they're fed and treated when they're young. I noted in my book: 'Very good, three stars, a grand walker.'

According to all these criteria, Galilee was a good buy. There was nothing in Dad's principles about a yearling needing to have a perfect conformation. The perfect horse hasn't yet been bred. Some buyers fall into the trap of seeking perfection and being turned off by any minor idiosyncrasy. Not me.

On top of that, I didn't think being pigeon-toed was necessarily a problem. (It never hurt Charlie Chaplin!) This colt's hooves came down onto the turf evenly. And nature has already provided the solution to pigeon toes. The outside ligament on a horse's leg is twice as thick as the inside one, so it's already taking most of the strain. Pigeon toes are nothing more than a cosmetic deformity.

So I paid 3500 guineas for him, a solid price but not as much as his breeding warranted. I bought him for Max Bailey, the Adelaide builder who owned Ziema, and his wife Venice. In the sale ring, Tommy Smith hopped into me. Tommy, already the champion trainer in Sydney, would be one of my main rivals through the next quarter-century. At this point, in 1964, he was well ahead of me: he had trained a Melbourne Cup winner, Toparoa, and the great champion Tulloch, probably the best horse to race in Australia since Phar Lap. But I would soon be catching up . . .

Tommy had a very high-pitched voice. In the sale ring, as soon as I'd bought the Alcimedes–Galston colt, Tommy came up and squeaked: 'It's a cripple! You bought a cripple!' But I thought I'd done all right. If you're waiting for the perfect horse, you'll be waiting forever. (Three years later, when the horse won the Sydney Cup, I saw Tommy Smith walking by and couldn't help myself. I sidled up to him and squeaked: 'The cripple's done pretty good, Tommy!')

The colt would be Galilee, a good Biblical name the Baileys chose. I held him back until the last month of his two-year-old season. In the meantime, we had him gelded, to take any excess weight off his lopsided front legs. Entire horses (colts and stallions) have more muscle in their shoulders and crested neck than gelded males and females. With half a tonne of total weight coming down on their tiny front hooves and skinny front legs, going at 45 miles an hour, one leg at a time, there's so much pressure per square inch on those hooves that it's a wonder they stand up at all. Gelding a horse takes about 30 or 40 kilos off its forequarter, so it's less likely to get injured. Also, once a male horse is gelded, he becomes less moody, less feisty, easier to handle and train. Take breeding off his mind and a male concentrates better on his work – it's pure commonsense, no matter what the species!

To geld colts before they had raced was much more common in those days than it is now. Among the top stallions, very few were Australian-bred. Most of our best stallions were brought in from overseas, and New Zealand stallions, as I'd found, were overshadowing ours in producing winning stayers. So there wasn't as much incentive to keep a colt an entire. Nowadays, with Australian sires a proven quantity, and equal to the best in the world at producing sprinters and milers in particular, you hesitate before gelding a colt. You usually try racing it first, because if it does well as a two-year-old it might be worth $10 million as a stallion. You will only geld it after giving it the opportunity to show its potential as an entire. This is what happened with champions such as Kingston Town, Saintly and Might And Power, who were tried out as colts, raced without success, and realised their potential after being gelded. But in Galilee's day, with his unpretty conformation, I didn't hesitate in recommending he be gelded.

Within a few months of gelding him we noticed the usual difference in his growth – he wasn't putting on as much weight in his front half. I had him ready for a two-year-old maiden at Gawler, in South Australia, in the winter of 1965. Gawler is a tight track with plenty of turns and a short straight, and he got too far back in the field. From twenty lengths behind on the turn, he stormed home into second place.

He had two more starts that spring, and then, on Victoria Derby day, while I was at Flemington puzzling over whether Light Fingers would be ready to run in the Melbourne Cup, Galilee was running in a 7-furlong transition race at Cheltenham in Adelaide. He won it by three lengths, then won twice more in Adelaide that spring.

The next autumn he won that Birthday Cup over 10 furlongs (2000 m) at Victoria Park on Golden Slipper day. I was more excited by Storm Queen's feat in Sydney, but I had a feeling I had a good one in Adelaide. I spelled him for the winter, and brought him back for the Melbourne spring carnival. He won a strong welter at Caulfield, then went up to Sydney for the Epsom Handicap, the glamour 1-mile race of the Sydney spring carnival.

John Miller, the West Australian who had ridden Ziema to so many second places the previous season, was Galilee's regular jockey now. Roy Higgins rode him in track work, but didn't quite have the feel for him. Roy would jump on him, and because of the way Galilee shuffled around arthritically on his pigeon toes, Roy would say, 'This horse isn't right, he's sore.'

'Just get out on the grass,' I said, 'and do what I tell you.'

Then, after galloping him, Roy said, 'He felt like a cripple walking, but once we were on the grass he felt like a Rolls-Royce.'

I said: 'That's why Miller's riding him in races, not you. You don't know him.'

Not that Miller was above making mistakes. In that Epsom, Miller rode Galilee into a distant second behind the top New Zealand mare Chantal. Galilee struck himself against the starting barrier as he came out, and on the home turn he was running seventeenth out of twenty. But he put on the magnificent closing sprint we were getting used to, and finished faster than any other horse in the field.

When he came in, Miller apologised, saying he'd thought he'd won.

'I got through the pack, I rode him hands and heels, and I thought I'd hit the front,' he said. 'To my surprise I then realised Chantal was five lengths out ahead of us. I hadn't seen her.'

It just showed, Miller was a gifted jockey but he didn't always have the same awareness as 'Roy the Boy'.

In any case, Higgins wouldn't be riding Galilee in the big spring races because he was committed to Light Fingers. She had come back well after her gruelling Melbourne Cup campaign the previous year, winning the St George Stakes in the autumn before being injured and rested. In the spring she was placed in the Underwood Stakes, Caulfield Stakes and Cox Plate. She was up against weight-for-age champions like Tobin Bronze and Winfreux, who were better suited at the mile-and-a-quarter of those races, so I was quite happy with her progress.

Higgins wasn't the only one who formed a poor opinion of Galilee from the way he walked. I became so worried that the stewards might get the wrong idea and scratch him for his ungainly action that I instructed Miller to walk Galilee onto the track on the far side of the clerk of the course's mount, to hide him behind the pony. I didn't want the stewards, watching from the mounting yard, to see his action before he warmed up.

One person who wasn't fooled was the handicapper. Galilee was given 8 stone 7 pounds in the Caulfield Cup, which I thought was a bit much given that he hadn't won any major Melbourne or Sydney races. But the handicapper had seen his potential. It was a wet spring in Melbourne, so I kept Galilee in warmer climes in Sydney until the week before the Caulfield Cup. Running in the Toorak Handicap over a mile, he was last on the turn but then powered down the outside and won going away.

He had suffered all his life from people sneering at his shuffle and thinking he was sore. So it was in the Caulfield Cup. Punters thought he was limping after the Toorak Handicap, and he drifted to 14/1 when unfounded rumours spread that he was injured. Tobin Bronze, the weight-for-age champion, was favourite at shorter odds than any horse since Tulloch in 1957. Tobin Bronze led the field into the home straight, but Miller was patient, holding Galilee in fifth or sixth place on the turn. Galilee seemed to be handling the distance at his first try, and he surged down the straight past the weakening Tobin Bronze, Gala Crest and Pharaon to win my first Caulfield Cup by a length and a half.

Galilee was certainly not underrated by the VRC handicapper, who hit him with a 6-pound penalty in the Melbourne Cup after his win at Caulfield.

Tobin Bronze dropped back to his favourite distance and

conditions and won the Cox Plate and Mackinnon Stakes on the next two Saturdays. Galilee finished well behind him in the Mackinnon, and poor Miller was dragged in before the stewards to answer a charge that he'd ridden the horse too 'cold', or not vigorously enough. The stewards were fired up by some newspaper reporters claiming that Galilee should have finished closer. What they didn't understand was that Galilee was being trained to run 2 miles, whereas Tobin Bronze was the best weight-for-age horse in Australia running over his favourite distance. If Miller didn't throw everything at Galilee, it was because he was well beaten. The horse was still trying his best, and I had the torn-up betting tickets to show that I'd been confident he would win.

The stewards, in their wisdom, accepted Miller's explanation and he was reprimanded. It would have been most unfair if he'd been suspended after his near miss the previous year. As it turned out, a suspension would have cost him a Melbourne Cup.

Galilee started 11/2 favourite for the Cup ahead of Tobin Bronze (who was questionable at the 2 miles under handicap conditions), Tea Biscuit, Gala Crest and Light Fingers. The champion Winfreux and the Metropolitan winner Duo were also in what was a very strong field.

Tobin Bronze led the pack down the Flemington straight the first time, but then Winfreux took up the pacemaker's role. Miller had Galilee well back, as usual, and Higgins had his 'Mother' close behind the leaders. As they entered the finishing straight, Duo took the lead, but Higgins and Light Fingers scooted straight past him at the furlong post. For a moment I thought Light Fingers might do it again – two Cups in a row!

What a mighty little mare she was. But Miller had been holding Galilee tight and he was cruising. He moved up on Light Fingers' flank and went past her, as Higgins later said, as if the mare was anchored to the ground. He said Miller grinned at him as he went past. If he did, that wasn't in my instructions. I know Miller was satisfied at having his revenge on Higgins after losing to him on Ziema the previous year, but Galilee was a different horse from Ziema. He finished the Cup like a sprinter. Higgins said it felt like Galilee must have been hiding out at the top of the straight while the others went around the circuit; he finished so fast, it was like he was fresh out of the barrier, galloping through with his head held distinctly high.

This was the day for the Baileys' red, gold and black colours. Galilee's two-length win was one of the most impressive in memory, and he might have been the best staying horse I ever trained. You can't compare them from different eras, but you can compare them when they're racing against each other. Light Fingers was a champion and he went past her like she was a second-stringer.

I'd become the first trainer to quinella the Melbourne Cup twice, and to have done it in successive years was special indeed. As usual, I smiled and accepted the backslaps and quietly plotted my next move. The reporters asked me if I might make it a hat-trick the next year, and just because I felt like creating mischief, I said yes, but not with Galilee or Light Fingers – instead I mentioned a dour young stayer who'd been injured in the Geelong Cup a few weeks earlier. They thought I was joking.

It was satisfying also to share the win with the Baileys, loyal owners who had been so close to victory the year before.

Wally Broderick had a second place to go with his win, and even he accepted that the better horse had got home on the day. Galilee was only the sixth horse to win the Caulfield–Melbourne cups double, and was still lightly raced. I genuinely believed his best was ahead of him.

He hadn't won at weight-for-age yet, though, and I set him for the C.B. Fisher Plate over 12 furlongs the Saturday after the Melbourne Cup. Tobin Bronze was entered as well, and this was a good chance to compare the two top horses of the season at a distance that was between Tobin Bronze's favoured 10 furlongs and the 16 Galilee had just covered in the Cup. Tobin Bronze had won the Cox Plate and every other weight-for-age race in the spring, including the Mackinnon, where he'd blitzed Galilee. But Galilee had outgunned him in the Caulfield and Melbourne cups. The counter-argument was that, in the cups, Tobin Bronze had had to carry bigger weights than Galilee. This time, they'd be racing at weight-for-age.

Galilee settled the matter in the Fisher Plate, bounding away to beat Tobin Bronze by two and a half lengths. Light Fingers over 2 miles on Tuesday, Tobin Bronze at weight-for-age on Saturday – a horse's greatness is always best judged by what he beats, and it was on this basis that the writers started calling Galilee the best galloper since Tulloch. John Miller, in typically colourful style, said: 'This ain't a bloomin' horse; he's an express train.'

We gave him a well-earned rest and brought him up for the autumn, when he confirmed his reputation by beating Tobin Bronze in the Queen's Plate at Flemington, then winning the Autumn Stakes at Randwick by ten lengths as 6/1-on favourite.

I entered him in the Sydney Cup, but heard rumours that Tommy Smith had a plan to box him in with the several runners he was entering. Everyone knew Galilee liked to start slowly and sit at the rear of the field before charging home. This could be exploited by other trainers and jockeys; they could obstruct his run while the leaders stole a march on him.

So Miller and I decided to race Galilee 'upside down'. He was carrying a big weight, 60.5 kilograms, but he could handle that; what he couldn't handle was being blocked and giving the leaders too much of a start.

That day he showed his greatness. Ridden near the front, not the way he liked, lugging that massive impost, he careered home to win the Sydney Cup by six lengths. This was when I couldn't resist reminding Tommy Smith that he'd called the horse a cripple.

In my mind, the only thing that could beat Galilee in the 1967 Melbourne Cup would be the handicapper. Or himself. A champion horse can sometimes try so hard he injures himself, and sadly this was the case with Galilee. When he came out of his box the day after the 1967 Sydney Cup, he had a pronounced limp – and it wasn't the usual Galilee shuffle. He was shin sore, a condition usually afflicting young horses with immature bones. But as he was fully grown, we had to investigate further. I patted his legs gently, calming the horse while probing him to find the soreness. Soon it was clear: he had a damaged splint bone, the finer of the two bones below the knee, in his near foreleg. Treve Williams operated twice, with Fred Monahan assisting, taking out the bone chips that were hurting the horse. In those days the operation wasn't done in a theatre. It took place on the grass in front of the stalls at our Adelaide stables.

It was a successful operation in that the broken pieces of bone were removed, but only time would tell whether Galilee would be the same force when he came back. He'd carried 9 stone 7 pounds to win the Sydney Cup, becoming the first horse to win the Caulfield, Melbourne and Sydney cups in one season. It would be a hard act to follow with an injured leg, as he'd be carrying the proverbial kitchen sink on his back every time he raced in a handicap from now on. That is, *if* he raced again. When he was bandaged up after his operation, we had no idea whether he would.

Light Fingers, meanwhile, had given us another trophy shortly after the 1966 Melbourne Cup, bringing home the Sandown Cup. It was the last of her fifteen wins. She came back for one race in the autumn before being injured, and then two unplaced runs in the spring. We decided to retire her, and she returned to her owners, Fred and Molly Dawson, as the second-highest stakes-winning female horse in Australian racing history. Only Wenona Girl had won more than Light Fingers' $109,370.

As a broodmare she wouldn't be as successful or co-operative as she was while racing. She only produced five foals in fifteen years at Pirongia Stud. She refused to mate with the New Zealand sire Sovereign Edition on two occasions. That one was easy to explain: he was a grey horse.

8

The ugly duckling

I WASN'T HAVING A BAD RUN. OUR STABLE HAD OTHER GOOD HORSES, such as Fulmen, who won the Adelaide and Brisbane cups, and I won my first South Australian trainers' premierships in those two seasons, 1965–66 and 1966–67. (The racing season starts on the 'horse's birthday', 1 August, when all horses change age regardless of what month they were actually born.) Aside from the stable stars like Galilee, Light Fingers and Storm Queen, I had dozens of good horses in Adelaide, and we racked up a record seventy-eight winners in 1966–67 alone.

🐎

BACK ON THAT 1964 NEW ZEALAND TRIP WHEN I'D BOUGHT Galilee, I had spotted another ugly duckling: lot 202 in the sale ring, a chestnut colt by Le Filou out of Red Might, being offered for sale by my friend Jack Macky from Pirongia Stud. As always, I was looking at the female side of the pedigree, and Red Might was a close relative of Redcraze, the Mackys' champion of the mid-1950s. Red Might had produced Water Waggon, a top New Zealand two-year-old of the time. There were several similarities between this colt's pedigree and that of Light Fingers, who was turning into a promising two-year-old at that time.

This colt, though, made even Galilee look pretty. His off foreleg was club-footed, and his head resembled a violin case. As a foal he'd been kicked in the face by another horse, and the nerves down one side of his head were paralysed. These nerves controlled the muscles that moved the ears, so he'd ended up with an ear that wouldn't stand up, but just flopped around limply. As I've said, I'm willing to overlook superficial deformities, but perhaps this one was taking it to an extreme.

Still, price is everything, and the colt's ugliness kept the asking price down. The club foot distracted observers, but in my experience a club foot is nature's way of redressing an imbalance between the legs; if one leg is slightly shorter than the other, the hoof compensates by growing a bit thicker. It's not a serious problem, but once again there were a lot of buyers searching for perfection. My winning bid was just 870 guineas, a quarter of what I paid for Galilee, himself a bargain.

I was acting for a group of Adelaide businessmen enjoying their first venture at owning racehorses. Brian Condon, a transport contractor, Bill Clarke, a jeweller, and Angus Tyson, a bloke who made ladders, had got together at a dinner and talked up the idea of being racehorse owners, but only to a point; they didn't want to spend more than 850 guineas. Like many owners, their hopes were high but their resources slim. As it turned out, the Le Filou–Red Might colt was more or less on budget for them.

They called him Red Handed, another play on Le Filou's thief theme. At 870 guineas, he turned out to be a steal.

As a youngster he wasn't very strong, and no matter what we did with him he was never much to look at. But he would stay all day. I knew from the start that he wasn't going to be a fast-maturing two-year-old sprinter, so I didn't race him at all until he was an autumn three-year-old, in March 1966.

He raced in restricted events on the country tracks outside Adelaide, like Balaklava and Murray Bridge, and won six races in his first preparation, culminating in the Alderman Cup against older stayers over 13 furlongs. When he won the Queen's Cup at Morphettville, over 10 furlongs, there were some who said he was even better credentialled than Galilee for the 1966 Melbourne Cup.

I took him to Victoria to get him ready. His main lead-up was the Geelong Cup, in which I entered him against my better instincts. It was a mistake. The Geelong track had a reverse camber on the home turn – the ground sloped towards the outside of the curve, placing tremendous pressure on the horses' legs as they accelerated. I complained about it then, and continued doing so for years until they fixed it. A reverse camber is terrible for the horses. I've complained about it at the Newcastle and Kembla Grange tracks in New South Wales over the years, too, but nothing has been done about them.

In that Geelong Cup, Red Handed was running behind a horse called Alecon, who buckled and fell on the treacherous turn. Red Handed fell too, breaking a small bone in the hock of one of his hind legs. Just like that, he was out for the spring, leaving me with 'only' Galilee, Light Fingers and Ziema in the Melbourne Cup. When Galilee won and I was asked about the hat-trick in 1967, I said, 'It might be asking a bit much, but Red Handed might be the one for next year . . .' They all fell around laughing, as people often do, for some reason, when I am speaking in deadly earnest.

IT WAS TEN MONTHS BEFORE RED HANDED RACED AGAIN. AFTER HIS injury we put him in a box in Pat Murray's stables in Sydney, and didn't let him move for three months. Percy Sykes attended him, and Red Handed was a calm patient, mature and relaxed. Most of the best horses I've trained were like that. They didn't have airs or graces. Even when he was injured, I liked to make Red Handed feel happy. In training, everything starts with a contented horse. We kept the stables clean and tidy – not that it pleased everyone. Once a health inspector came to visit and said, 'You've got too many flies here.'

I couldn't work out what he meant, and replied with a question: 'How many should I have?'

For stable staff, we hired the horsemen who shared my view that the horse's happiness came first. You really have to love the horse and read its moods. A lot of trainers don't put themselves inside the horse's skin, and don't ask themselves why horses are behaving a certain way. Horses are always sending you messages, and you need to learn their language. Unless they're Mister Ed, they won't tell you in English. You need to have empathy.

How they are stabled has always interested me. If you cage them up like wild animals, they behave like wild animals. You've got to think like a horse. So I have them where they can all see each other and enjoy each other's company. They have to like their neighbours. Some horses, when you put them next to each other all they want to do is fight. If I saw this happening, I'd switch them around until I found horses that liked being next to each other. It sounds like commonsense, but so many trainers don't do it I suspect it must be a secret. Some horses get lonely, so I'd put a mirror in their stalls so they could look at themselves. Once they had the mirror, some of them just liked looking at it all day – they thought it was great!

I was continuing to refine my feeding methods, too, always following Dad's rule of hand-mixing our own feed rather than buying pre-mixes, and experimenting with new high-protein supplements. I knew that Light Fingers could have eaten a tonne of oats and not got the protein she got from our feeds. As for Red Handed, he needed all the help he could get, and good feeding was just the start.

But the base line is, it's all about the will to win. Whether it's the trainer, the jockey or the horse, everyone should have that will to win and it's the trainer's job to nurture it, by good feeding, sensitive training, and making the horses feel liked. Then they'll relax, and by the time they go out to race they should be wanting to race. Then their will to win takes over. All you're doing as a trainer is removing the obstacles.

AFTER THREE MONTHS RECUPERATING IN SYDNEY, RED HANDED went down to Melbourne for another few months of rest. At this stage Galilee was carrying all before him, and we were thinking he'd be our stable leader for the 1967 Melbourne Cup. But another lesson Dad had taught me was, if possible, to have back-up plans, good horses in training to step in when another got injured or lost form. So it was when Galilee had his leg operation; as he went out for a long, long spell, I had Red Handed coming back into work.

His first race back was over the straight 5 at Victoria Park. Glynn Pretty was riding him, and he told all his jockey mates that Red Handed was a special. A betting plunge ensued, and like Light Fingers two years earlier, Red Handed showed that a staying horse can do very well in a 5-furlong sprint if it's run down that long, energy-sapping straight.

Red Handed went to Melbourne and was placed three times in top company. He chased Tobin Bronze home in the Toorak Handicap and the Caulfield Cup, without any luck in the latter race, as he came from barrier 20 and only carried 7 kilos less than the established weight-for-age champion before rushing home for a fast-finishing fourth.

The next week, Tobin Bronze won his second Cox Plate and

was sold to America. I couldn't help wondering what Galilee might have done that spring.

Red Handed was no weight-for-age star; he didn't have the sprint. He was a grinding, one-paced stayer. In the Mackinnon Stakes he came in fourth behind Winfreux, another run that suggested he was crying out for more distance. Accordingly, the bookmakers installed him as 4/1 equal favourite for the Cup, skinny odds considering he hadn't won anything at Group One level. But this Cup didn't have the class of the previous two years, so maybe he had a chance.

In a good omen, Red Handed was stabled in the same stall as the great Carbine, winner of the 1890 Melbourne Cup carrying 66 kilos, a full 24 kilos more than the second-placed horse. On two occasions Carbine won two different races on the one day. They certainly don't make horses like that anymore! The Mersey Lodge stables had been built for Walter Hickenbotham, Carbine's trainer, nearly a century earlier, and were more recently leased by Stan Boyden, the trainer of the 1948 Melbourne Cup winner Rimfire. We used those stables for a couple of years. Maybe there is such a thing as a lucky stall – you'll have to ask the horses.

Reporters asked me after our fourth in the Mackinnon if I could make it a hat-trick of Melbourne Cups, and I said, 'Red Handed isn't worried about me trying to be the first trainer to win three Melbourne Cups straight, and he is the one who will be running.' A good thing the horse was listening to me and not believing his own press.

Now that Light Fingers was no longer racing, Roy Higgins was riding Red Handed. Higgins had matured to become the top jockey in Melbourne, if not Australia, and had ridden more than a thousand winners by now. On Cup day, he and the strapper arranged for Red Handed to wear the same bridle as Higgins' favourite, the just-retired 'Mother'.

As I said, there was no horse of the quality of Galilee in the field, but as well as Red Handed I had my Brisbane and Adelaide cups winner Fulmen, and six-year-old Ziema was in there for another try, carrying the top weight. He'd just won a cup, finally – the 1967 Werribee Cup – for Max and Venice Bailey.

The other stables also had their contenders. General Command, the equal favourite with Red Handed, had won the Metropolitan at Randwick in a national record time for 13 furlongs. Red Crest, the top New Zealand entry, had won the Wellington Cup. And there was Swift Peter, the winner of the AJC Derby. All up, it wasn't the strongest Melbourne Cup ever run, but it wasn't the weakest either.

That year the spring was dry in Melbourne, the roses had failed to flower, and the track was brown and patchy with drought. From barrier 15, Higgins took Red Handed towards the rails in the back half of the field as they went up the straight the first time. Just as they passed the post, Swift Peter almost fell, knocking Red Handed off balance. Higgins kept him on his feet and improved his position along the back of the course.

He kept moving up around the long home turn, but when Higgins took Red Handed into the lead at the top of the straight I thought he'd gone too early. Patience. Patience is everything – and it looked like Higgins had broken the golden rule and ruined our chances when Red Crest, the New Zealander, emerged from the pack and ran past Red Handed. Our horse seemed gone, but Higgins pulled the whip and he lifted, kept lifting, while Red Crest started to fade on his run. Red Crest's jockey, Ron Taylor, didn't ride all that often and he tired too, falling forward on the horse's neck.

But Red Crest was still in front. There are few sights more thrilling in racing than when a horse who has been passed turns the race around and comes again. Higgins would later say that at this point he 'remembered who trained Red Handed'. I don't know about that. Red Handed didn't know about my Cup training record. He just kept plugging away, with that indefinable will to win. Twenty metres from the post he got his nose in front of Red Crest, and he got across the line by a neck. Fulmen came ninth, Ziema twelfth.

So: three Melbourne Cups. This was the first in which the winning rider carried our stable colours of diagonal green and gold stripes. I'd designed those silks myself and registered them in 1958. I am a proud Australian, and wanted to make a statement of my love for the nation. Those colours have been good to me.

It was said that in Light Fingers and Galilee I had champion racehorses, whereas Red Handed needed much more of the trainer's skill. I suppose that's a fair call. Comparisons are odious, but Light Fingers was mighty and Galilee was a world champion who would have won anywhere on the globe between 1966 and when he was injured in 1967. Red Handed wasn't as good as either of them, and he'd had his problems, but we got him right and he won a Melbourne Cup. Not bad going for a horse with a club foot, a paralysed ear and a head like a violin case.

9

The headline horse

JUST WHEN EVERYONE WAS SAYING I'D WORKED OUT THE SECRET of winning Melbourne Cups, it would be seven years before I won another one. Some years I didn't have the horses; other years I didn't have the luck. And our best chance in all those years, the horse that should have won, was undone not by the sport of racing but by an act of human bastardry.

🐎

By 1968 it was time to branch out. We had owners coming to us not just in Adelaide but in Melbourne and Sydney, and increasingly our focus was on the big interstate carnivals. With the children growing up, Valmae was keen for us to move to one of the bigger cities so that I could be closer to the action, but for the time being I was content to keep up my routine of travelling all week and coming home on Saturday nights.

But it was only a matter of time before we would become national in our mentality and expand beyond Adelaide. At Flemington I bought and developed Roy Shaw's property, with space for twenty-four boxes and a spare block next door. Before long I was the only trainer with self-contained stables in Adelaide, Melbourne and Sydney. I was an Australian trainer, not just a South Australian trainer. Results were looking after themselves. In 1968–69 I won my third South Australian trainers' premiership in a row, and my first Victorian premiership. I was even training successful jumpers, such as Embason, the winner of the South Australian Grand National Hurdle. I had one stakes-winning jumper, called Bogan Cloud, whom the flat jockey John Letts rode over the hurdles before coming back, all flushed and panting, saying, 'Phew, that was the ride of my life!'

Letts was a nice young fellow who had been riding since 1959 in Adelaide. But in the late 1960s he was having a run of outs and his confidence was very low. Like a lot of jockeys, his personal self-esteem seemed to rest entirely on how many winners he was riding. So I took him home to our place and reassured him that he could still ride. I put him on Bogan Cloud, who won several big hurdle races in fast times. Letts thought it was terrific. Not only was it good for the horse and the stable, it was good for John Letts too. Realising he could ride horses to win big races again, Letts went on to win Melbourne Cups on Piping Lane in 1972 and Beldale Ball in 1980. He now does television interviews with the jockeys during the Cup carnival and is well known around the country for his excitement as he rides around the back of the course with his microphone.

Eventually I would scale down my training of hurdlers. This was not because I had anything against jumps races, but because we were having so much success on the flat. Preparing hurdlers had historically been part of the trainer's repertoire, and my father was one of many who trained both flat and jumps horses. Hurdling has gradually declined in popularity, however, and nowadays there is a move from greenies and animal-liberation types to ban hurdles racing altogether. I think they have missed the point. Because they wanted to lessen the number of injuries, a few years ago they successfully had the height of hurdles and steeples lowered. The problem with this was, it allowed the horses to go too fast, and thus increased the number of falls and injuries. I can see that these activists have horses' welfare at heart, but they know nothing about the racing industry and would ruin it if given free rein. Inadvertently, by having the hurdle heights lowered, they caused more horses to be injured; if hurdling needs any reform, it should be to raise the heights of the fences to what they used to be, and then we'd see fewer falls.

IN THE AUTUMN OF 1968, I WON THE FIRST OF MY THIRTEEN (at time of writing) Australian Cups at Flemington. The horse was Arctic Coast, and the owners were three Adelaide busi-nessmen: the stockbroker Hubert Harvey, Bill Wylie, who made shock-absorbers for cars, and a young newspaperman named Rupert Murdoch. One day Valmae met Murdoch coming up the street; he was heading to the shoemaker's to get his shoes resoled. Valmae came home and said, 'Things must be going bad for Rupert – I saw him going in to have his shoes resoled!' I reassured her, saying that from what I knew of Rupert, this didn't mean he was in desperate straits. He was careful with every cent that went out of his pocket, that was all.

We had all sorts of owners in those days, and mixed socially with them. We had Wilbur Joynt, the Adelaide gynaecologist, who darted between the racetrack and the maternity ward. We had Charles Farren-Webb, a chief inspector for the National Bank and one of the founders of BoysTown, the institution set up to help underprivileged young boys, but also a very lonely man whose lack of family and friends we didn't really appreciate until one Christmas Day when he turned up on our doorstep to ask if we would let him in. He had nowhere else to go, and of course we welcomed him. We had one of the daughters of the Penfolds wine family, who was married to a very puritanical Methodist gent, and his disapproval of racing was so stern that she had to race her horses on the sly. They were all interesting people, and gave us a great exposure to the wider world.

Valmae and I were able to take some overseas trips in those days – North America, Britain, Europe – although I often treated them as busman's holidays, no doubt to my wife's occa-sional chagrin. On one trip to Canada in the middle of the year, we met George Gardiner, the chief executive of General Electric in Canada and the chairman of the Woodbine Turf

Club near Toronto. We spent some enjoyable time at his farm, and he showed us several of his horses and some of his secrets. He told us that for the meeting a few days later, he would have five runners in five separate races, and they would all win.

Valmae always had an independent mind, however, and when the races came up, she decided to back anything other than George Gardiner's horses. She would bet on 20/1 shots, 25/1, 33/1, as long odds as you like, when Gardiner's were running as short-priced favourites. And wouldn't you know what happened! In three of the five races, Valmae's horses got up over Gardiner's. He was beside himself, almost seeming to believe she had some special magic powers.

Maybe he was still in a state of confusion when he came to Australia in the late 1960s. We invited him to a party at our place, and in all the parties we've held, this was the only occasion when someone has left before it started. Poor George was so drunk on arrival – an hour early – that he quickly got himself into such a state that a friend had to help him home to dry out. He must have thought Mrs Cummings had put a curse on him!

Our upbringing, Valmae's and mine, had been fairly sheltered, so it was a real eye-opener to meet such a variety of people from so many walks of life. Few of those owners would leave quite as lasting an impression, however, as the Gawith brothers from Melbourne.

I WOULDN'T SAY PRIDE CAME BEFORE A FALL – I DON'T THINK I EVER succumbed to hubris – but such are the ups and downs of racing that as soon as you think you've got it made, disappointment is inevitably around the next corner.

After more than a year out, Galilee was coming back into training for a tilt at the 1968 Melbourne Cup. He didn't race at all as a five-year-old, a tragic shame as he was in the prime of his life. We were bringing him back as a six-year-old, on suspect legs, and the handicapper would show him no mercy.

In the spring of 1968 he ran in the weight-for-age lead-ups, coming third to Winfreux in the Liston Stakes before winning the Memsie and Turnbull stakes. The great horse was back, but for the Melbourne Cup the handicapper gave him 68.5 kilograms – 68.5! It was unbelievable. Recently, Makybe Diva won two Melbourne Cups, a Sydney Cup, a BMW International and several other races, and for her third Melbourne Cup she was handicapped, if that is the right word, with 57.5 kilograms, pretty much the same as Light Fingers got after winning one Cup. And Galilee, who had won one Cup, had 68.5 kilograms. It was as if they didn't want him to run.

On Derby day he ran third in the Mackinnon Stakes behind an Adelaide horse, Rain Lover. My other Melbourne Cup starters, Lowland and Arctic Coast, were unplaced. But our focus was on Galilee. Max Bailey loved the champion so much that he wanted some kind of assurance that if Galilee ran in the Melbourne Cup under 68.5 kilos he wouldn't break down again. On the Sunday, Percy Sykes inspected Galilee, and said he couldn't guarantee that the champion could run out the 2 miles. I sat on the fence; I felt the horse would be all right, but didn't want to contradict Percy. On the Monday afternoon, VRC vets John Bourke and Leo McNanammy examined

Galilee and he looked fair, but they said they wanted to see him in his track work the next morning.

So at six thirty am on Cup day, there we were at Flemington with 2000 spectators, punters and press, some of them still in evening dress from their Cup eve parties the night before, as the stewards watched John Miller work Galilee. They pronounced him fit, and he would start as 7/1 equal second favourite, with Rain Lover, behind the equal favourites Lowland and Arctic Coast.

It was a rough old race. An outsider named Wilton Park fell in the straight right after the start, and Galilee clipped his legs as he jumped over him. As he landed, he almost buckled down onto his nose under all that weight, but Miller kept him going. Rain Lover avoided all the trouble and ran away to win the Cup by eight lengths. My horses all missed the placings, Galilee finishing a brave eighth, beaten by bad luck and punitive handicapping.

I spelled him, and tried to bring him back for the 1969 Cup, but after two unplaced runs it was plain to see that he'd had enough. He retired with a record of eighteen wins from thirty-six starts. I can't play favourites, but in fifty-six years I've not trained a better horse.

If I had learnt one lesson from the previous few years, it was that having a champion racehorse in one season gave us no guarantees about the future. Galilee, who had the talent to win three Melbourne Cups, won one. You never know what is around the corner. For this reason, you have to seize the moment when it comes, and take the opportunity when it arises. Who knows – if we had exercised more prudence with Light Fingers in 1965 and Galilee in 1966, and saved them for the next year, the 'next year' may never have arrived. Luck can so often intervene.

The other step we had to take was constantly replenishing our stables. If I didn't keep looking for the champions of tomorrow, I would be yesterday's man in no time.

When I'd gone to New Zealand for the January 1967 yearling sales, there was one colt in particular that I wanted, being put up by my old friend Jack Macky at Pirongia Stud. The colt was sired by Le Filou out of Pink Lady, who was a daughter of Light Fingers' dam Cuddlesome. This made the yealing colt a three-quarter brother to Light Fingers.

Of course, by now I couldn't hide my interest in a yearling with this pedigree, and others went against me in a stout bidding competition until I got him for 3500 guineas. In Melbourne I sold him to Charles and George Gawith, a notable pair of Victorians who had become wealthy through a bread-baking company they had founded. Charles became a member of the Upper House in the Victorian Parliament. He was opinionated and forceful and didn't care if people liked him or not. George, meanwhile, was a much quieter fellow, who I think did most of the hard detailed work in the background while Charles was the public face of the business. But that didn't mean George was totally happy with the arrangement. Once I remember George saying to me, 'Charles has always been luckier than me.'

'Why?' I asked.

'Because he's got me for his brother, and I've got him for mine.'

The Gawiths were exacting owners, but were willing to put their money where Charles's mouth was. At the same sales I bought two other yearlings for them, who would race as Alrello and King Pedro.

I didn't race the three-quarter brother to Light Fingers as a two-year-old, but brought him out at three. He was a lean, gangly bay, with a cheeky temperament. He liked to take a nip at people if they walked too close to his stall. Big Philou, as he was called, showed staying promise immediately and won five races from his eleven starts as a three-year-old. The way he was going, and with his breeding, he'd be absolutely ripe for the 1969 Caulfield and Melbourne cups.

In the Sydney spring carnival, Roy Higgins felt the sting of the Gawiths. He rode their horse Alrello in the Epsom Handicap at Randwick. Higgins tracked the race favourite, a horse called Black Onyx. Unfortunately, Black Onyx bled during the race and slowed suddenly. Alrello was held up, but stormed home to finish second.

It was only bad luck, but Charles Gawith accused Higgins of adopting tactics which cost him the race. Higgins and I were staying in the same hotel in Sydney, and apparently there was an argument between the jockey and Charles Gawith in the bar on the Saturday night. The next morning, Higgins came to me and said, 'I will never ride for that pig of a man again and I don't care what he's got in the stable. I will not ride it.'

I calmed him down and acted as a mediator between the pair. Higgins agreed to keep riding Gawith's horses, but the two men still wouldn't talk to each other.

One of those horses was Big Philou, whose spring campaign was tuning up steadily. A week after the Epsom, he was backed from 20/1 into 12/1 in the Caulfield Stakes before running second to Hamua. It was a good run, but now I was struggling with jockey problems on a second front. I was training General Command, one of the beaten brigade in the 1967 Melbourne Cup, and he came eighth in the Caulfield Stakes after drifting in the betting. The Victorian Amateur Turf Club (VATC) stewards hauled in the jockey, Geoff Lane, and me for a three-day inquiry to answer the charge of not allowing General Command to run on his merits. There was no evidence, but they still found us guilty on suspicion and fined us $500 each.

For the Caulfield Cup the next week, Big Philou's Caulfield Stakes effort had attracted the punters, and he started as 9/2 favourite. He drew barrier 17, but Higgins angled him straight in to the fence to save ground in the running and he stayed there just behind the leaders until the home turn.

As they entered the straight, Des Lake rode Nausori into the lead. As soon as he was clear, Lake cut across towards the rail. But Lake didn't see Higgins, who had kept Big Philou on the fence all the way, and was now bursting through. At the furlong post, Nausori appeared to cut Big Philou off. Checked, Higgins had to slow and balance Big Philou, then go around to the outside of Nausori, before resuming his charge for home. He did accelerate again, but finished a neck behind Nausori.

I thought Big Philou was unlucky not to have won, but wasn't certain about what had happened. When Higgins came back on the horse I asked him if he was going to protest.

'Yes, for sure,' he said, 'and we are sure to get it.'

I was pleased by his confidence, and the siren was raised. All bets had to be held as we went into the stewards' room: Higgins, Charles Gawith and myself, as well as Nausori's connections. Before we entered, Higgins begged me to prevent Gawith from speaking up. As the owner, it wasn't as if he could have prejudiced the proceedings against us, but Roy distrusted him so deeply after the Epsom that he saw Gawith as a loose cannon who might find some way to muck it up.

We sat before the stewards and, following the normal procedure for protests, Roy lodged his objection first. Then Lake replied with his version, and the stewards asked the two jockeys some questions. At one point during the twenty-minute hearing, the stewards asked Gawith if he had anything to say. He started, then suddenly stopped, courtesy of a sharp kick in the ankle from yours truly.

There seemed little doubt: Nausori had cut Big Philou off and cost him more than the finishing margin. For the second time in history, and the first time since 1893, the result of the Caulfield Cup was reversed on protest – Big Philou was awarded the race, with Nausori second.

Punters who had backed Nausori booed and catcalled the presentation, when the Victorian governor, Sir Rohan Dela-combe, gave the trophies to Charles Gawith, Higgins and me. There were many others cheering, though; Big Philou had been backed heavily to win the Caulfield–Melbourne cups double, as Galilee had done three years earlier, and it soon emerged that some bookmakers stood to lose hundreds of thousands of dollars – something like $5 million in today's money – if Big Philou completed the double.

Higgins went to shake hands with Charles Gawith, willing to bury the hatchet over the whole Alrello affair, but Gawith simply said: 'You still cost me the Epsom.'

Two weeks later Big Philou ran in the Mackinnon Stakes,

losing by a nose to Roman Consul, who flashed home at long odds. It was an excellent final trial for the Cup, and I couldn't have been happier with him. On Cup morning Big Philou worked for a leisurely 2 furlongs, and when Higgins brought him in he said to me, 'You've got no idea how good this horse feels. We'll probably never get him as good as he is today, and it happens to be Melbourne Cup day.'

I felt as confident as I'd ever been with a Cup horse. His preparation had gone like clockwork. I went to Flemington and might even have told some reporters how confident I was. I hate to tempt fate, and if I expressed such confidence as I was said to have, I don't know what got into me.

Big Philou's strapper was a very reliable eighteen-year-old named Ron 'Smoky' Dawson, an English lad who would work for me for many years, serving ably as my stable foreman in Sydney. He was the first to notice that something wasn't right with the horse. Normally such an impudent customer, Big Philou was hanging his head in his stable. When Smoky walked past him, expecting the usual nip, Big Philou just ignored him. At ten o'clock on Cup morning, Smoky saw the horse passing some soft-looking droppings at our stables. Then, at midday, when Smoky led him to his float to go to the track, the droppings had turned into an attack of 'scouring', or diarrhoea.

Smoky didn't think it was anything too sinister, however – or not yet. But by the time they got to the Flemington exercise ring, Big Philou's eyelids were swollen and his coat gleamed with sweat. He was projecting diarrhoea uncontrollably. Smoky told our stable foreman, Noel Spiers, and John Bryden, our Melbourne stable vet, who relayed the message to me: Big Philou was scouring.

At the time, I was enjoying a drink with my brother Patrick in the winners' circle. His horse Storm Ruler had just won the third race for us. When Spiers and Bryden came to me and murmured the news, I took them into the alleyway off the mounting yard and said, 'Just stop and tell me that again.'

Bryden told me that the horse was unhappy and running a temperature. He was scouring and his mucus membranes were inflamed.

We walked calmly to the horse's stall, where Smoky was looking morose and worried. I'll never forget the trouble the horse was in. He was just exploding with diarrhoea and writhing in pain. He was in an awful mess.

The VRC's chief veterinary steward, John Bourke, joined us at the stable, but it was a mere formality; I had no hesitation in agreeing with him that Big Philou had to be scratched from the Cup. I didn't say any more. I just walked back to the grandstand to get ready to watch the race.

By now it was almost two pm, and the race was due to start at two forty pm. Roy Higgins was in the jockeys' room putting on his silks when the assistant VRC judge, Les Benton, saw him and said, 'That's bad luck, Roy.'

'What?' Higgins hadn't been told.

'About Big Philou being withdrawn.'

Higgins thought he was joking, and didn't believe it until at 2.01 pm, thirty-nine minutes before the race, the warning siren went off and Joe Brown, the course announcer, told 85,000 people at the track and the rest of the nation that the favourite, horse number 6, Big Philou, was a scratching from the Melbourne Cup.

The race went ahead with millions in a state of shock. Rain

Lover won for the second year in a row, under 60.5 kilograms, but I still thought Big Philou would have beaten him. Already I harboured a suspicion that our horse wasn't actually sick but had been nobbled. Laxatives are often the poison of choice for those who want to keep a horse running but not at its best. The idea is to give the horse a dose of laxative that upsets his bowels, but isn't noticed before the race. If the nobbler is even more foolish than he already is, he might give the horse too much laxative, causing a scouring attack such as Big Philou had suffered. It backfires on the nobbler, because when the horse is scratched the bets on it are cancelled and repaid. But in this case, with the bookmakers standing to lose heavily in doubles bets if Big Philou won the cup, they would have been satisfied simply to return the wagers and avoid such a crippling payout.

Big Philou's urine was tested, and two weeks after the Cup I was called in by the stewards to hear the results. My suspicions were confirmed. Someone had given Big Philou a laxative called Danthron, but had given him too much and made him ill.

The question was, who?

In conjunction with the Victorian police, the VRC stewards started an investigation. Charles Gawith offered $5000 as a reward for information leading to a conviction, but nobody was tempted. His brother George was so saddened by missing out on a chance at the Melbourne Cup that he fell ill, and his declining health over the next few years, leading to his death in 1974, was said to have resulted from his heartbreak over Big Philou.

I couldn't work out how it had happened. Smoky Dawson

had been with the horse all the time, and he was above suspicion. He slept less than 2 metres from Big Philou, on the other side of a weatherboard partition. Noel Spiers was in a room in the stables, and checked the horses every hour before he got up at four o'clock in the morning. Neither had seen anything. The only time that anything could have happened was during Big Philou's transfer to and from the Flemington racetrack for his morning work.

Very soon the authorities had a suspect. For a brief time in mid-1969 I had employed a stable hand called Les Lewis. A shifty, unreliable fellow with flaming red hair, Lewis hadn't impressed me and I'd dismissed him in July. He was an odd bod, and I didn't like the look of him at all. If you can pick a horse you can pick a human, and Lewis looked the way he performed. He was a drinker and a gambler and a loudmouth. Since I'd dismissed him, somehow he had managed to keep some friends around the different stables and hadn't disappeared completely.

Lewis came to the officials' attention because a bookmaker, Jack Hurry, had heard him shooting his mouth off in the Racecourse Hotel the Friday night before the Cup, boasting that he had a 'job' to do, which was to stop Big Philou and another favourite, the Hotham Handicap winner Tails, from winning the Melbourne Cup. On the Sunday, Lewis was mowing Hurry's lawn and allegedly told Mrs Hurry that Big Philou couldn't win the Cup. Lewis had also been seen flying to and from Sydney, returning to Melbourne with great wads of cash.

Another of my strappers, Helen Klowss, came forward and told the investigators that Lewis used to pay her money to do his shift while he flew to Sydney. He kept this secret from me. Then yet another strapper, Robert Davis, said Lewis had offered him $700 to help him nobble King Pedro in the 1969 Duke of Norfolk Stakes, during Lewis's brief time in my employ.

By early 1970, the police were ready to charge Lewis with doping King Pedro and Big Philou, and with inciting Davis to help him dope King Pedro. At first Lewis couldn't be found. He'd flown to New Zealand on a false passport and hoped to disappear. But he was tracked down and extradited within weeks, to face trial in the Victorian County Court.

I was called to give evidence, but didn't know anything more than I've said here. One of the interesting things to come out of the trial was that Lewis had paid a woman in Ascot Vale to let him use her phone to make calls to a company in Sydney, Stanlight Investments, which was owned by the bookmaker Bill Waterhouse.

But no evidence in the trial could place Lewis directly in Big Philou's stall or vicinity on Melbourne Cup morning, and he denied everything. He was acquitted of nobbling Big Philou, but the jury found him guilty of attempting to incite Davis to nobble King Pedro in the Duke of Norfolk. The judge sentenced Lewis to six months' jail, and the stewards warned him off racetracks for life.

After such frustration – a thirteen-month investigation and trial leading to only a minor conviction, and nothing to do with the Big Philou doping – the authorities still had to look like they were taking action. I was reprimanded for the level of my stable security, though it was tighter than anyone else's at Flemington. The sorry truth was that if a criminal was determined enough to get in and nobble a horse, they would find a way, be it in the stables or between the stables and the racecourse.

Lewis had been lying – and continued to lie in four appeals he made against his warning-off. Many years later, in 1997, when he was dying of cancer, he signed a statutory declaration admitting that he had doped Tails and Big Philou between three and four o'clock on Cup morning 1969. He said he'd been paid $10,000 to do it, and that this was his main source of income; he'd accepted $1000 a pop to nobble up to ten other racehorses that year, including King Pedro. He said that his paymaster had given him the air ticket to New Zealand for free.

As the Bible says, whoever creates the temptation is worse than the person who commits the act. Lewis wasn't smart enough to do it unassisted. He had help, he needed money, and he was acting on someone else's instructions.

What has never been revealed publicly is who paid him to nobble Big Philou. Before Lewis's confession, at a Christmas party in the early 1990s, on a boat on Darling Harbour in Sydney, an acquaintance of mine told me the whole story, including the name of the mastermind behind the crime. This person had managed to steer clear of prosecution, and for defamation reasons I am not allowed to name him here. I have no doubt at all that this person was the one who ordered and paid for Lewis's actions.

The shame of it was that Big Philou deserved a chance to win the Melbourne Cup. His owners deserved it, the jockey deserved it and, after all the work we'd put in, the stable deserved it. There was only one way Big Philou could be stopped, and that was illegally, by someone who stood to lose a great deal if the horse won the race.

THE VETS SAID THAT DANTHRON SHOULDN'T HARM A HORSE permanently, but Smoky Dawson, Higgins and I all felt that Big Philou was never quite the same after that day.

After spelling him in Adelaide, we brought him back for an autumn campaign in 1970, and he squared off against Rain Lover in the Queen Elizabeth Stakes over a mile and a half at weight-for-age at Flemington. Those two horses were so superior at the time that all the other entries pulled out, so it was effectively a match race. Big Philou pulled as usual, but in a very exciting finish he outlasted the Melbourne Cup winner by a short half-head. Higgins said it was poetic justice, but I didn't think justice would be served until Big Philou got another chance at the Melbourne Cup.

I was preparing him for the race in the spring of 1970 and again he was shaping up well, winning the Underwood Stakes and being installed as 3/1 favourite for the Caulfield Cup. But on the Tuesday after the Underwood, he struck himself during a gallop and went lame. I flew Percy Sykes down from Sydney, and he confirmed that the horse couldn't run in the Caulfield Cup.

Charles Gawith was furious – not so much that Big Philou was injured, but that he'd been scratched. Gawith wrote to the stewards saying none of his horses could be scratched without his permission. He took Big Philou out of my stable. Not that it helped him – the VATC veterinary stewards affirmed what Percy Sykes and I had said about the horse. He was injured, and couldn't run in either the Caulfield or the Melbourne Cup that year.

He was a fine galloper, though. As a six-year-old he came up again, finishing third in the Caulfield Cup and then, in his only Melbourne Cup start, running eighth behind Silver Knight. Gawith kept him racing for another three years before retiring him.

The Big Philou affair of 1969, and its aftermath, is one of the few sour memories I have from a life in racing. You might say that with twelve Melbourne Cups, I might not mind too much missing out on one. But that is not the way I am. I like to win, or at least have a chance to win, when I have a good horse and have put years of work into it. I like my owners to win. Every big race means as much to me as every other one, and to have been denied a chance by greedy and cruel criminals, low types who had no qualms about putting a horse in terrible pain, is something that still rankles. I could train for another fifty-six years, and still I would never forget the terrible state that poor horse was in that day.

10

The princess and the thief

BECAUSE SO MUCH ATTENTION IS PAID TO THE MELBOURNE CUP, the early 1970s are regarded as 'quiet' years for my stable. It's true that in the seven years after Red Handed's win, I did not have one horse in the placings for the Cup. In 1972 I didn't even have a starter.

But fortunately, the Melbourne Cup isn't the only race on the Australian calendar. And during those 'quiet' years I had some of the best younger horses I have ever trained.

Dayana was, and still is, the only three-year-old to win four derbies in one year. I'd bought him as a yearling in New Zealand, and in 1972 he won the Victorian, South Australian, Western Australian and Australian derbies. The last two were run in Perth, and to top off his visit he won the Perth Cup too. He was named Australian horse of the year, though as an older horse he was never able to recapture the form of his classic year.

We had probably the best sprinter in the country in those years, the colt Century, who won most of the feature sprints, including the Newmarket Handicap. Century went on to establish a reputation as one of Australia's leading stallions, siring Rubiton, Double Century and Century Miss among many others.

Not destined for stud was a big, heavy, precocious gelding with bad legs called Tontonan, who became my second Golden Slipper winner in 1973. The favourite was the unbeaten Imagele, but he fell in a three-horse pile-up and Tontonan ran on to win the race from Latin Romance. He showed it was no fluke by winning the AJC Sires' Produce Stakes a week later. As a three-year-old he broadened out into a top sprinter-miler and won the Doncaster Handicap at Randwick, on a day notable for the presence of two streakers running across the track. Tontonan wouldn't be put off, winning with a record weight of 56 kilograms. He later showed his unflappable temperament again by retiring into a life as a popular and useful police horse.

UNTIL 1973 I HAD NOT WON THE W.S. COX PLATE, THE SO-CALLED weight-for-age championship of Australia. Certainly Galilee and arguably Light Fingers and Big Philou had the talent to win the Cox Plate, but because I was setting these horses for the Melbourne Cup I tended to bypass the Cox Plate. It is a real anomaly in the Australian racing calendar that there is no weight-for-age race of a mile and a half (2400 metres) in the lead-up to the Melbourne Cup. I always considered the Caulfield Cup, over that distance, to be the best preparation for the Melbourne Cup, so generally ran my horses in that instead of the Cox Plate. But if you had a horse as good as Galilee, it would be handicapped out of the Caulfield Cup, and if you didn't want to bring it back for the unsuitable distance of the Cox Plate, you were stuck without the ideal preparation. I complained about the absence of a 2400-metre weight-for-age race for many years, with no result. The best they could do was to make the 2500-metres Queen Elizabeth Stakes at Flemington a set-weights race, but being run a week *after* the Melbourne Cup, it's not much help!

The result was that the Cox Plate very often attracted horses prepared specifically for it and not the Melbourne Cup, sprinter-milers who might stretch out to the 10 furlongs and middle-distance horses who specialised at weight-for-age. Tobin Bronze, who won two Cox Plates, had run in the Melbourne Cup, but only because his class gave his connections hope that he would stay the distance. In truth he was a mile to mile-and-a-half horse, perfectly suited to the Cox Plate but not the Melbourne Cup.

Another type of horse that can go very well in the Cox Plate is the early-maturing three-year-old. Many of these have won Cox Plates, including Alister, Surround, Red Anchor and Octagonal. In 1973 I had just such a horse in Taj Rossi.

Taj Rossi was sired by Matrice, a popular South Australian entire whom Pat Glennon had ridden to many wins. Matrice also sired the Golden Slipper winner Pago Pago and Manihi, the father of Manikato, so he was clearly passing on his sprinter-miler's blood. Australian sires were just gaining recognition, and Taj Rossi's dam was Dark Queen, by Coronation Boy. It was a blueblood sprinter's pedigree. At the Adelaide yearling sales in 1972, held in the showgrounds owned by the Coles company, I bid the top price for Taj Rossi, $18,000, buying him for the Melbourne owners Victor and Lila Peters.

A handsome dark bay in colour, he ran six times as a two-year-old, improving each time until he won his last two starts. I was intent on setting him for the Caulfield Guineas and possibly the Victoria Derby, if he could be trained to stay the distance, in the spring of 1973.

Taj Rossi won the Ascot Vale Stakes over the Flemington straight 6 in the second start of his campaign, but he could be a fractious individual and had a habit of throwing his head about inside the starting barrier. He did this in the Caulfield Guineas and ran home fourth behind Imagele with a concussion. We had been wondering what was wrong with him until he returned to scale with a lump on his head the size of a cricket ball.

Still, he was ready in time for the Cox Plate, in which we had another star three-year-old, Leica Lover, who had won two guineas races in Adelaide and would later add the Australian Derby in Perth. We'd bred Leica Lover ourselves, so I was particularly fond of him. Leica Lover set a fast pace on the tight track, but didn't quite go the distance. Taj Rossi, ridden by the apprentice Stan Aitken, burst home over the top of Leica Lover in the short home straight and won from a very good New Zealand horse in Swell Time, a Caulfield Cup winner.

There was nothing Taj Rossi couldn't do that spring. After the Cox Plate he won the VRC Derby, over 2500 metres, and the George Adams Handicap, coming back to a mile. He topped off his campaign by winning another mile, the Sandown Guineas, from Imagele in a virtual match race of the star three-year-olds. I thought Taj Rossi was the best three-year-old ever to have raced, certainly the best I'd trained, and believed that the sky was the limit for him. But he caught a stomach virus the next autumn and just wasn't the same. He was well beaten in the 10-furlong Australasian Champion Stakes at Randwick, finishing six lengths behind Asgard, another of my three-year-olds. But I knew Asgard wasn't as good as Taj Rossi at his best, so there was clearly something amiss with the champion. Taj Rossi retired to stud as a four-year-old, standing at Spendthrift Farm in the USA. Later he returned to Australia and stood at Turangga Stud near Scone, and we kept the connection going into the next decade, with his son Taj Quillo and his daughter Taj Eclipse winning stakes races for us before he died after an operation to remove a tumour in 1986.

THANKS TO HORSES SUCH AS DAYANA, CENTURY, TONTONAN, LEICA Lover, Asgard and Taj Rossi, in 1973–74 I became the first trainer to win a million dollars in stakes in one season, edging out Tommy Smith by about two hours when I won a race in Brisbane during the winter just before he won one to pass the milestone in Sydney. It pleased me that our stable won so many of these big events with Australian-bred horses, but I was as active as ever in the New Zealand yearling sales, and in 1972, the year I had no Melbourne Cup starters, I had made two purchases that would turn the tide.

Andrew Peacock, a parliamentarian from Melbourne who was then a young member of the McMahon federal government, came with me to inspect yearlings in New Zealand in January 1972. Peacock was a dashing fellow who has passed on his passion for racing to his daughter Jane Chapple-Hyam, now a successful trainer in England, and it was good to see a high-up politician with an interest in the racing game. There should be more of them! We didn't talk politics at all, as far as I can remember. Racing is a more important subject anyway, and I was pleased to discover that Peacock shared this view with me. Peacock knew Tom Williams, who owned Te Parae Stud near Wellington, where the leading sire Oncidium stood. Peacock had asked Williams to keep an eye out for a promising yearling, and Williams responded that Oncidium had sired a nice dark brown filly out of the good race mare Lei. A courtly gentleman named Ian McRae, a neighbour of Williams, owned both Lei and the filly. Peacock came with me to New Zealand, and we stood at McRae's property to watch the filly running around in the paddock. We asked if she was for sale, but McRae, like the Dawsons with Light Fingers many years earlier, would not sell her. He wanted to bring her back as a broodmare, but he would agree to lease her out for racing.

Like Light Fingers, she was lightly framed but had a

good girth and a nice fluid gallop. Lei, a daughter of one of my favourite sires, Summertime, had won sixteen races in New Zealand from 6 to 10 furlongs. Lei was a mudlark, particularly strong on wet tracks, and very often these characteristics are passed on in the horse's genes.

So it would be with her daughter, who would race as Leilani for Peacock and a businessman named Ian Rice. Rice had owned one of the first Kentucky Fried Chicken franchises in Australia, and did very well out of it before becoming a Melbourne city councillor.

Usually I had an owner in mind when I bought or leased a yearling at the sales. But I had nobody lined up when, on the same visit, I bought a bay colt by Sobig from Sarcelle for $10,000 from Wynthorpe Stud. It was a spur-of-the-moment purchase, not really typical of my way, but not the first time either. I just liked the look of him, and he had good staying blood. His brother Duglig had won seven races in Australia, including the Parramatta Cup, and he had another brother, who raced as Sungei Wang and won ten races in Singapore. I thought I would have no trouble finding an owner for him back at home.

A few weeks later, I was at a hotel on Sydney Road in Melbourne. The jockey Glynn Pretty wanted to introduce me to a distinguished real estate developer he had met in Kuala Lumpur.

Tan Chin Nam was one of sixteen children in a family that had migrated from China to Malaysia between the wars. He had planned to go to university, but when the Second World War broke out he had to work as a roadside vendor of chickens, fruit and vegetables. As he built up his capital he invested in property, and after the war ended he built an empire of low-cost housing for the poor in Kuala Lumpur. He had nick-names in the Malaysian press like 'Mr Lowcost Housing' and 'Mr Condominium', as he was instrumental in bringing afford-able apartment living to people in his country. By 1972, when I met him, he was one of the biggest property developers in Malaysia.

We were close in age – he was only two years older than me – and enjoyed an instant rapport. He and Pretty came to look at horses in Adelaide, and back at our house a game of two-up started. Chin Nam cleaned up, throwing seven heads in a row. I liked him even more! Luck, good and bad, seems to follow people around, and this was a lucky guy.

Although I don't remember this exact conversation, Chin Nam says he was very upfront about what he wanted from me. One thing I have always liked about him is that he does not leave me trying to guess what he's thinking.

'I want you to buy me a horse to win the Melbourne Cup,' he claims he said.

I do know what happened next. I told him I already had the horse he wanted. He bought a share in the Sobig–Sarcelle colt sight unseen.

A few months later, he was having dinner in Melbourne with a friend of his, a Queensland land developer named Rick O'Sullivan. Chin Nam has always been careful with a quid, and liked to share the risk around by bringing in other owners. Typically confident, in his version of the story Chin Nam said: 'Do you want to join me in owning a Melbourne Cup winner?'

According to Chin Nam, O'Sullivan said that for all the

slow horses he'd owned, he was due three or four Melbourne Cup wins, to which his wife Joan said, 'That's typical, you're always thinking big.' They shook hands and named the colt Think Big – or so Chin Nam's story goes.

As a racehorse, Think Big was always going to get better as he matured. We had him gelded, which was still par for the course. He raced eight times as a two-year-old and won once. As I had horses like Taj Rossi, Asgard, Tontonan and Leica Lover in the stable, Think Big attracted little attention. He always seemed to be one of those horses that snuck under the radar. As a three-year-old he won a hat-trick of races, finishing with the Carbine Club Stakes on VRC Derby day, but even then he was overshadowed, as this was the day Taj Rossi won the feature race. Think Big didn't do much in the autumn, only winning the Ballarat Miners' Cup, but then he went to Queensland for the winter and beat my former horse of the year Dayana in the Sir Winston Churchill Stakes over 10 furlongs. But Dayana was well past his best. Think Big finished his three-year-old season with placings in the Grand Prix Stakes and the Brisbane Cup. He was an iron horse, one of those stayers who relished heavy racing, but there were question marks over his ability.

He was seen as a workmanlike stayer in a stable of stars, one of whom was the filly Andrew Peacock and Ian Rice were racing. Leilani, as they called her, hadn't raced as a juvenile but as a three-year-old she became the outstanding filly in the country, being placed in each of her nine starts and winning four, including the AJC Oaks by five lengths. Like her mother Lei, she loved it wet; the Oaks was run on a bog track. But it came at a price. Her will to win carried her through the pain barrier, and her ability to ignore stress only aggravated any injury she was carrying. Leilani pulled up after the Oaks with a hairline fracture in her hock bone, and she was spelled, her leg put in plaster.

The enforced rest did her good. Always lean and wiry, like Light Fingers, she put on a bit of muscle during her break. She had chronic soreness in her back, though, which I noticed one day when I was giving her a rub and she dipped in pain when I touched her sacroiliac joint. We had to keep on attending to that throughout her career. When their backs are hurting, they won't perform on the track. Nowadays we would use a chiropractor, but nobody had heard of them in the early 1970s so we had a vet treating her.

When we got her right, she came good – real good. She returned in the spring for a fourth over 5 furlongs at Cheltenham, then a third in a Caulfield welter, before the rain came down for weeks, turning all the tracks to mud. Peacock and Rice went around with big grins. Leilani won the Turnbull Stakes at Flemington in 2 minutes 13.3 seconds, about 10 seconds slower than the usual winning time for that race. The track was that heavy. The next week at Caulfield, we had icy driving rain and she won the Toorak Handicap by three lengths. As the rain kept falling, the bookmakers installed Leilani as 9/4 favourite for the Caulfield Cup, the shortest-priced female in history.

She was handicapped to carry 52 kilos. Roy Higgins, whose constant problem as a jockey was keeping his weight down, couldn't make himself that light, so Mick Mallyon rode her. Mallyon was a committed rider and a good fellow, who sometimes invoked the stewards' ire by celebrating too exuberantly as his winners crossed the line. He was always copping a fine for nothing more serious than waving his whip as he passed the post. Mallyon had been booked to ride High Sail, a good stayer who had run third in the Metropolitan at Randwick. He asked that horse's owner, Bill Stanley, if he could switch to Leilani, and Stanley said, 'If you think she can win the Caulfield Cup, then you ride her.' Owners aren't always that generous.

I also had Leica Lover and Asgard in the Cup. On the heavy track, Asgard went into the lead a long way from home, and Leilani took up a good position just behind him and on his inside.

At 500 metres, Asgard tired and the charge was on. Mallyon pushed Leilani forward, but Gay Icarus went past her. She was just getting going, though. At the furlong post she bolted away from Gay Icarus and was easing up on the line to win by two and a quarter lengths.

Her win was impressive enough for the VRC handicapper, Kevin Ryan, to give her the maximum penalty of 3 kilos for the Melbourne Cup. She went up to 55.5 kilos, a full 3 kilos more than Light Fingers' weight-carrying record for a mare. Once again, I was unimpressed to say the least. Handicaps are meant to level the field, not stop the in-form horses from winning. She was only a small thing, and I felt the handicapper had overreacted to her Caulfield Cup win.

But maybe Leilani was good enough. On the Saturday before the Melbourne Cup, she won the Mackinnon Stakes from Battle Heights, the New Zealand champion 2-miler who had won the Wellington and Sydney cups and was the early favourite for the Melbourne Cup. It was still open to question, though, whether such a lean, light mare could run out the two miles under such an onerous weight.

THAT SPRING, LEILANI WASN'T OUR ONLY STABLE STAR. LEICA LOVER won two weight-for-age races and another of our home-breds, Leica Show, won the big three-year-old fillies' races. Kenmark, Cap D'Antibes and Ein Prosit all won stakes sprint races for us.

One horse who was not impressing was the colt, now gelded, that Tan Chin Nam and Rick O'Sullivan had bought.

Until Derby day, Think Big had failed in all his starts since returning from Brisbane. He pulled up lame after coming last in the Metropolitan on the October long weekend. We thought we got him right, but then through that sodden month he ran unplaced twice more in Melbourne. O'Sullivan and Chin Nam might have been thinking big, but by now the horse was hardly encouraging them.

But I only had to be patient with him. I knew he had a good pedigree, stamina and constitution; he just needed to be injury-free. He also didn't seem to like wet tracks, which were everywhere we looked that spring. What was good for Leilani, it seemed, was terrible for Think Big. After he ran, unplaced again, in the Moonee Valley Cup, I eased him along, and then on Derby day he surprised everyone by coming home from the rear of the field in the 2500-metres Hotham Handicap to win by a length.

It's obvious that in racing you never know what's going to happen next. But in the stable we were pretty confident that Leilani was our main chance in the Melbourne Cup. We hoped that Think Big, if everything went well for him and the track kept drying out as it had been for a few days, might be able to chase her.

Certainly Harry White thought so. Harry wanted desperately to get onto Leilani. We were having a bit of a jockey shortage at the time. Roy Higgins and Mick Mallyon were both suspended after infringements in the Caulfield Cup, and I'd booked Peter Cook for Leilani in the Mackinnon and the Melbourne Cup. Peter was the son of a great rider in Billy Cook, and at the time was emerging as one of the very good younger jockeys. I wouldn't be moved on this, and to Harry's (temporary) chagrin, he had to ride Think Big. After the Hotham Handicap win, however, Harry began to have second thoughts; maybe he was on a good thing after all.

If a horse's temperament reflects that of the trainer, often it picks up something from the jockey too. Harry was an extremely mellow character. There were times when we had Harry riding one of our horses, and ours would be the only horse in the mounting yard without a jockey. I'd send someone into the jockeys' room, and they'd have to wake Harry up! He'd say, 'Where is everyone?' Our person would say, 'They're out there getting ready to start.'

As a rider he had good soft hands and great patience. Some jockeys have 'itchy arses' – that is, they can't wait. Often the itchy-arsed jockeys seemed to come from Queensland, I don't know why. The more relaxed ones came from Victoria, in my observation, and none of them was more relaxed than Harry.

On Cup morning he had a grim face. It bucketed down, and Leilani shortened even further in the betting, starting at 7/2 favourite ahead of Battle Heights, who had won the

Cox Plate easily before coming second behind Leilani in the Mackinnon. Think Big was kept safe at 12/1. I thought those relative odds were a fair estimation of our two horses' chances in the race.

On the heavy Flemington track, the outsider High Sail set a good pace and the field strung out behind him. Soon all the riders' silks, and the horses beneath them, were spattered with mud. Leilani was racing forward, and everything seemed to be going right for Cook.

Not so for Think Big. White had let him drift to the rear, and at the half-mile a number of tired horses were falling back on him from the front portion of the field. To his credit, White held his nerve and guided Think Big steadily through the weakening pack, avoiding the worst of the interference. But he didn't get clear until the furlong.

Meanwhile Leilani had put on her sprint. Battle Heights had taken the lead at the top of the straight, but began to wilt under the 61.5 kilos he was lugging. Another New Zealander, Captain Peri, overtook Battle Heights, but then Leilani cruised past both of them and I thought she had it won. She went three lengths clear at the furlong post, with Cook riding her very well close to the fence. The crowd, most of whom were on her, cheered her red-white-and-blue colours.

Incredibly, once White got him clear the only threat to Leilani was Think Big, in my green-and-gold diagonals and white cap. I was watching as calmly as I could, but I had no doubt Leilani would win – until Think Big bowled up alongside her in the last 50 metres and won going away, by three-quarters of a length.

Cook came back and said that he thought he'd won it,

'but then in the last little bit Think Big went whoosh, straight past me'.

White said he didn't give himself a chance until the 300-metre mark, when Think Big 'was really starting to wind up, so I pulled him out wide, put my head down and hoped for the best'.

I was pleased, of course, especially for Tan Chin Nam and Rick O'Sullivan. It was a great thrill to win the Cup again after so many years. But unlike my other Cup quinellas – Light Fingers and Ziema, Galilee and Light Fingers – I wasn't so sure that the better horse had won. Leilani carried an extraordinary handicap for a four-year-old mare, and it was probably the weight that beat her. She'd have had to be a 3-kilogram better mare than Light Fingers, and she very nearly was. But my other horse had beaten her. So be it. When the reporters asked me what I thought, all I could say was, 'I beat myself.' I won't deny it – a part of me was disappointed that Leilani got beaten. But it's a nice consolation when the winner is the stablemate.

At the presentation, Rick O'Sullivan and I both spoke, and we couldn't help mentioning how game Leilani had been. Leilani was a sentimental favourite of mine, and I'd later name my Sydney stables 'Leilani Lodge' after her. I never felt I could name it 'Light Fingers Lodge'. Such was the legacy of naming so many horses after a thief. But if anyone had come and pinched something from under our noses, it was the ever-underestimated Think Big.

11

The one day of the year

By AUTUMN 1975 THE STABLE'S SUCCESS WAS PULLING ME ALL OVER Australia. While Valmae gave the children a home base in Adelaide, I was jetting several times a week to Sydney and Melbourne, Perth in summer and Brisbane in winter. Not to mention New Zealand in January! Throughout, I made sure I came home to Adelaide on Saturday nights and stayed there through Sunday, to go to church and spend time with the family. Often some owners would come over for a visit, and add some colour.

159

All of this made it essential that I had trustworthy staff and thorough record-keeping. My brother, Patrick, was involved with the stable in Adelaide, running the office and keeping an eye on track work and the actual training when I wasn't there. In Sydney and Melbourne I relied on strong foremen and senior staff, many of whom were with me not just for years but for decades. I was in constant touch with all my offices via phone and telex, and had index cards for every horse. My methods were, and are, simple: I write everything down in a clear and systematic way. I note the date that the horse comes into the stable to start training, and then there will be four weeks before it starts serious track work. With the horses in training, I list their feed, their medication, their temperature, their track-work distances and times, and how much they eat again at the end of the day, and that's all I need to know. So a typical horse's card might show that it's eaten two dippers of oats (about 2 kilos), cleaned out its feed bin, recorded a normal temperature, been given an anti-ulcer medication, galloped 2 furlongs in even time (30 seconds) under a 60-kilo track-work jockey on the grass track (or sand or dirt), gone on the bit for the second furlong, then eaten another two dippers of oats in the afternoon. I file it away on a card, and it's all there for me to refer back to. It's a simple system; plain commonsense. And it's foolproof – you can't make mistakes. I don't know why every other trainer doesn't do it the same way. Everyone seems to think I have some kind of top-secret method for training horses, but the answer is right there under their noses. I suppose there is also an element of instinct in judging what yearlings to buy, and interpreting a horse's moods – but this is not a method, this is just something you've either got or you haven't. I'll never believe that my success owes anything to any mystery. It's just a thorough and painstaking application of the old-fashioned methods I learnt from my father, and a basic love and affection for the thoroughbred. Everything else follows from there.

Elementary, it was, and it was bearing fruit. That 1974–75 season was the fourth year I won the Victorian trainers' premiership, and our nationwide winnings passed a million dollars again. At the Flemington meeting on 8 March 1975, our horses won four races in a row, which hadn't been done since 1888.

The first of those four was Leilani, who was now acknowledged as the best racehorse in the country. The Queen's Cup was her first start since the Melbourne Cup, and it started a winning run of five races ending with the Australian Cup, in which she carried 58.5 kilos, a massive weight for any mare, let alone one as lightly framed as she was. Everybody seemed to love her, not least because she brought a touch of glamour to the track, thanks to the wives of the owners, Liz Rice and Susan Peacock. While I enjoyed the sight of nice two-legged fillies almost as much as the four-legged ones, what I most appreciated with these owners was how exuberantly they enjoyed the unique euphoria that comes with winning big races.

Leilani went for a spell that winter. She was tuned up for a big 1975 spring, and perhaps redemption in the Melbourne Cup, when she came back with a third in the Warwick Stakes in Sydney. But as she was being loaded onto the plane to fly to Melbourne, she reared up, slipped on the tarmac and fractured some bones in her spine. It was a freak injury, and ironic, in that the main reason I favoured air travel between cities was because it was safer for the horses than going by road or train.

The disappointment was immense, probably my greatest feeling of a lost opportunity since Galilee in 1967 and Big Philou in 1969, but I wasn't left without runners in the cups. Leica Lover became one of the weight-for-age stars of the Melbourne spring, and the four-year-old mare Cap D'Antibes was probably the best sprinter-miler in the country that season.

And then there was Think Big. After his 1974 Melbourne Cup win, I hadn't spelled him immediately. He entered the Sandown Cup and came ninth. He ran three times in Perth, his best result a third behind Runyon in the Perth Cup. He didn't race in the autumn or winter, then plodded home a long way behind the winners in three races in Sydney. The week before the 1975 Caulfield Cup, he surprised everyone by running third in the Caulfield Stakes over 10 furlongs. He ran all right, but it's worth noting that only five horses were in the race, so you could also say that he finished third-last.

Leica Lover, Think Big and Cap D'Antibes started in the Caulfield Cup, with mixed results: Leica Lover came second to Analight, Think Big ran on well for tenth, and Cap D'Antibes broke down in the running.

As the rain teemed down in another torrential mid-1970s Melbourne spring, Think Big's odds for the Melbourne Cup kept lengthening. His form in the wet was dismal; many thought he just didn't like soft ground. A lot of horses don't, as is proven by their form. If only Leilani was running; she absolutely loved the wet. But there was one exception in Think Big's record – the small matter of the 1974 Melbourne Cup.

Still, this didn't sway the punters, who regarded that win as a fluke, and besides, this time he would be carrying 58.5 kilograms on a track shaping up to be considerably heavier than in 1974.

Cox Plate day saw another deluge. The New Zealand star Fury's Order won the feature race in front of Princess Margaret in an absolute quagmire, and then the Moonee Valley Racing Club (MVRC) cancelled the meeting before it was finished, the first time that such a step had been taken. The jockey Larry Olsen had bleeding eyes from a clod of mud that had hit him in one event, and as a group the riders were angry that the stewards had kept the races going as long as they had.

In the Moonee Valley Cup, run before the Cox Plate, my strongest Melbourne Cup chance emerged from the slop. During the winter, I'd advised one of my owners, a Mr Morison from Sydney, to go in with some others to buy a share in a New Zealand three-year-old he was considering. Holiday Waggon, by Battle Waggon from Dolly Gold, had a modest record but a good pedigree. He'd won three from thirteen starts in New Zealand but I could see him improving with age and distance. After I started training him, he won a restricted-class Randwick race at his fourth start and then came fourth in the Geelong Cup, when Harry White didn't ride him the way I asked. It was a slow-run race and he got too far back. I was very annoyed with Harry, and let him know.

Holiday Waggon seemed to like the mud when we galloped him at Flemington, and he ploughed through the bog to win the Moonee Valley Cup running away. Princess Margaret was there to present the cup, and lost her shoes in the mud walking to the podium! One of the winning part-owners was,

I believe, an SP bookie from Queensland who wasn't present on the day – either that or we didn't deem it proper for him to go and shake hands with royalty. I can't remember. Instead, I sent down Mr Davis, a friend of mine who was one of the founders of the Carbine Club, to accept the trophy on the absent owners' behalf.

Holiday Waggon won the Moonee Valley Cup so convincingly that the punters took a big interest in him for the Melbourne Cup. Punters love a 'swimmer', because this kind of horse seems to have special powers that elude all of its competitors. A week later it was still raining, and Holiday Waggon ran third to another boom New Zealander, Suleiman, in the Hotham Handicap. His strong run was enough to push Holiday Waggon up to third favourite for the big race, behind Suleiman and the Cox Plate winner, Fury's Order, both of whom had proven themselves wet-track specialists.

Think Big, meanwhile, showed his usual distaste for bad weather and failed in the Mackinnon Stakes. There were three good reasons why he drifted out to 33/1 for the Melbourne Cup. It was raining non-stop. His form was bleak. And he was carrying 58.5 kilos. I know I complain about the handicappers over the years, but this was ludicrous. Think Big had not won a race since the 1974 Melbourne Cup, he hadn't won much before it, and yet he was asked to carry more weight than Galilee in 1966. The only thing that had changed for Think Big since the previous year was that the former Prime Minister of Malaysia, Tunku Abdul Rahman, had joined Tan Chin Nam and Rick O'Sullivan as an owner. Maybe the trappings of power earned Think Big all that excess weight.

It kept raining. It rained as we saddled our three horses,

Think Big, Holiday Waggon and Leica Lover. It rained as they paraded in the ring. It rained as I wished Harry White, riding Think Big, a safe trip. Harry had needed to be woken up, again, in the jockeys' room. The VRC club doctor had been the one to rouse him, asking if he was in the race. Harry slurred, 'Yeah, I'm in this race.' The doctor misheard him, thinking he'd said, 'Yeah, I'll win this race'. The doctor went out and grabbed the 33/1 odds on offer.

But as it teemed down, I had much more hope for Holiday Waggon, who was being ridden by John Duggan. Our top stable jockey, Roy Higgins, had chosen Leica Lover.

It stopped raining while the horses went out to the starting gates.

Then, as they moved into the barrier, it pelted down again.

It rained while a rank outsider called Medici, carrying 46 kilos and a young lad called Malcolm Johnston, tried to lead all the way. Our threesome raced midfield, in a bunch. Medici had appeared to fade, but then he came again at the top of the straight and went three lengths clear. John Duggan on Holiday Waggon moved up on his flank, for all money to splash his way to immortality. Leica Lover had fallen right back. It was hard to see where Think Big was.

Then, wearing my green-and-gold colours but with red sleeves to distinguish him from Leica Lover, White angled Think Big towards the rail. It was an all-or-nothing move. In such muddy conditions, the ground near the rail would either be significantly worse or significantly firmer than the wider running.

White guessed right. Think Big strode straight up to Holiday Waggon and mowed him down in the straight. Duggan might have gone a little too soon. Think Big fought off Duggan's mount in the last 100 metres and won by three-quarters of a length. The next horses, Medici and Suleiman, were five lengths behind Holiday Waggon. I could scarcely believe it; we'd done another Cup quinella. I'd beaten myself again!

I was as mystified as anyone by Think Big's ability to lift for this race. He only seemed to be able to win on this track at this distance, on this day. It was the only race he liked. If he had to choose any race, it wasn't a bad one. And I have to concede, Think Big showed that he merited the handicapper's high opinion of him.

Tunku Abdul Rahman led him in, and White was all smiles amid the rain and mud. Chin Nam later received the title 'Dato', which is a Malaysian equivalent to a knighthood. It's my understanding that he received it for his contribution to the Malaysian community, not for winning his former leader a Melbourne Cup.

As for me, I'd equalled Etienne de Mestre's record of five Melbourne Cup wins. I know I have talked a lot here about races won and landmarks achieved, but that's only because I am laying down a record of events. I don't boast and I don't gloat. I don't even think about patting myself on the back for what I've done. Yes, it felt like a big achievement to have equalled a record that had stood since the last century. But I'm telling the honest truth when I say I didn't really think about it unless someone else reminded me. I was too busy looking forward to waste my time looking back.

THINK BIG RACED ANOTHER NINETEEN TIMES AND, TRUE TO FORM, didn't win once. I tried to get him up for a third Melbourne Cup in 1976, but he broke down. Tan Chin Nam and Rick O'Sullivan were kind enough to give the horse to Harry White, and he retired to Harry's farm at Gisborne in Victoria where he lived for many more years.

Leilani, meanwhile, came back for the 1976 autumn before breaking down in the Tancred Stakes at Rosehill. Aside from an unsuitable sprint at Cheltenham in 1974, this was the only time in twenty-nine starts when she had missed a placing – and those were nearly all Group races. She retired as the highest stakes winning mare in Australian racing history, and remains on the top rung. Personally, although I try never to show more affection for one horse than another, with Leilani I might have bent my rule a little.

12

The heartbreaker

BACK ON MY 1973 TRIP TO NEW ZEALAND, I'D DONE A PRE-SALE inspection of a yearling colt whose first-season sire reminded me in some ways of Le Filou. In The Purple was a French import, untested as a stallion, but he'd won at Longchamp over 3100 metres, so he could clearly stay and might be a good sire of distance horses. The colt's dam was Gem, who came from a family of stakes winners and had Hyperion on both sides of her pedigree.

I bought the colt for $4000 for an Adelaide ceiling fixer named Jack Harris and his wife, Mary. As you might have noticed by now, my owners varied all the way up and down the social scale, from Cabinet ministers to city councillors and race club committeemen all the way to small business people, successful and struggling. When it's said that racing is the greatest leveller, it's no empty cliché. It doesn't matter who they are – Andrew Peacock or Queen Elizabeth or Jack and Mary Harris – as far as I'm concerned they're all making the same investment in hope and excitement, and when they're watching their horse enter the home straight in a Melbourne Cup, the adrenaline running through their veins is all the same.

Jack, who wasn't a wealthy man, said he wanted a partner in the ownership of the In The Purple–Gem colt.

'What do you want a partner for,' I said, 'when it only cost $4000?'

But Jack insisted and I found the partner in a Sydney quantity surveyor, Hugh Gage, and his wife Gloria. Hugh Gage would later be an AJC committeeman. Earlier in his life he'd worked as part of the team designing and building the rocket range at Woomera in South Australia, and who do you think was also working there but Jack Harris!

Jack said, 'I know that bastard, he was my boss at Woomera.'

I said, 'Well, you were the one who wanted a partner.'

Jack and Hugh argued from that day on, but winning a Melbourne Cup together went a long way towards bringing about a reconciliation.

As I've said before, just as a dog is a reflection of its owner, a horse is a reflection of its trainer. I'm a patient person by nature, and I'm patient with the way I train horses; I don't bring them on too early or work them too hard too soon. Sometimes they need hard racing, but I'll only make that decision after months or years of close observation. My hope is that my patience will then be picked up by the horse, who will be relaxed and happy. The more patient the horse is, the better it's going to be in a race, whether over the 6 furlongs of a Golden Slipper or the 2 miles of a Melbourne Cup.

Gold And Black, the In The Purple–Gem colt, was a case in point. After having him gelded, we eased him very slowly into racing. He didn't run as a two-year-old, but showed some promise over distance as a three-year-old, finishing third to Galena Boy in the Victoria Derby in 1975.

The next autumn, Gold And Black learnt more about racing and showed us that while he was out of his ground in sprints he liked the races when they got past 10 or 12 furlongs. He won the Sydney Turf Club Cup over 12 furlongs at Rosehill before going away for another spell.

He seemed a classic Melbourne Cup horse, but when I entered thirty starters in the first acceptances for the race, I wouldn't have said Gold And Black was a star of the stable. We entered Think Big and Leica Lover, but our real champion of that year was Lord Dudley. I'd bought him in Melbourne for about $3000. He was a top-class two-year-old, winning the Blue Diamond Stakes at Caulfield, but we didn't overrace him. So many excellent two-year-olds don't go on the next year because they are raced too hard too young, but Lord Dudley repaid our prudent handling at three, winning a string of weight-for-age races culminating in the Australian Cup over 2000 metres and then the VRC St Leger Stakes, over

2800 metres. He was Australian horse of the year in 1975–76, my fourth in a row after Dayana, Taj Rossi and Leilani. It was an incredible run of great names in racing. It's little wonder that the 1970s, a decade which ended with two of the greatest champions of all, Kingston Town and Manikato, is thought of by those who can remember it as the most stellar of racing eras. I don't know why there was such a run of great horses concentrated within those few years, but certainly, from my own perspective as a trainer, the 1970s were a decade of many wonderful names.

Outside our Melbourne Cup hopes, we had the best juvenile in the country, Vivarchi, who won the Golden Slipper and Champagne stakes, the first and third legs of the Sydney two-year-old triple crown (the AJC Sires' Produce Stakes is the middle leg). I'd bought Vivarchi as the top-priced yearling at the Sydney Easter sales; her sire, Wilkes, had been the father of Wenona Girl, Vain and John's Hope among other champions. Vivarchi was a rare case of top breeding and high price ending up with a Group One win. They don't often happen. If you think you get what you pay for, you should get involved in something other than horse racing! We also won the Epsom Handicap with La Neige, my first Epsom after five second places, including the infamous Alrello race in 1969, and one of the big Melbourne sprints, the Craven 'A' Stakes over the straight 6, with a young filly called Maybe Mahal. Maybe Mahal had been a weedy little yearling who filled out a little to win seven races as a two-year-old in 1975–76. We were going to hear a lot more of her down the track.

UNFORTUNATELY, AS WE APPROACHED THE 1976 MELBOURNE Cup, my hopes fell away one by one. Lord Dudley broke down in training and went off to stud. Leica Lover and Think Big found the rigours of their preparations too much to bear and didn't make it through the first weeks of October.

Gold And Black was coming along all right with John Duggan riding him, running home third in the Metropolitan at Randwick and then fifth behind How Now, another of In The Purple's progeny, in the Caulfield Cup. Everybody seemed to expect me to pull a Melbourne Cup rabbit out of my hat, but Gold And Black was seen as too dour. The surprise package came on Cox Plate day when my three-year-old Oncidium colt Ashbah easily won a 10-furlong race for three-year-olds. I'd not started a three-year-old in the Melbourne Cup since Sometime in 1961, but the punters were keen on this one and they pushed him up the betting. Perhaps they remembered Dad's audacity in running Comic Court in the Cup as a three-year-old; but perhaps they'd forgotten that Comic Court didn't actually win the race until he was five.

By Derby day, Gold And Black and Ashbah were my last remaining entries for the Cup. They enjoyed contrasting fortunes on that Saturday. Ashbah, odds-on favourite in the Victoria Derby, ricked a muscle in the running and was unplaced. Gold And Black ran in the Mackinnon Stakes at the realistic odds of 40/1. A plodding handicapper with only two wins in his career, he was up against proven weight-for-age stars such as How Now, Battle Heights and Better Draw. I don't know how he did it, because he was being trained for a much longer race, but they went hard at the front and he flashed home to beat Better Draw by a short half-head, with

Duggan sticking to the fence all the way and darting through in the last furlong.

The other interesting result on Derby day was in the Hotham Handicap, which was won by a little-known six-year-old called Reckless. He'd been racing for four years before he won his first race, and barely made it into the 1976 Melbourne Cup, because his achievements were so scarce and his handicap was so light. But the public took to him immediately; he was trained by Tommy Woodcock, who had been the strapper of Phar Lap nearly half a century earlier. Tommy loved Reckless, and the public couldn't help falling in love with them both, trainer and horse alike.

We'd had some wet Melbourne Cups in the previous few years, but 1976 will never be forgotten by those who were there. All sorts of antics were going on with spectators, drenched through by drink and rain, letting go of their inhibitions, and when the puddles began to fill up in the viewing areas, dinner suits were turned into swimsuits.

It poured in the morning, dumping an inch of water on Flemington, then eased off again before it absolutely bucketed down half an hour before the Cup. There was lightning, thunder, and the most torrential rain you've ever seen – just as the horses were brought out to parade in the mounting yard, water was filling up the entire area, from the betting ring to the lawn to the racetrack. People were turning the wooden seats into bridges over the lakes that were forming within minutes.

We were fairly confident about Gold And Black's liking for a wet track, and we liked his handicap – he was down 7 kilos from the Mackinnon to carry 50 kilos – but this amount of water was unprecedented. The clouds were so low and black you couldn't see the far side of the track from the grandstand. You could hardly even see the near side. As a spectacle, the early races were atrocious. The stewards said they would postpone the start of the Cup and it looked like the race might not be run on the first Tuesday in November for the first time since 1916.

But as soon as the scheduled start time, two forty pm, arrived, the rain stopped and the stewards inspected the track. It had drained better than any other part of the precinct, and the race would start at two forty-seven. Gold And Black was 5/1 second favourite behind Van Der Hum, a New Zealand swimmer who had impeccable wet-track form and was sired by the European import Hermes.

It's difficult to say too much about that Cup, because the sky was so dark and the mud was flying so thickly that most of the jockeys' silks were a uniform glistening mud-brown as they entered the finish straight. Reckless went briefly to the lead, but Van Der Hum motored through the mud and passed him at the furlong. Gold And Black came out to chase Van Der Hum, but never looked like getting closer than the two-lengths final margin.

I WAS SURE THAT WITHOUT ALL THAT RAIN, GOLD AND BLACK would have won. After a summer spell he showed he was still improving in his Sydney campaign in the autumn of 1977, finishing second to the New Zealand champion Balmerino in the Autumn Stakes.

But was he improving as rapidly as Reckless? Somehow Tommy Woodcock was getting the best out of his stallion as they both got older. He flew Reckless from Melbourne to Sydney on the morning of the Sydney Cup, and in the afternoon it beat Gold And Black. Tommy was seventy-one by then, and Reckless was about the same in horse years, but it didn't matter. They went on to Adelaide to win the Cup there, and to Brisbane to win the Cup there too. If there was a Cups King that year, it wasn't me, it was Tommy. By Melbourne Cup time, Reckless loomed as the major threat to Gold And Black, and certainly in the public's eyes he was the sentimental favourite.

While Gold and Black was shaping up well, we had some other good winners in the summer and autumn. A grey gelding with a big personality, Ming Dynasty, won three in a row in restricted company, showing he might develop into higher company the next spring.

Belmura Lad won the AJC Derby and Ngawyni won the Australian Cup. Belmura Lad would mature into one of the country's best and most versatile gallopers in the next few years, while I was particularly proud of my training efforts with Ngawyni. Trained and owned in Western Australia before he came to me, he was bred only to sprint, and lived up to that as a two-year-old. He had shelly feet, far from solid, and I had to train him very carefully, but he won the West Australian Derby as a three-year-old. He won the Australian Cup, the Queen Elizabeth Stakes at Randwick and the Moonee Valley Cup among an amazing run of victories as a four-year-old. He also came second to Reckless in the Brisbane Cup, over 2 miles – not bad for a sprinter! When he retired, Ngawyni had

My father, Jim, as a young man, on one of the rare occasions he was fitted out in collar and tie.

As a cheeky young fellow with my sister, Teresa, and brother, Patrick (right).

I'm on the right riding Comic Court. My sister, Teresa, is leading one of our strappers on Comedy Prince.

Dad on Comedy Prince (middle) in October 1949, with St Comedy on the left and Comic Court on the right. Thirteen months later Comic Court would be a Melbourne Cup winner.

ABOVE: I'm a very snappily dressed strapper parading Comic Court at the track at Murray Bridge after he won the 1950 Melbourne Cup.

LEFT: My son Anthony, a nuisance around the stables from an early age, and my daughter Margaret riding Stormy Passage – my first derby winner! – at the Adelaide stables.

A rare moment of family time between race meetings. I'm reading one of my favourite works of literature with Valmae and (left to right) Anthony, Sharon, Anne-Marie, John and Margaret.

Not just a win, but a quinella! The 1965 Melbourne Cup:
1st – Light Fingers; 2nd – Ziema; 3rd – Midlander.

With (from left) Wally Broderick, Roy Higgins, strapper David Edwards and Lord Richard Casey, the Governor-General, following Light Fingers' victory in 1965.

I did my duty and stayed in Adelaide for the Birthday Cup in March 1966. We won – and I heard that Storm Queen won the Golden Slipper the same day. Jockey John Miller looks on as I meet the Queen Mother. Eight months later, he and his mount that day, Galilee, would win a Melbourne Cup.

With Patrick at the 1966 Caulfield Cup. I'm the horse trainer, he's the tax accountant.

John Miller and Galilee winning the 1966 Melbourne Cup. I haven't trained a better stayer.

I have eyes only for Galilee. His co-owner, Venice Bailey, seems pretty
pleased with the trophy.

Roy Higgins gets Red Handed home in the 1967 Cup. Higgins said he lifted to beat Red Crest when he remembered who had trained his mount.

Roy Higgins said I might have won two fewer Melbourne Cups without his riding on Light Fingers and Red Handed. I said that without my training, he wouldn't have won any! Owner Angus Tyson, owner Bill Clarke (obscured), me, Higgins and owner Brian Condon. The Cup belongs to Red Handed.

I've had a long association with another racing family, the Windsors. Here, in April 1970, Princess Anne presents me with a trophy after Gay Poss won the AJC Oaks.

Roy Higgins on board Dayana, in the 1972 Victoria Derby. The horse won a record four derbies that season and was horse of the year.

Taj Rossi (No. 2) and Higgins pip stablemate Leica Lover in the 1973 Victoria Derby. Taj Rossi had won my first Cox Plate the week before and was the best three-year-old I'd trained.

Leilani and Mick Mallyon the day they won the 1974 Caulfield Cup. She should have won the Melbourne Cup too …

… until Harry White and Think Big got up and stormed past her. I beat myself!

With Think Big and strapper Guy Walter, who went on to become a very good trainer in his own right. Everyone seemed a bit apologetic about Think Big upsetting our favourite.

I trained some handy two-year-olds as well: here Lord Dudley wins the Blue
Diamond Stakes at Caulfield in 1975.

Maybe Mahal, the weedy filly who won more Group Ones than any other of
my horses, winning at Flemington.

At 33/1, Think Big wins the 1975 Melbourne Cup, his second. We got another quinella, with Holiday Waggon chasing him home.

The Malaysian PM Tunku Abdul Rahman had come into the ownership of Think Big since 1974, and cashed in with the 1975 Cup. Tan Chin Nam would become a 'Dato', the Malaysian equivalent of a knight.

John Duggan brings Gold And Black (left) down the straight to win the 1977 Cup. Tommy Woodcock's Reckless, the people's favourite, was runner up.

Sir John Kerr, Duggan and me after Gold And Black's win. They booed the Governor-General. I told him, 'Don't worry, they're all commos.'

With my friend Peter Mason and a couple of mates we'd reeled in at the Bay of Islands, New Zealand, January 1978.

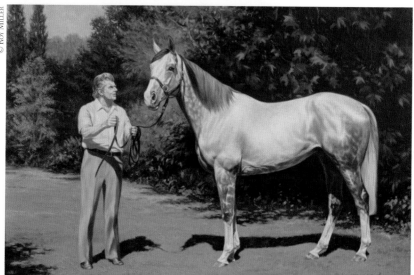

© Roy Miller

A painting of me with Ming Dynasty, winner of two Caulfield Cups and one Australian Cup. When he was retired, he wandered back into the stables looking for his old stall after escaping the AJC clerk of the course.

Hyperno (Harry White) edging out Salamander (Roy Higgins) in the 1979
Cup. Higgins hadn't liked Hyperno from the start. He liked him even less
that day.

Harry White
sometimes needed
to be woken up
before a race. He
was fully awake
by the time of
the presentation,
though. Hyperno's
win was White's
fourth Melbourne
Cup in six years.

won nineteen races from forty-three starts, one of the better-performed Group One winners of that or any other era.

NEARLY ALL OF MY MELBOURNE CUP WINNERS HAVE HAD TO overcome some serious health obstacle, and Gold And Black was no exception. After his second place in the Sydney Cup, we were taking him for his spell to a stud near Oakbank, in South Australia, and he contracted pneumonia so seriously he nearly died. He had a lung weakness throughout his life, and was susceptible to bronchial complaints. For a time in the winter, while Reckless was winning his historic treble of 2-mile races, we wondered if Gold And Black would ever race again. He was a rising five-year-old, headed for the prime of his racing life, and here he was suffering an almost-fatal illness.

I took him very slowly, but it didn't help my morale when the VRC handicapper gave Gold And Black 57 kilos for the 1977 Melbourne Cup. The horse had only won three times in more than thirty starts. He'd come second in the Cup with 50 kilos, but hadn't won a race since, and was down with pneumonia. And he was given 57 kilos!

When he was ready to race, he finished seventeenth in a field of seventeen down the straight 5 at Victoria Park. We took him to Melbourne for the weight-for-age races, and he trundled along unplaced in all of them: sixth in the Memsie, last in the Craiglee, fifth in the Underwood and eighth in the Caulfield Stakes. In hindsight it looks like a typical slow-building Melbourne Cup preparation, but we didn't really know how his stamina had recovered from his illness.

His first big staying test was the Caulfield Cup. He started at 25/1 in a strong field that included Family of Man, Sir Serene and Unaware, all Group One winners. Our grey gelding Ming Dynasty was backed in to 9/1, with Harry White aboard. He'd certainly taken the step up in class since the summer, charging home to win the Craiglee Stakes, and didn't surprise us when he took the lead halfway down the Caulfield straight and ran away with the Cup. It was my fourth win in the race, which nobody else had done.

Ming Dynasty's success was all the more satisfying for my having bought him for $3000. Valmae was racing him as owner, in partnership with some others. Lloyd Foyster, the breeder, had come up to me after the sale and said he wanted a share in the horse. This other man, standing next to Foyster, said, 'I want a share too!' I got it organised, thinking the other man was Foyster's friend. In fact he wasn't at all. They'd never met. And now they were racing Ming Dynasty in partnership.

While Ming Dynasty was coming into Melbourne Cup calculations, we weren't sure if he'd go the distance. Gold And Black caught my eye, however, when he ate up the ground and came home very strongly in the Caulfield Cup for another fifth place, the same as 1976.

Only two horses had ever won the Melbourne Cup after finishing second the previous year, and one of them was the great Carbine, so Gold And Black had to be very, very good. But I thought he was, and he gave me great heart by flashing home for second to Sir Silver Lad in the Mackinnon on the Saturday before the Cup.

The public, of course, were red-hot for Reckless. Tommy Woodcock had given him an unorthodox preparation, racing him so solidly in the winter and then giving him just four starts, well spaced, during the spring. But if anyone knew this particular horse it was Tommy, and nobody was prepared to rule them out.

The difference between the bookmakers' odds and those on the tote was extraordinary, reflecting just how much Reckless was a 'people's horse'. Tommy Woodcock even let children sit on Reckless in the birdcage half an hour before the Cup. Bookies frame their odds based on their opinions. That Melbourne Cup had the strongest field in a while – Van Der Hum, Ming Dynasty, Unaware, Family of Man, Salamander and an up-and-comer called Hyperno were all in it – but Gold And Black and Reckless were the outstanding favourites. With the bookies, Gold And Black started 7/2 while Reckless was 11/2. The tote odds, meanwhile, are driven purely by popularity, and on the TAB Reckless was 3/1 favourite with Gold And Black 11/2. It takes a massive amount of money, millions of dollars, to generate that kind of difference between tote odds and bookies' odds. I can't think of a Melbourne Cup where sentimentality has created such a wide spread between the two.

On a good surface, John Duggan rode Gold And Black confidently. After being the top Sydney apprentice under Theo Green in the early 1970s, Duggan had finished second for us in the past two Melbourne Cups, on Gold And Black and Holiday Waggon. But he'd won the Golden Slipper for us on Vivarchi, leading all the way, and I'd made him our first pick when we were racing in Sydney. When he was focused and at the track, Duggan was an extremely good rider; but when he was off horseback, he needed a lot of help. The same applies to a great many jockeys.

As they moved into the home straight, Geoff Murphy's Hyperno burst clear. I would get to know this horse, with his enormous talent and difficult personality, a lot better in years to come. Having raced in midfield, Duggan hooked Gold And Black wide and came after Hyperno. He hauled him in at the 300-metre mark, but the roar went up – here came Woodcock's Reckless. Everyone, or almost everyone, wanted Reckless to win. I doubt I've ever trained a more 'unpopular' horse. But of course Gold And Black wasn't unpopular for us in the stable, and certainly not for the owners. Hugh Gage, who was at the track having missed the Cup while having open-heart surgery in 1976, must have been the good-luck charm. Gold And Black, with Duggan in his black cap with gold and black hooped silks, held off Reckless and won by a length, with Hyperno another two and a half lengths back in third. The time was an astonishing 3 minutes 18.4 seconds.

There were many reasons for satisfaction as we unsaddled Gold And Black. For the Harrises and the Gages, it was the end of a long and patient journey – this was only Gold And Black's fourth win in forty-one starts. For Duggan, it was vindication after his two second placings. For my son Anthony, who had just started working full time for the stable, and my new Melbourne stable foreman, a former jockey and baker named Leon Corstens, it was the first authentic taste of Melbourne Cup success. Anthony had been the only one of my children to make a real nuisance of himself following me around the stables from a young age, and was now making as if he wanted to work in the racing industry. My three daughters, Margaret, Sharon and Anne-Marie, had enjoyed having ponies when they were young, but only Anthony showed an inclination to go into racing professionally. He said he remembered viewing an autopsy on a horse when he was five years old. I suppose something like that is either going to turn you off horses forever, or the opposite. Anthony claims that as he was growing up working in the stables, he earned $60 a week but was fined $20 for every morning he turned up late. The result, often, was that he was paying us money to work for us. Sounds to me like a good deal both ways! Anthony went to university for a short time, but like his father he was bitten by the horse-racing bug and he didn't stay there very long. He had wanted to be a vet, but didn't get the marks and decided to study science instead. Then, one day, I called him and said I needed a float driver. He dropped his studies like that, came to drive the float, took the horses on trips interstate, and that was the beginning of his career in racing. So I suppose Gold And Black was to Anthony what Comic Court had been to me.

I'd come a long way since strapping Comic Court. This was Cup number six, and I'd done it: I'd passed Etienne de Mestre's record, set exactly ninety-nine years earlier. This is one of those achievements that I almost let pass me by. First of all, I'm not one to look back and tell myself how clever I am. And second, the crowd around the enclosure was strangely quiet. They were all looking at Reckless, and Tommy Woodcock, and feeling understandably sad that the fairytale hadn't come to pass. A lot of them would have done their dough as well.

And finally, there was the presentation, which added to the unusual feeling in the air. The Governor-General, Sir John Kerr, was booed by the crowd as he had been ever since his dismissal of the Whitlam government in 1975.

The crowd was full of trade unionists, as far as I could see. I said to him, 'Don't get upset, sir, they're all commos.' He gave a bit of a grim laugh. It must have all been pretty awful for him, having been a supporter of the left in the past but now having turned into their number-one public enemy. I went on: 'It's a race meeting, sir, not a political rally. Don't worry about it!' He laughed away, thankful for some light relief in a dark time.

It was commented that Sir John's speech was made in a state of drunkenness. If that was so, he fooled me. I stood close by him, and accepted my trainer's trophy from him; they said he was blotto but I didn't think he was too bad. He seemed quite sober to me. But perhaps I was distracted. It was beginning to sink in. I had won six Melbourne Cups. It was, to that point, the proudest moment in my racing life.

13

The wild bastard

It was as if Gold And Black lived his whole life for those two days when he ran in the Melbourne Cup. Like Think Big, he hardly won a thing outside that race. He deserved to win two, just like Think Big. Horses can have an affinity for a track and a distance, and they can also have an affinity for a day in the year, such as the second Tuesday in November. Sometimes, I'm sure of it, they just know.

Gold And Black went into retirement for eighteen months,

but we would decide to bring him back for a crack at the 1980 Melbourne Cup. We campaigned him in the autumn of that year. He ran unplaced a few times before coming third behind Tommy Smith's new champion, the three-year-old Kingston Town, over 12 furlongs. Then, in a slow-run Sydney Cup, Gold And Black tailed off for twelfth, and we figured that he'd had enough.

He retired comfortably, first as a clerk of the course mount in Adelaide and then to a farm at Gawler, where he lived until 1985 when, suffering from kidney stones, he died after complications during surgery. In an incredible coincidence, his sire In The Purple and his one-time conqueror, the In The Purple mare How Now, both died the very next day on separate stud farms in New Zealand.

It was in 1976 that we moved permanently to Sydney. The big city was the centre of the action as far as racing was concerned, but the authorities in Adelaide gave us a little push when the West Beach Trust withdrew their permission to let me take the horses onto the beach and into the water. Swimming and beach-walking were at the centre of my training regime, and I couldn't understand such pettiness.

Still, it was probably inevitable that we would relocate to Sydney sooner or later. The children had either finished school or were close to it, and Leilani Lodge was where most of my horses were. Since the 1960s I had been encouraged by the Thompson family, who owned the famous Widden Stud near Scone in the western Hunter Valley, to move to Sydney. Frank

Thompson and his son Bim were keen to see some competition for Tommy Smith in Sydney. They helped me secure the lease on the new stables that would become Leilani Lodge, and gave me every assistance to get set up. I don't know why they wanted someone to knock Tommy off – maybe it was just the belief that competition was always good for sport, and Tommy was winning the premiership with a frequency that was becoming monotonous. Anyway, I didn't need a second invitation. I would never say that Tommy and I had a 'friendly' rivalry. I loved beating him, and am sure he loved beating me. We loved beating each other! But that's the way it should be.

So off we went to Sydney at the beginning of 1976. For the last few years I'd kept up a long-term rental on some rooms in a house in Wunulla Road, Point Piper, and now we bought a house in Vaucluse, in the eastern suburbs, and made the harbour city our home. Valmae had wanted to move to Sydney since the mid-1960s, so she took no persuading. We left twenty-year-old Anthony in charge of the Adelaide operation, which was sixty horses strong.

We enjoyed Sydney and already had many friends there. One of our neighbours was Bruce Rose, a former RAAF pilot who had lost one of his legs in the Second World War. He had had some property dealings with John Singleton up at Mount White, north of Sydney, but that was as near as Bruce got to the horse-racing caper. Nevertheless, he offered to become my taxi service to country meetings – in his helicopter! Bruce and his wife, Pam, lived in a two-storey waterfront house on Point Piper. You could walk down a concrete path from the house to the harbour, and step out onto Bruce's helipad. He was the only person to get permission to set up his private helipad on the harbour. He told me it had been in recognition of his war record. He was keen to use it whenever he could, and if I had a country meeting coming up, at Scone or Gosford or Kembla Grange for instance, Bruce assured me it would be a lot easier if I just popped down with him to his helicopter and he'd run me up. And he was right. We never had any problems with traffic.

GOING INTO 1978, THAT WEEDY LITTLE FILLY MAYBE MAHAL WAS causing a few of us to scratch our heads. She'd raced so well as a two-year-old, but at three she was still growing and had no energy. We tested her blood and there was nothing noticeably wrong with her; winless in nine starts as a three-year-old, she was retired to stud. But she couldn't get in foal, so we brought her back to the track.

Just as well. At four, she won the Craven 'A' Stakes (1200 metres), the George Adams Handicap (1600 metres), the Lightning Stakes (1000 metres) and the Doomben 10,000 (1350 metres). At five, she was Australian horse of the year, winning the Lightning Stakes again, the Newmarket Handicap (1200 metres) and the Doncaster Handicap over a mile at Randwick. Tommy Smith, who'd trained the beaten favourite, was blueing about Maybe Mahal's handicap, saying she should have been carrying another stone. Always complaining when he lost, was Tommy. I just had to chuckle.

When I've talked about the virtues of patience, I'm not just referring to staying horses. It's obvious why patience is necessary with a 2-miler. But what a lot of people don't understand is that patience is equally vital with sprinters. It's the finishing burst that wins, not the burst out of the starting gate. Even more than stayers, in a way, sprinters have to be kept quiet and relaxed. Maybe Mahal was like this. Although her wins were up to a mile, she had that same patient quality as Think Big, Gold And Black and the other great stayers. She ended up winning seven Group One races. My Melbourne Cup winners might have earned more fame, but alongside Storm Queen, Maybe Mahal won more Group Ones than any other horse I have trained – so far.

She captured the imagination of the racing public in the autumn of 1978, as did Ming Dynasty, who won the Australian Cup at Flemington and later in the year the Metropolitan at Randwick. Our three-year-old Stormy Rex, meanwhile, nearly equalled Dayana's record of four derbies. Stormy Rex won three – the Victorian, South Australian and West Australian derbies – but, like Dayana, never matured into a successful older stayer.

Stormy Rex was one of our four entrants in the 1978 Melbourne Cup, the most fancied of whom was Panamint, an imported horse owned by Robert Sangster. It wasn't our year, though. Panamint, coming ninth behind Arwon, was our best-placed runner.

Probably the form horse in the stable at that time was a middle-distance galloper called Lloyd Boy. He became a notorious horse, through no fault of his own or, for that matter, mine.

In the spring of 1978 Lloyd Boy came third in the Epsom Handicap and won the Caulfield Stakes, but wasn't quite up to the standard of the Cox Plate winner, So Called. We spelled him, then he came back in the autumn to finish second in the Futurity Stakes over 1400 metres and win the Carlyon Cup at Caulfield, the main lead-up to the Australian Cup.

He'd caught a virus after the Futurity and I'd considered spelling him, but he picked up well and won the Carlyon Cup by three lengths. Then, disaster: Lloyd Boy's urine test after the Carlyon returned a positive swab to oxyphenbutazone, an anti-inflammatory painkiller.

Immediately there was a VATC stewards' inquiry. Oxyphen-butazone was, and is, a perfectly legal medication, but the stewards had to be notified when it was administered and it couldn't be given to a horse within five days before a race. I'd been in Sydney, not Melbourne, at the time, and my Melbourne stable foreman Leon Corstens was in charge of feeding and medicating the horses. At the inquiry, Corstens said Lloyd Boy's feed bin must have been mixed up with that of another horse. He said it was an innocent mistake. We backed this up by showing that neither the owners nor myself, nor anyone who had anything to do with us, had backed Lloyd Boy in the Carlyon Cup.

Nevertheless, the stewards disqualified the horse, and banned me from training anywhere in Australia for three months. As with Cilldara eighteen years previously, I argued my innocence strenuously. A three-month suspension was a severe blow to me and the stables. We had 120 horses in work, and sixty-five staff in Adelaide, Melbourne and Sydney. The horses would need to be sent somewhere else and the staff would need to find other employers. Three months may sound like a short period, but with the logistics of closing down three stables and the damage to my reputation, I felt that it was a huge overreaction from the stewards. Corstens had been careless, true, but this was one of hundreds of thousands of feeds he had overseen, and he'd never made the mistake before. Plus, the medication hadn't improved the horse's performance.

Ever since the trauma of 1969 and Big Philou, I'd been at the forefront of the anti-nobbling movement, supporting a new dope-detecting method using gas chromatography that the AJC had imported. I'd increased stable security since Big Philou, and it felt unjust that I was having to carry the can for a genuine human error, a technical kind of mistake.

I appealed the ban, and was allowed to keep training for another few weeks. Lloyd Boy went up to Sydney and won a stakes race, the Ajax Quality at Rosehill, at his next start. The same day, a two-year-old filly I was training called Century Miss qualified for the Golden Slipper by running a race record over the Slipper track and distance, flying home from tenth on the turn in the Magic Night Quality. I was as excited as always about training for the big carnivals, and the last thing I needed was a suspension.

We had bred Century Miss ourselves, and I was a silent part-owner, with my good friend Malcolm Wuttke also involved. So we had a lot at stake in her succeeding. A Golden Slipper-winning filly would be worth hundreds of thousands of dollars in those days (millions nowadays) as a broodmare. She started 9/2 favourite for the Slipper, even though she was being ridden by an eighteen-year-old apprentice. No apprentice had ever won the Golden Slipper, so there were plenty of pundits who thought I was mad even to think of it. Peter Cook had ridden her in her previous start, but he had a prior commitment to the colt Mighty Kingdom, so I called Wayne

Harris to see if he was interested. Sometimes jockeys, like horses, can be precocious talents, and Harris was one of the best apprentices ever seen. I instructed him to let her settle, even if that meant dropping to the rear of the field, and set her up for one run only, from the top of the straight. It was the same tactics we'd used for Storm Queen in 1966. The funny thing was, it worked, yet few others thought to do the same. Golden Slippers are notorious for the cut-throat jostling at the front of the field, because everyone thinks you can't win from the tail. But my view was, if that's the way they want to play it, they're welcome; my horse can wait at the rear, avoid the trouble, and save itself for the last shot.

Harris rode Century Miss very patiently, just as I asked, and she tore down the outside from way back in the field to win by a head from Dawn Command. It was my fourth Golden Slipper after Storm Queen, Tontonan and Vivarchi, equalling Tommy Smith's record. (Incidentally, Century Miss never won another race in five more starts, retiring when she broke her jaw banging it against a stall, and was no good at all as a broodmare, which just shows there is no such thing as a certainty in racing!)

But the highs and lows have always followed each other. That's racing. A week after Century Miss's Golden Slipper I had to go back to the Victorian stewards for my appeal on the Lloyd Boy affair. I suspected that there were substantial interests, including rival trainers, who were lobbying the stewards to put me out of the game. I argued that as I wasn't in Melbourne at the time, I shouldn't be punished so harshly for a harmless mistake made by one of my staff, a mistake from which I had not substantially benefited. The committee decided, however, that as the boss I was responsible for all mistakes made by my staff.

So on 11 April 1979, I was given exactly fourteen days to dispose of all 120 of my horses, and forty-eight hours to find trainers for the sixteen horses who were racing the next weekend. All this in the middle of the second-biggest carnival of the racing calendar.

Before I was able to finalise things, three days after my failed appeal, the Doncaster Handicap was run. Belmura Lad had drifted badly in the betting, in a race that was expected to go to the champion three-year-old Manikato. But in a boilover, Belmura Lad burst clear and won in race-record time. Uniquely, he became the first horse to win a Group One race without a trainer being listed in the racebook. I suppose he trained himself!

We were able to make satisfactory arrangements over the next few days. A good Sydney trainer, Malcolm Barnes, took over Leilani Lodge. Ron Dawson remained as foreman, and my son Anthony worked as an assistant to Ron. I closed our Melbourne stables at Fisher Road, Ascot Vale – on which I'd just spent $27,000 in renovations – and sublet the Adelaide stables to Colin Graves. I stayed in Sydney to spend some time with the family, and then took off for overseas.

Each winter now I was travelling to the Northern Hemisphere, to look and learn. That year Valmae and I travelled to England, Europe and the USA, inspecting stud farms, racetracks and training facilities. We especially enjoyed France. We stayed at the George V Hotel in Paris, and to Valmae's enduring credit she didn't just go shopping while I went to the racetracks. She shared my curiosity about the racing scene and came along with me. The training facilities were impressive, to say the least. Some of the stables at Deauville and Chantilly were as grand as palaces. I looked at Valmae and said, 'We'd better smarten up Leilani Lodge!' We were invited to garden parties and cocktail parties, and the locals kindly spoke English to us. They really knew how to do things. I met Alex Head, one of the top trainers there, and had long conversations about training with him, often in his car, which he drove down the French roads like a rocket. I thought I was a fast driver, but these rides had my knuckles turning white on the door handle. His establishment was like something out of a fairytale, a palace that had been seized by the Gestapo in the Second World War and used as their headquarters. I suppose there were elements of government who always resented the racehorse industry having the use of such fine properties, and when the French Socialists won power in the 1980s a lot of these palaces were taken away again.

On these trips I also loved to go to the Keeneland yearling sales in Kentucky, to see what was going on and to hear the thoughts of the American trainers. Or, over on the west coast, I would make my way to the Hollywood Park racecourse near Los Angeles International Airport. There I would meet the great trainer Charlie Whittingham, a sensible and kind man with whom I had a long association. We would sit up at night and talk for hours, or Charlie would talk and I would listen. I enjoyed visiting him immensely, and for a few years made it an annual pilgrimage. He taught me a lot about his training methods and the different vitamins the Americans put in the horses' feed, pelletised forms of which weren't available in Australia.

The whole set-up was different in the United States, much

more entrepreneurial. For example, when trainers came from interstate to race horses at Hollywood Park, the race club offered them free accommodation for themselves and free stabling for the horses. After a few years, it shot up to the grand sum of $20 a week! The idea was all about creating an incentive to come to the course and win races. That, in turn, would increase betting turnover and benefit the clubs. The clubs did the same in Japan, letting out apartments and stables to trainers for next to nothing. In Australia, by contrast, trainers have always had to pay exorbitant fees for their stabling. Here at Randwick now, we pay rent of $47,272 a year for twenty boxes. It's quite a difference! I think it says a lot about the conservative way Australian race clubs approach the sport. Modernising their approach, and thinking innovatively, will become more and more important in the future if they want to keep racing relevant and vibrant.

One thing that surprised me in America was how much racing they did on dirt, artificial and other non-grass tracks. If you ask me, grass is the only natural surface to race horses on. Grass and coarse river sand for training, and that's about it. Dirt and artificial tracks are hard and dangerous, and create havoc for the horses. Their injury rates say it all. In America, the hard dirt tracks caused so much lameness that the trainers were allowed to use butazolidin, a medication which was illegal in Australia. But they had to use it because the dirt tracks were so tough on the horses.

I came back impressed with some things, particularly the technological innovations in therapy and medicine, but more convinced than ever that the very simple, commonsense methods centring on *thinking like a horse* that I had learnt from my father remained the best foundation for training successful thoroughbreds.

🐎

MY SUSPENSION ENDED ON 11 JULY 1979, WHEN A MAIDEN CALLED Show A Smile won a race. I was still away. I'd missed Panamint's win in the Adelaide Cup, which was a great achievement for Colin Graves but a bittersweet moment for me.

Malcolm Barnes had entered twenty of my horses in the 1979 Melbourne Cup. Not included among them was Hyperno, the 1977 third placegetter. Malcolm couldn't enter him for the simple reason that he was still being trained by one of my Victorian competitors, Geoff Murphy.

Hyperno had a bit of a name as an underachiever. He'd come back after his 1977 Melbourne Cup placing behind Gold And Black to win the 1978 C.F. Orr Stakes and the Adelaide Cup, but then he'd only had two starts in the 1978–79 season due to leg problems and a difficult temperament. Nobody doubted that he had talent, but he was a puzzle to which it was hard to find the solution.

Early in my suspension, while I was cooling my heels in Sydney, one of Hyperno's owners, Dr Ray Lake, approached me to ask if I would take over training the gelding. At first I said no. Hyperno was a rising five-year-old with attitude problems, I was suspended, and he had a good trainer already in Geoff Murphy. Dr Lake kept asking – well, to be frank, he was begging me. I told him that it was hard enough to win big races with sound horses, let alone those as injury-prone and cantankerous as Hyperno. Besides, I was under a training ban.

Murphy had bought Hyperno at the 1975 New Zealand yearling sales for $6500. The brown colt was by the recently imported British sire Rangong out of a mare called Mikarla. Murphy had bought another Rangong yearling, and brought them back to Melbourne to parade before a group of prospective owners.

Those owners included Tom (later Sir Thomas) North, then the head buyer for Coles, the property developer George Herscu, businessman John Pizem, and their wives. They selected the second Rangong colt, who would race as Fashion Beau. They also noticed the Rangong–Mikarla colt, or more immediately they noticed his strapper, who was bruised and lacerated over one eye. Herscu asked the strapper what had happened.

'This wild bastard did it to me,' the strapper said, indicating the colt.

Herscu said he liked wild horses, and bought it. (Herscu had a wild side himself, that ended up with him serving time in jail for financial crimes before he took off for Canada.)

The 'wild horse' was gelded and named Hyperno. Later, Ray Lake took over John Pizem's share in the galloper.

Hyperno only raced once as a two-year-old, but improved steadily in his three-year-old season and won six of fifteen starts. It seemed that Geoff Murphy had done with the gelding what I would have done in his shoes: patience, patience, patience. As a four-year-old Hyperno was an outsider in Gold And Black's Melbourne Cup, but wasn't far from winning it. Clearly he was one to watch for 1978.

In the autumn he was even better, winning the C.F. Orr Stakes at weight-for-age at Sandown. The Moonee Valley Cup was run in the autumn that year, and Roy Higgins was aboard. Hyperno looked certain to win, but Higgins stopped riding him just short of the line, the horse stopped running, simply gave up, and he was pipped. Higgins was suspended, but he always blamed the horse, saying Hyperno had ceased trying in a way that was unusual for a thoroughbred, indicating that he had an attitude problem. Higgins called him a 'rotten dog' of a horse.

Dr Ray Lake, an extremely nice gentleman, kept at me to take on Hyperno when I came back from my ban in 1978. But I still wasn't persuaded.

Hyperno's two runs as a spring five-year-old were promising, with placings in top-class races, but after his third in the Toorak Handicap he was found to be lame in one of his legs and went for a spell again. He didn't come right for the autumn either. But Ray Lake kept asking. Reluctantly I was drawn in. Persistence can overcome most obstacles, and Ray Lake was nothing if not dogged. I looked at X-rays of Hyperno's legs and his ligaments looked normal to me. There was no problem with his conformation, so his injuries weren't stemming from some structural abnormality. I went and saw him in his spelling paddock, and finally, after so much coaxing that felt like Ray would go on forever, I agreed to train the horse.

When I took him on he'd only raced twice in fifteen months and was broken down. My approach to him was to wait, wait, and then wait some more. I didn't want to do anything with him until I'd figured out how his mind worked.

He was complicated. I watched him and learnt what I could. When I took on older horses from other stables, I just wanted to find out what they liked and disliked, and why. This had worked with Ngawyni recently. With Hyperno, I noticed that he galloped, raced, did a lot of things, with his tongue hanging out. There needn't be anything amiss with this habit. A lot of people stick their tongue out of the corner of their mouth while they're exerting themselves, playing sport or concentrating.

Previously with Hyperno, his flopping tongue had been addressed with a tongue-tie, holding the tongue down so it wouldn't wave about. But I noticed that the tongue-tie irritated him. He hated it. Having his tongue out was one of his favourite things. When you walked past him in the stables he'd drop his tongue out for you to give it a tug. He loved nothing more than having his tongue pulled. So the first thing I was going to do, racing him, was take away the tongue-tie.

We started him in the weight-for-age Craiglee Stakes at Flemington in September 1979, and he ran tenth behind Dulcify, the champion four-year-old trained by Colin Hayes. Roy Higgins rode Hyperno. Maybe the jockey was the issue. Higgins never liked the horse, and quite probably the feeling was mutual. So we tried Gary Willetts on him, and Hyperno ran fifth in a Flemington handicap. Willetts was at the top of his game then, enjoying great success on Manikato. At Hyperno's third start for me, in the Caulfield Stakes, we tried Brent Thomson on him. Brent was the new wunderkind who did a lot of the riding for the Hayes stable, but he couldn't find the key to unlock Hyperno's talent. The horse ran fifth.

We tried Higgins again, in a Moonee Valley handicap, but Hyperno plodded home for sixth.

Somewhat desperately, I considered the use of blinkers. Ever since Cilldara I'd had mixed feelings about blinkers, but with Hyperno it seemed that anything was worth a try. He really was a riddle.

The rules on blinkers stated that you had to trial the horse in them in front of the stewards before they would give you permission to use the equipment in a race. I chose Higgins as the trial jockey, and we fitted Hyperno with the blinkers on the Tuesday before Derby day, exactly a week before the Melbourne Cup.

I asked Higgins to go quietly on him, and Hyperno promptly went out and ran half a mile in 49 seconds. That's anything but quiet – he flew! The stewards were obviously happy to green light the use of the blinkers.

Higgins came in and I said, 'Do you want to ride him in the Mackinnon and the Cup?'

Roy screwed up his face and said, 'No, but I'll find you a nice apprentice to ride him.'

I couldn't work it out at first. I thought, 'Something's not quite right here.' Imagine putting an apprentice on this horse for the Melbourne Cup! It turned out that Higgins was engaged to ride Salamander for Tommy Hughes. Higgins didn't like Hyperno as a horse, and he didn't want him to win. Or he might have been pulling my leg.

Instead of letting Higgins find me an apprentice, I called up Harry White. Harry and I had had a falling-out the previous spring, when he'd ridden a horse of mine called Dancairo at Moonee Valley. It had been backed very strongly, we thought it was a strong chance, and under Harry it had finished twelfth in a field of fifteen. There were lots of stories going around about Harry at the time, and I'll admit I might have been influenced by them. For all I knew, they might have been spread by other jockeys, jealous of all the Melbourne Cups he'd been winning. Leon Corstens gave him the message that I wasn't pleased with his ride on Dancairo, and Harry and I didn't talk for a while. In the interim, he'd won his third Melbourne Cup, piloting Arwon.

The hatchet was well and truly buried when I called him to offer the ride on Hyperno for the 1979 Mackinnon and Cup. The owners were happy. The only person who was going crook about it was Roy Higgins, who must have feared what Hyperno could do under another jockey.

The star of the season was unquestionably Dulcify. As a three-year-old he'd been horse of the year, winning the Victoria and AJC derbies and the Australian Cup. In the spring he was unbeatable at weight-for-age. He won the Craiglee and the Turnbull stakes, then the Cox Plate by an incredible seven lengths. The VRC handicapper had more or less gifted him the Melbourne Cup, with a very light weight of 56 kilos. Imagine a horse like that, being rated inferior to Think Big and Gold And Black! As long as Dulcify was fit and could run the distance, it was hard to see anything beating such a champion. Hyperno, carrying the same weight, seemed distinctly disadvantaged given their respective records.

But on Derby day, although Dulcify won the Mackinnon, he seemed to struggle to hit the line. Hyperno ran on for fourth place, a pleasing trial similar to so many of my Cup horses.

Dulcify still attracted most of the money for the Cup, and closed in to start at 3/1 favourite. Hyperno was fourth favourite at 7/1, behind Warri Symbol and Cubacade. Higgins' ride, Salamander, was next at 10/1. Even leaving aside the business with Higgins, Salamander and Hyperno had a rivalry going way back; in his last run for Geoff

Murphy, Hyperno had finished close behind Salamander in the Toorak Handicap.

There was a function for the annual Calling of the Card at the Victorian Club in Queen Street on the Sunday night before the Cup. Valmae didn't come, so I took my old friend Malcolm Wuttke. A bookmaker, an old friend of my father's, invited us to have a drink at the bar before we left. He told us that he had heard from a vet that Dulcify had an injury which would stop him from running in the Cup. This rumour was apparently all over the place after his Mackinnon Stakes run, so on Cup day we were amazed, given the rumours, that he was still in the field.

Rupert Murdoch backed Hyperno. According to Ray Lake, who was a good friend of Murdoch's, the media owner gave him $15,000 in cash to put on Hyperno. Ray didn't know where to put it safely, so he stashed it in his freezer. He thawed it out on Cup morning, took it down to the track, and placed it on Hyperno at about 7/1.

Hyperno and Dulcify ran in midfield, then both loomed up on the home turn. All of a sudden Brent Thomson pulled Dulcify up. He had been galloped on, and was later found to have broken his pelvis. It was a shocking fate for a champion horse, but everything happened very quickly and I wasn't aware of the commotion at the back of the field until after the race.

On the turn, Hyperno cruised up from fifth place to take the lead from Red Nose. On Salamander, Roy Higgins was riding a brilliant, and lucky, race. He never left the rail and every run he needed opened up for him.

Salamander scooted through on Hyperno's inside. Their duel

was reminiscent of Light Fingers and Ziema, or Red Handed and Red Crest. Hyperno, with Harry White in the owners' pink, black and gold colours with gold cap, was holding on, just. But on his inside, Higgins' bare brown metal helmet – his red cap had flown off – was bobbing up and down, refusing to let our horse win. Hyperno and Salamander crossed the line together, and nobody in the grandstand could call it, certainly not me or the owners.

Harry was sure he'd won, and told Higgins so as they were slowing down. Higgins said he was hoping for a dead heat. The developed print came through, and Hyperno had won by the skinniest possible margin, a short half-head.

Another Melbourne Cup! And the stable still wasn't running at full capacity after my suspension. This was such a heart-stopper, but extremely satisfying given that I'd only had Hyperno for a few months and he came with such untapped potential. It's enormously satisfying to pick a yearling and train it up for years until it wins a Melbourne Cup, as I had with all the others, but this was a very special feeling indeed, to fix a problem horse. And he beat the boy who had called him a 'rotten dog'.

Valmae had a humorous moment with Dr Lake up in the grandstand and encouraged him to rush down and bring Hyperno back to scale.

He took the steps three at a time, just as I had many years earlier to get to Comic Court. He deserved it, too. If not for his persistence, Hyperno would never have come to me and may not have won a Melbourne Cup.

14

The winners between the wins

WITH FOUR MELBOURNE CUPS IN THE PAST SIX YEARS, SEVEN CUPS in all, four Golden Slippers, 134 Group One wins and a string of trainers' premierships, I finished the decade with every expectation that the rivers of gold would keep on flowing. I celebrated in 1980 by buying a 53-foot fishing boat, which I called the MV *Leilani*. We moored it at the Royal Motor Yacht Club in Sydney and took guests out on the harbour. When the mood took me, I'd go out into the open sea to fish for something bigger. A day of fishing adds a day to your life, and every time I fished it brought back memories of those wonderful days on Lake Taupo or in the Bay of Islands on my New Zealand trips.

The 1980s dawned bright. Yet I would not win a Melbourne Cup at all, nor a Golden Slipper. The premierships would dry up. I don't look back on the eighties as a bad decade for me, as I won sixty-three Group Ones and had some of my best horses, but it certainly ended badly, with the worst crisis, financially and personally, of my training life.

The decade started with no hint of trouble. We certainly seemed to have unlocked the secret to Hyperno. His Melbourne Cup win was not the end of his run, but just the beginning. A few days after such a torrid Cup, he'd come out at Flemington again and won the Queen Elizabeth Stakes, over 2500 metres. In the next two years he won the Caulfield Stakes, the Australian Cup, the Rawson Stakes, the Blamey Stakes twice, and was second in the Caulfield Cup under 59 kilos. He was a terrific horse and, remarkably, Australian horse of the year for his performances during his seven-year-old season, in 1980–81. He won nineteen races and a dead heat, the majority of them in the years after he had been declared a broken-down rogue.

Harry White continued to ride Hyperno, which impacted on the decline of my partnership with Roy Higgins. The Hyperno business in the spring of 1979 was only a part of it. Roy's chronic problem was his weight – he was naturally a few kilos on the heavy side for a jockey, and constantly had to waste to get down to his required riding weight. If I had a lightly weighted horse I couldn't even consider Higgins as the rider, which limited our options. In January 1980 he wanted to waste for a two-year-old called Silver Shoes, but I didn't think she was worth it. He wasn't himself at that point, as he was taking appetite suppressants and these were affecting his mood. He also suffered from another of the curses of the successful jockey: a lot of hangers-on who wanted to lead him astray off the racetrack.

We went our separate ways that autumn, after a sixteen-year association that started with Light Fingers. He had won 103 stakes races on my horses, and for his balance and his intuition, I will always rate him among the best jockeys I've seen. But for us as a team, that was it. Not too long after, Roy would retire.

We have since made up again. We had too many good memories in common. Roy said to me a few years ago, 'You know, you've won a lot of Melbourne Cups but my rides on Light Fingers and Red Handed were pretty good – if it wasn't for me, you'd have won two fewer Melbourne Cups than you have.'

I shot back: 'And if it wasn't for me, you wouldn't have won any.'

MIDGE DIDHAM WAS THE REGULAR RIDER OF MING DYNASTY, WHO continued to surprise as he grew older. Valmae led him in to scale when he won the 1980 Australian Cup, the first horse to win that race twice since Craftsman in 1965 and 1966. He hadn't won a race for eighteen months, the old grey, but Ming had a tremendous will to win and obviously focused his energy on the big races.

That autumn and spring were dominated by one horse, Tommy Smith's Kingston Town. I couldn't help gnashing my teeth a little. At the yearling sale when Kingston Town was first offered up, there was little interest and he was passed in at around $12,000. His owner, David Hains, kept him to race in his own colours and sent him to Tommy. What kept gnawing at me was that I'd been late arriving at those sales, and would have bought the nice black Bletchingly–Ada Hunter colt for $12,000. Without a doubt he was the one that got away.

As a three-year-old Kingston Town was unbeaten in Sydney and Brisbane, before going down to Melbourne for the spring carnival and the cups. Even though Hyperno upset him by a neck in the Caulfield Stakes, Kingston Town was a short-priced favourite for the 1980 Caulfield Cup, ahead of Hyperno at 5/1. I remember the day distinctly. Tommy Smith's daughter Gai was a cadet journalist at the time. She had a microphone and as the horses paraded she said how sad it was that old Ming Dynasty was forced to race at his age. He hadn't been running well and was going to the post at odds of 50/1. She said he should be leading a quiet life as a clerk of the course's mount.

He must have heard her! In a classic Caulfield Cup, Kingston Town challenged in the final furlong, but Ming Dynasty came steaming home. For good measure, Hyperno finished second, ahead of Kingston Town in third. I suppose it didn't hurt that with my fifth Caulfield Cup I'd passed Tommy's record.

That was Ming's last win. He sustained some cuts on his legs in the Caulfield Cup, and against my own reservations I ran him in the Cox Plate the next week, when he ran sixth behind Kingston Town, who proved himself a true champion in that race, going on to win it three times, a feat that has not been matched.

Hyperno ran unplaced as favourite in the Melbourne Cup behind Colin Hayes's Beldale Ball, but was horse of the year for that season, winning the St George Stakes, Blamey Stakes, Australian Cup, Rawson Stakes and AJC Queen Elizabeth Stakes in the autumn.

I always had to be careful with how I treated him. Like all the champions, he was a highly intelligent horse, and I think his strong personality was a sign of that intelligence. Sometimes when he knew it was race day, he got himself worked up with nerves. His normal race day routine would be to gallop over 2 furlongs on the grass in the early morning, then have a rest at the stables before coming back to the track. This was nothing unusual – many horses would have the same routine. But they don't all react to it in the same way, and we noticed Hyperno was getting more and more anxious when he knew it was race day, so we decided to trick him. On the morning of the Blamey Stakes, we told his track jockey Bob Ball to give Hyperno his *Sunday* routine – that is, trot and canter him on the sand track. When this happened, Hyperno thought it must be Sunday and went back to the stable and cleaned out his feed bin. He didn't have time to get worried, and must have been astonished when we came around later in the day, took him to the racetrack, saddled him up and sent him out. He beat a very good New Zealander, My Brown Jug, over the mile of the Blamey, then won my eighth Australian Cup from the same horse and Turf Ruler. His autumn in Sydney, in the injured Kingston Town's absence, was his finest campaign.

Our stables were expanding and improving. I bought Brian Gilders' stables at Flemington, which adjoined ours, and the entire facility grew so I could have several dozen horses in training at the same time. For $2000 I imported a new machine I'd seen in America, which circulated ice water around the horse's legs while it stood there. Nowadays it's common knowledge for human and equine athletes that ice water can be a great restorative after hard work, particularly in hot conditions, but at the time I was the only trainer to use such a machine in Australia. We also took good care of our spelling horses, and I'd often be visiting them at Princes Farm, a beautiful 120-acre property of improved pasture at Castlereagh, just north of Penrith at the foot of the Blue Mountains. The Nepean River runs alongside the farm, and with its plentiful shade and lush grass it was nirvana for horses. It could support more than a hundred at a time, from foals and weanlings to spellers, pre-trainers and retired horses. It had a 1100-metre track for breaking in and tutoring young racehorses. It was owned by Sir John Austin, the head of Blue Metal Quarries, before he sold it to the advertising man John Singleton. I knew Singleton through racing, and always found him a good businessman and a bit of a character. He has a horse in training with me now, a Melbourne Cup hopeful called Joe Blow. Singo named him after his son. After he bought Princes Farm off Sir John Austin, Singo lived in the staff quarters while he had the house rebuilt. He put in a swimming pool and a spa. At the time he was married to a former Miss World, Belinda Green, so I suppose he needed to put in the pool and spa to keep her up to scratch. In 1988 I bought the property, including the new house overlooking the Nepean River, at Castlereagh. I had loved the farm from the first moment I saw it, and going there brought me great calm and happiness. We got great use out of Singo's swimming pool, where my children and grandchildren could come – the Cummings family tree was branching out fast – and we had a little statue made of a jockey wearing my green-and-gold diagonal striped silks. He stood guard at the front of the main homestead.

The winners kept coming. After what I'd done with Hyperno, more and more owners of proven horses were switching them to me if they were unhappy with their present training arrangements. On behalf of a syndicate involving John Singleton and Gerry Harvey, I bought the champion juvenile of that season, Best Western, after the colt had won several times as a two-year-old for Neville Begg. When I took him over, Best Western won the Sydney three-year-old spring triple crown of the Peter Pan, Gloaming and Spring Champion stakes, emulating what Kingston Town had done two years earlier. An amusing footnote was that there was a solid gold cup awarded to the owners of horses who won the spring triple crown. After Kingston Town won it the racing clubs were up for $250,000 to make another one for Best Western only two years later. Of course, they had this covered by insurance. Insurance companies will cover a gold cup being won, just as they will cover it if it gets lost. But after Best Western won it, the insurance premiums went through the roof. It looked like someone was going to win this gold cup every second year, it was too easy! So the race clubs stopped making the gold cup. Sure enough, the triple crown has never been won since then, gold cup or no gold cup.

Best Western might have turned into as good a racehorse as Kingston Town, but he was injured after the Spring Champion Stakes and only raced one more time, winning again for me. Gerry Harvey and John Singleton felt that as a colt, he was too valuable to risk injuring again, and he retired to become one of Australia's most influential sires. I was particularly pleased to see so many good local stallions coming through. The days of second-rate English sires being thought of as superior to Australians were coming to an end. Like many businessmen, Gerry liked to control every factor down to the minutest detail, and when you're racing thoroughbreds you have to give up control to the trainer, first of all, and then to the racing gods. Nothing can be guaranteed. That didn't sit too comfortably with Gerry. Ever since the Best Western days, whenever I see him he makes noises about giving me horses to train, but he never does. It's probably best that way. I might have to charge him extra for the advice he wants to give me!

No Peer was another good galloper who got up to win five races as a four-year-old in the spring of 1981. He started favourite in the Caulfield Cup, in which I also had Hyperno, who had come in third behind Kingston Town in the Caulfield Stakes. Kingston Town was being saved for the Cox Plate and Melbourne Cup, and No Peer looked to have the Caulfield Cup sewn up until Silver Bounty flashed through and pipped him by centimetres.

But No Peer was looking for the 2 miles of the Melbourne Cup, and we had a very strong contingent lined up. Hyperno was in good form at eight years old, as was my other veteran, Belmura Lad. Having won an AJC Derby four years earlier,

Belmura Lad was an incredibly durable and versatile race-horse. He flashed home for fourth in the Epsom Handicap on the Saturday of the Randwick spring carnival in 1981, over 1600 metres, and then on the Monday stepped up to 2600 metres and won the Metropolitan. Then he went down to Flemington for the Cup, and on Derby day was expected to chase home Kingston Town, who had just won his second Cox Plate and was 5/2-on favourite for the Mackinnon. But Belmura Lad became my second 50/1 old-timer to beat Kingston Town in successive seasons, making me a bit of a 'hoodoo' trainer for Tommy's champ.

We had every reason to be confident for that Melbourne Cup, in which No Peer started at 4/1 favourite ahead of Kingston Town, Hyperno and Belmura Lad. It was one of the strongest fields in years. Koiro Trelay had won the New Zealand and Wellington cups, Arwon had won a Melbourne Cup, and Our Paddy Boy, Just A Dash, Pelican Point and Magistrate had all won 2-mile cups in other cities that year.

In the running, all of our horses copped bad luck. No Peer was caught wide and couldn't get into the race. Hyperno was blocked when he was looking for a run and came sixth. Belmura Lad split them with a brave seventh. Kingston Town had had enough and tailed off, but Tommy managed to win his second and final Melbourne Cup with Just A Dash, a relative outsider, surprising the more fancied runners. With Kingston Town failing, Tommy must have felt, as I sometimes had, that he had beaten himself.

IT WAS TWO OR THREE YEARS BEFORE I HAD ANOTHER GOOD CROP of horses. As our numbers of big winners fell off, there were some who questioned my commitment to training, but you can't work with blunt tools. You need the horses, and as Hyperno, Ming Dynasty, Belmura Lad, Best Western and others retired, I would inevitably have to go through a leaner period. The game was getting more and more competitive, with new trainers and owners coming through, and there were enough people copying my methods that I could no longer drive around New Zealand in January on my own and be confident I wouldn't run into other Australian trainers. The sport had always been highly professional, but the money coming in now was astronomical and I was having to think up new ways to stay ahead.

The rising New Zealand sire was now Sir Tristram, owned by Patrick Hogan at his stud at Cambridge. Patrick had brought the stallion out from Europe in 1971, and a stable fire in quarantine nearly killed him. Having paid $160,000 for him, Patrick tried to syndicate the ownership, but there were few takers so he ended up owning most of the horse himself. Sir Tristram's first big winners were full brothers: Sovereign Red, who won the 1978 Victoria Derby, and Gurner's Lane, who won the Caulfield and Melbourne cups in 1982, edging out Kingston Town in the latter.

Patrick is a superb horseman and a cheeky fellow. I first met him back in the late 1960s at the property he owned at the time, Fencourt Stud. I was in New Zealand on my usual January buying tour, and I rang Patrick to ask if I could come and look at a couple of yearlings by Hermes, who would become a leading sire later but was still relatively unknown.

Unbeknown to me, Patrick and his brother John got scared at the idea that a Melbourne Cup-winning trainer was coming to look at their young horses. They didn't even have a parade ring, so they arranged for a truckload of sand to be poured into a circular area of bare ground in front of their cow shed. They raked it smooth, and when I arrived they brought out the first yearling.

Its legs sank straight into the sand. I said to Patrick, 'Son, I wouldn't mind seeing his pasterns and fetlocks. Take him out of the sand and put him on the dirt over there so I can take a better look at him.'

I liked to have a bit of fun with Patrick; we shared an Irish sense of humour. Once he sent me one of his horses to train, but unfortunately it died of some illness or other while in the stable. I called Patrick and told him, and gave him my sympathies. A year or so later, he sent another horse to me, and I sent him an invoice for the horse's rug and head collar. Patrick phoned me up to query it.

'Well,' I said, 'your horse has to have a rug and a head collar.'

'Yes, JB, but don't you recall that I lost a horse at your stable? A horse that had a rug and had a head collar? Don't you recall that?'

I had a good answer for him.

'I do,' I said, 'but I'd like to ask you something. Do you blokes in New Zealand bury your dead naked?'

Patrick said that the laugh he got was worth the price of the rug and head collar.

He tried to get me back, a few years later. As I've said, the size of a yearling's girth was one of the principal factors influencing my decision to buy it. The bigger the girth, the more room for heart and lungs. I started sending my staff to inspect yearlings with a string to run around the horses' girths to measure them up. Patrick put one over them, offering to help but slipping his hand under the string to add a few inches onto the measurement. At the sales, when I saw some of Patrick's yearlings, I had a sense that the measurements we'd written down were inflated. I went back to Patrick myself the next day and told him I'd be doing the measuring myself.

When we got to the first horse, Patrick stood on the other side, waiting to 'help' me. I asked him to come around to my side.

'But, JB,' he said, 'I can't slip my fingers in behind on this side.'

'No, you can't,' I said. 'I knew there was something wrong here.'

There's one other Patrick Hogan story worth telling. In the early 1980s, I was visiting his new property, Cambridge Stud, where Sir Tristram was standing. It was a beautiful farm for horses, but the quarters for the human inhabitants left something to be desired. I saw a filly I liked, and said to Patrick's wife, Justine, 'I'll buy her, but only if Patrick promises to build you a new house.'

I bought the filly for $130,000, a record price at the time – ample money for Justine to have a new home by the next year, when I visited again. On my return, the first thing I said to Justine was, 'Aren't you going to take me to show me your new house?'

Well, Patrick was a little like me. If he got some money, he reinvested it straight back into the horses.

Justine said drily: 'Sure. My new house is running around in the paddock down there.'

THROUGH HIS CAREER SIR TRISTRAM WOULD SIRE FORTY-THREE Group One winners, a world record, and he was the leading Australasian sire for five years in a row in the 1980s. I would enjoy great success with Sir Tristram's progeny, including Oaks winner Tristanagh, Noble Peer and Our Tristalight. The first of my successful Sir Tristrams was Trissaro, brought to me by Sri Lankan businessman Upali Wijewardene.

Wije, as he liked to be called, had bought up a lot of palm groves from the English in Malaysia. They'd been listed on the local stock exchange, but had been let run to waste; Wije was able to buy them for a few cents a share, and did very well out of restoring them.

Wije purchased Trissaro, a gross, hard-to-handle son of Sir Tristram, for $200,000 after the horse had won five races in New Zealand, and sent him to me for the autumn of 1983. When he came to Australia, Trissaro was absolutely dominant. In Wije's red silks with gold crossed sashes, he won the Blamey Stakes, Carlyon Cup and the H.E. Tancred Stakes at Rosehill on Golden Slipper day, the weight-for-age highlight of the Sydney carnival. A big, temperamental horse, Trissaro was unbeatable when he put his mind to it. He came back the next year and won a Sydney Cup. But I can't help thinking of his career with a twinge of sadness for his owners.

I liked Wije and his wife Lakmani; they were very clever and generous people. Wije had his own private plane, and once he flew me over his palm groves to show me how he was growing cocoa trees under the palms. He got double the value for the land, he said, because he was able to grow both crops together. Then, after showing me around, he'd sit up all night playing the world's stock markets which he had on a number of screens in the study of his magnificent homestead. He had great energy and enthusiasm. But when I thought of Wije, I would always remember something Rupert Murdoch said, which was that the safest way to fly was on a commercial aircraft. You don't hear of commercial planes crashing very often, but you regularly hear of private planes going down. So it was with Wije. He died when his plane crashed on a flight between Malaysia and Sri Lanka, and Lakmani took over the ownership of his horses.

IT'S INTERESTING TO REFLECT ON THE ROLE THREE-YEAR-OLDS played in keeping me going in the 1980s. As Australian stallions were achieving prominence, breeders were criticised for focusing too much on the quick returns offered by two-year-old racing. There was a certain economic logic in trying to produce a precocious youngster who could win the huge amounts of money on offer now in the Golden Slipper, Blue Diamond and so on, then quickly send them off to stud where for massive fees they could sire new two-year-olds. By accelerating the whole racing–breeding lifespan of the horse, it enticed owners to think they could make their money back quicker. But the focus on two-year-olds did nothing for the breed as a whole, and many of us were worried that

Australia's three-year-old classics and semi-classics would fall to overseas-bred horses – not to mention the cups for older horses, which were already in the hands of the foreign-breds. Just A Dash was the only Australian-bred horse to win the Melbourne Cup between 1973 and 1984. I won nine Melbourne Cups with New Zealand- or overseas-bred horses before I won one with an Australian, and that was one I would breed myself. I think it says a lot about the Australian breeding industry that trainers had to look elsewhere to find Melbourne Cup winners.

Speaking for myself, although I had done well in sprints and juvenile races, there was nothing that quite matched the satisfaction of training a horse to win a three-year-old classic or a 2-mile cup. If you spend that long with a horse to build it up for those races, your relationship is deeper and more fulfilled. In my so-called 'lean years', meaning the years I didn't win a Melbourne Cup, I won a number of oaks races, the mile-and-a-half classics for three-year-old fillies, with Sheraco, Taj Eclipse (the daughter of Taj Rossi), Royal Regatta, Leica Show, Round The World and Tristanagh.

I had developed a good touch with female horses ever since Light Fingers and Storm Queen, but in the 1980s the three-year-olds that really stood out were the males. They came in two clusters. First, in 1983–84, there was Prolific and Bounty Hawk. Then, in 1987–88, there was the best crop of three-year-olds I ever raced: Sky Chase, Campaign King and Beau Zam.

BOUNTY HAWK AND PROLIFIC WERE BOTH DERBY HORSES WHO headed in different directions. Bounty Hawk naturally wanted more distance, Prolific less. But for one season, they were fierce rivals.

Having done little as a two-year-old, Bounty Hawk, a son of Balmerino, started slowly again at three, coming last in the Spring Champion Stakes at Randwick. But when we took him down to Victoria he thrived on the anticlockwise going under Harry White, coming second in the Geelong Derby Trial Stakes and winning the Victoria Derby at Flemington by two lengths from another of our three-year-olds, Cobbobonee. White, who had won four Melbourne Cups, had never won the Derby, so it was a nice day for him too. After the Derby, we took Bounty Hawk to Perth where he won the Western Mail Classic and then the Australian Derby.

Racing in three states – New South Wales, Victoria and Western Australia – in the spring and summer must have taken too much out of Bounty Hawk for the autumn, when he plugged on well without rediscovering his earlier form. This was when Prolific came through to dominate. Prolific, by the then boom sire Vice Regal, had been a sluggish juvenile, failing in the spring when he raced as an entire. During his summer spell, I convinced the owners to have him gelded, and as so often it wrought a profound transformation. He came back to win five races from 6 up to 12 furlongs. Even though he won the Tulloch Stakes over 10 furlongs, I thought Prolific was at the full extent of his stamina and wanted to bring him back in distance to the Doncaster, over a mile. Bounty Hawk, who had battled on well for a second to the New Zealander Beech-craft in the Canterbury Guineas, was more of a natural stayer and I didn't think Prolific could beat him over the 12 furlongs of the AJC Derby at Randwick. There is a rise in the long Randwick straight that makes distance races there particularly demanding, and to win an AJC Derby a horse really needs to be good for 2600 metres rather than the 2400. But the owners desperately wanted Prolific to run in the classic, so their wishes prevailed. Just as well – Prolific won the Derby, with Bounty Hawk finishing a game fourth.

Going into the spring of 1984, the pair were both weighted at 55 kilos for the Melbourne Cup. The VRC handicapper couldn't split them, but agreed that they were the top rising four-year-olds in the country. They both won at weight-for-age in the spring, but Bounty Hawk was looking for longer and Prolific didn't train on.

As favourite in the Caulfield Cup, Bounty Hawk was ridden by Harry White. Mid-race, a horse called Colonial Flag stopped suddenly, right in front of Bounty Hawk, and nearly knocked him down. White said it was a miracle Bounty Hawk had kept his feet. White rebalanced him and sprinted for home to finish second, by half a length, to Affinity. Bounty Hawk was my unluckiest Caulfield Cup runner, and deserved the race.

Two weeks later he won the Mackinnon Stakes, meriting his Melbourne Cup favouritism. But after looming on the turn in the Cup he tired, and finished fifteenth behind Black Knight (who had been bred in Western Australia and was a son of the 1971 Cup winner, Silver Knight). Black Knight was trained by the very successful Victorian-based horseman George Hanlon, who had also trained the Cup winners Piping Lane and Arwon. George had grown up in Adelaide, and was about my age. I knew him as a kid. He worked at the local bakery and came and parked his baker's cart outside our stables. He hung around and quietly asked questions of my father, hour after hour, day after day, three or four times a week. George was more interested in the horses than the bread. At the time I didn't know why he was there so much. Eventually I found out: he was climbing his learning curve as a would-be trainer. He turned into one of the better ones, unorthodox but wise, and I think he owed a lot of his success to what he gleaned from my father. Between the two of us, we protégés of Jim Cummings won half of the Melbourne Cups that were run between 1965 and 1984.

As the top-rated Australian middle-distance horse, Bounty Hawk was invited to the Japan Cup in Tokyo. This was a new adventure for Australian and New Zealand horses, having been inaugurated in 1981 as a true international race, and a lot of attention and anticipation went into the selection of our champion of the spring. It took nearly a decade before Horlicks (1989) and Better Loosen Up (1990) won the race for Australasia, and Bounty Hawk was among those who didn't perform at their best. He developed a wind-sucking habit during his trip to Tokyo – not that that mattered too much, as even the great Tulloch was a wind-sucker. But after his trip, Bounty Hawk needed an operation on his neck muscles. He'd never quite regain his old form again.

I was training Prolific to sprint, meanwhile, and he was looking to become the first horse since Heroic in 1926 to win the AJC Derby and VRC Newmarket. Little wonder it was such a rare feat – the Derby is over 12 furlongs for classic horses who might develop into 2-milers, while the Newmarket is a 6-furlong dash. But I always feel that good horses will win what you train them for. It's their talent that comes first, and then as their trainer you work with that. Prolific's talent got him through the Derby campaign as a three-year-old, but if I could keep him fresh and keen then he was a chance down the straight 6, which is a tough race that finds out the weaker sprinters.

Alas, Prolific didn't have the zip, finishing fourteenth, and his career was nearly over. I brought him and Bounty Hawk up for the 1985 spring, but Prolific went amiss after a bizarre Missile Stakes. The starting barrier was bogged so they set off from a flag start and the race was won by another of my horses, Plus Vite, at 200/1 becoming my longest-priced stakes winner. It was a thrilling win for the veteran jockey Peter Myers, but our immediate attention was on Prolific, who had broken down. The spring only got worse after that. Bounty Hawk, after getting his tongue over the bit and disappointing in the Chelmsford Stakes, sustained a stone bruise running seventh in the Caulfield Cup, and was more or less finished.

So for the first time since 1972, I didn't have a starter in the Melbourne Cup. The 1985 race was won by What A Nuisance, a hardy one-paced stayer who was trained by John Meagher and owned by an up-and-coming Melbourne businessman named Lloyd Williams, who had also owned the 1981 Cup winner, Just A Dash. Williams' horses would later win many Group One races, including another Melbourne Cup with Efficient in 2007, and he would own some of them in partnership with Kerry Packer. Williams of course became best known as the driving force behind the Crown Casino in Melbourne and one of the city's most prominent business faces.

But for me the name Lloyd Williams evoked different memories. I was at Flemington one morning, at the clock tower, and someone was talking about this big wheel Lloyd Williams, and I said, 'That's the boy who was Ray Borg's chauffeur.' The fellow I was talking to said this couldn't be true, Lloyd Williams was a big businessman, the Crown Casino man, he couldn't have been a chauffeur. But a few weeks later, the fellow ran into Williams and said, 'Bart Cummings said you used to be Ray Borg's chauffeur. That's not true, is it?' Apparently Lloyd smiled and said, 'Bart's got a very good memory.'

Back in the 1960s, Ray Borg was the head of a big Melbourne department store called Bon Marche. Ray had started out at Bon Marche as a window cleaner, then a window dresser, then rose up to be a floor walker and finally a manager before he was appointed the general manager. Eventually he controlled the whole operation. He had interests in several racehorses, and I met him through the sport. Once he introduced me to his chauffeur, who was a young kid with the face of an altar boy. His name was Lloyd. I assume that proximity to Ray was Lloyd's real education in business. Ray was up to all sorts of tricks, though. He had a friend, a Lebanese man from Queensland, who could sell the bridle off a nightmare. This fellow would travel between Victoria and Queensland with a truckload of fur coats which he'd got from somewhere. When he owed the bookmakers a debt, he'd pay it in fur coats.

Ray had all sorts of colourful acquaintances, and owned a big house in Toorak, the fanciest suburb of Melbourne. He'd entertain racing people at his parties there, and that was where I met the man with the fur coats. Lloyd was no doubt there too. Unfortunately it all went badly for Ray in the end, as he was found to be taking his shareholders' money and using it for his own ends. Like many high-flying businesspeople who get involved in racing, he was an institution one minute, and the next he'd fallen off the face of the earth. I believe that, like Hyperno's part-owner George Herscu, he went to jail and then ended up in Canada.

ALTHOUGH I HAD NOTHING RUNNING IN WHAT A NUISANCE'S Melbourne Cup, there was no need to despair: a better crop was just coming through. At the New Zealand sales that year, I paid $200,000 for a colt by Zamazaan from Belle Cherie. The purchase prices were rocketing up, and I sold a quarter share, then a half share, in the horse to a Melbourne businessman named Jack Eastgate. Jack made furniture, while his wife was a very nice Scots lady who came from a family that owned one of the big whisky distilleries over there. Jack made me a bar for my house, and it was a very useful one too. His favourite saying was, 'I couldn't agree with you more!' He was like a cockatoo, the way he kept saying it. And I couldn't hear it enough. 'I couldn't agree with you more!' If only I could train all owners to say that.

We didn't have the Zamazaan colt gelded, as I might have done in earlier years; the stud values for well-bred colts were so high now that it would have been irresponsible to geld him before he had raced.

Beau Zam, as we called him, won twice as a two-year-old. This was the season made famous by Kerry Packer's betting plunge in the Sydney autumn carnival. The exact amount of his wagers was never made public, but the turnover reported by bookmakers, which had not once exceeded $9 million and was $8 million the previous year, rocketed up to $40 million that year. This was believed to be solely due to Packer. The entire NSW TAB that year turned over $21 million, so he must have bet, all on his own, more than the rest of the population of New South Wales combined!

I never had anything to do with Kerry Packer, and when he owned racehorses he sent them to other trainers. Punters and trainers don't necessarily mix that closely, and I didn't cross paths with him. But I did have one brush with his father, Sir Frank Packer, back in the 1960s.

Sir Frank, who owned a newspaper, television and magazine empire, was a pretty formidable presence. It was said that he once had to bail out young Kerry to the tune of $10,000 for debts the son had accumulated with illegal off-course bookies. Sir Frank also owned racehorses. Once, when a horse of his called Foresight won at Randwick, Sir Frank had missed the report on the Channel Nine news. As he owned the station, he rang them up and demanded they show the race again that night, just before the Saturday night movie started. They did, and then Sir Frank called once more: 'Run it again, I was on the toilet.' So they did.

His reputation for fiery put-downs preceded him, and being a shy person, I'm always one for flight, rather than fight, in these situations. One day in the early 1960s I had wandered into the Champagne Bar at Randwick along with Tommy Smith. Trainers weren't allowed in there, but we both wanted to speak to a couple of owners. Tommy went off into the crowd, but no sooner was I in the bar than I felt a gorilla-sized hand around my collar.

'WHAT'S THAT BADGE?'

I looked up, and there was Sir Frank Packer looming over me. He was glaring down at my badge, which showed that I was a trainer and therefore not entitled to be in the Champagne Bar. My mouth opened and closed silently as I tried to think of something to say, knowing that if I didn't come up with something he would literally throw me out the door. Luckily, his attention was distracted at that moment.

'And where's that T.J. Smith? Is he in here too?'

I might have nodded in the direction Tommy had gone. Sir Frank rumbled off in search of Tommy. Tommy was smaller than me, so maybe Sir Frank really did fancy his chances of picking him up and hurling him through the window. While Sir Frank charged away, I took the opportunity to fly out the door.

That was the only time I met him.

AFTER HIS QUIET START AS A TWO-YEAR-OLD, BEAU ZAM FLOURISHED as a spring three-year-old, winning the weight-for-age Hill Stakes against the older horses at Rosehill and then the Spring Champion Stakes over 10 furlongs against his own age group. He was ridden by John Marshall, who had become my main stable jockey in Sydney. John was a studious, intense fellow, a well-balanced and patient rider originally from Western Australia. Never openly hungry for success, he had needed his mother to give him a push out of Perth and set his career running: she rang a priest, Father George Russo, who organised for young John to move to Sydney to go into the stables of the trainer Pat Murray. Marshall didn't have the flamboyance of many jockeys, which suited me just fine. He was a quiet and dedicated professional.

Beau Zam was going so well that we entered him for the Caulfield Cup. This was unusual for me – the last three-year-old I'd raced in the Cup was Sometime, way back in 1961. He'd finished fourth to Summer Fair and I'd never had a spring three-year-old since then whom I regarded as mature enough to take on the older horses in such a rugged race. Mighty Kingdom, in 1979, was the only three-year-old to have won in recent memory. But Beau Zam looked the goods, despite his relatively small stature at 15 hands, and the field didn't look overly strong, so we took the plunge and started him. When I told Jack Eastgate about my idea, he chirruped: 'I couldn't agree with you more!' The bookies agreed, making him 7/4 favourite.

The rain tumbled down and turned the Caulfield track into a bog, reminding me of all those wet springs in the 1970s. I told John Marshall that the horse to watch was Lord Reims, an out-and-out mudlark being ridden by Brent Thomson. I pointed to him across the parade ring and said to Marshall, 'Follow him.'

The race was a typically rough Caulfield Cup. Beau Zam would be mentioned in the stewards' report three times as a victim of other horses buffeting and bumping him and falling about in the mud. He cut and bruised his near hind hoof and was squeezed at the 3-furlong mark, just as they were entering the home turn. Faced with a wall of horses fanning out across the home turn looking for firm ground, Marshall had the opportunity to cut the corner and come home the short way, following Lord Reims. But he wasn't sure of the going or that there would be a way through, so he went wide. Meanwhile, Thomson on Lord Reims did cut the corner and came home close to the fence. The other horses fell away in the straight and it came down to Lord Reims, who hadn't wasted a yard darting through close to the rails, and Beau Zam, who had lost ground going wide. They battled down the straight and past the post. Marshall's goggles were so coated with mud that he had to ask Thomson who had won. Our horse was desperately unlucky – he'd come second by half a head, in unsuitable conditions and copping a fearsome pummelling for any horse, let alone a three-year-old.

The honest racehorses who love nothing more than winning are also the ones most susceptible to injuring themselves, and I was concerned about how Beau Zam would pull up after such a bruising affair. Remarkably, he seemed to come through the race fit and healthy, however, and I kept a close eye on him in the lead-up to the Cox Plate, run a week later. I also had Campaign King running, though the 10 furlongs would be at the outer limits of his endurance. By Saarond from Acid Queen, Campaign King, another three-year-old, had won the Chelmsford and George Main stakes in Sydney that spring against the older horses. Earlier in his career Campaign King had run a few times for a Melbourne trainer before I bought him to race him for the Sydney property developer Leon Fink. He was showing early signs of the promise on which he would deliver the next autumn.

I also considered entering two other three-year-olds. Sky Chase had won the Champagne Stakes as a juvenile and came back well in the spring to win both the Up and Coming and the Gloaming stakes. Sky Chase, by Star Way out of Vice Reine, was another of my purchases at the New Zealand sales in 1985; I paid a little bit more for him than I paid for Beau Zam the same week, but both horses had more than amply recouped the outlay. The fourth three-year-old I toyed with entering in the Cox Plate was a staying type named Omnicorp; but in the end I settled with Beau Zam and Campaign King.

The betting was dominated by Rubiton, a son of my former sprinter Century. Rubiton had come from nowhere to utterly dominate the weight-for-age races in Melbourne. As it turned out he was a class above all the others in the Cox Plate, winning easily. Beau Zam laboured home for fifth and Campaign King tenth. The next weekend, we started Beau Zam in the Victoria Derby, but he was over the top by then and finished seventh as favourite to Omnicorp. If anyone had to win, I was happy for it to be my second-stringer, Omnicorp, but Beau Zam didn't deserve to have his reputation tarnished by his runs in the Cox Plate and the Derby. Clearly I'd been mistaken when I'd thought he'd pulled up well from the rigours of the Caulfield Cup, and it had taken more out of him than I'd observed to be the case. This is why three-year-olds tend not to run in the race. But his second place, so unlucky, was a sign of his talent. All I had to do was take care of the colt during his summer spell and the racing world would see what he was made of in the autumn.

So in 1987 I looked like being without a runner in the Melbourne Cup again. At least the successes of my three-year-olds stopped anyone writing obituaries for me. But a few weeks before the race, I was approached by the American billionaire Nelson Bunker Hunt, who asked me to purpose-train his stallion Rosedale, whom he was bringing to Australia for the race.

This was in the early days of the VRC's endeavours to ease the way for Northern Hemisphere horses to compete in the Melbourne Cup. Up to then, the travelling distance, the quarantine and various other hardships limited the Melbourne Cup's appeal to them. But now that the race's prize money had shot up past a million dollars, connections from the UK, Europe and the USA were showing an interest and the Australian authorities responded by smoothing out the logistics for them. The VRC handicapper also offered a sweetener, allocating the European horses what I've always thought were not so much handicaps as invitations.

Bunker Hunt was an interesting fellow who made and lost a fortune trying to corner the international market in silver. His stock in trade was originally oil. He had huge oil holdings in Texas, and had assisted the discovery of 'black gold' for Colonel Gaddafi in Libya. As a way of thanking him, Gaddafi nationalised the oilfields, taking everything away from him.

'Bunker' was a very large man, and he'd drive along in a big car with a huge tub of ice-cream between the front seats. He'd sit there and talk with a spoon in his hand and help himself to the ice-cream until it was all gone or he reached home.

Bunker Hunt also owned the 8000-acre Bluegrass Farm at Keeneland, Kentucky, which had been home to some of the world's greatest racehorses, winners of the biggest races in America, Britain and Europe. By 1988, Bunker Hunt would run into terrible financial difficulties brought on by his venture into the silver market. At the time when he thought he had the world's supply in his grasp, pushing the price up, Spanish-speaking people from Central and South America realised that all the trophies and trays and goblets they had sitting on their shelves, family heirlooms from generations in the past, were made of very valuable silver. These people weren't necessarily rich, so they traded in their silver, melted it down and sold it at the high price. Just when Bunker thought he had the market cornered, suddenly thousands of ounces of South American silver flooded the market and ruined him. To stave off bankruptcy he would have to sell 580 thoroughbreds, raising $US46 million, the biggest such sale in the world (and a fore-runner for my darkest day, just a year later).

I'd met Bunker Hunt a few times in America, and was eager to see his facilities and hear what he had to say. I found him an extremely kind and friendly man, and would feel terribly sorry for him when he met his financial Waterloo. He and I already had an indirect connection. Jim Shannon, who'd acted as an agent in Australia and New Zealand back in the sixties and was involved in the lease of Light Fingers, had been in Kentucky at sale time one year and was hitchhiking along the road when Bunker Hunt picked him up. They got talking, and the American offered him a job.

Long before I knew him, Bunker Hunt had set an important precedent for Southern Hemisphere breeding. In 1970 he had bought Waikato Stud at Matamata in New Zealand, and for six months of the year he brought his French stallion Pretendre to stand there, before taking him back to the Northern Hemisphere for their breeding season. Pretendre had been the highest-priced racehorse in training in the entire world in the mid-1960s, but he had broken down and stood at stud in the UK. Bunker Hunt had phoned me from Kentucky, saying he had no stallions to stand at Waikato Stud. I encouraged him to have Pretendre sent down to fill the gap. He would sire Leica Pretender, the dam of Nothin' Leica Dane, who became a great rival of my champion Saintly in the 1990s. It is only logical to exploit the stallion's full potential by letting it serve mares throughout the year, rather than saving it for the season in just one hemisphere. What had prevented it from happening was a combination of quarantine restrictions, lack of resources and will, and a perception that Australasian racing wasn't lucrative enough to invest all the time, money and risk in bringing top European stallions down under for a few months of the year. These factors would all change, though, and the practice of 'shuttling' stallions from north to south between the seasons, landing them at the Cocos Islands in the Indian Ocean to undergo quarantine, would become standard. But Bunker Hunt was its pioneer.

By 1987 Bunker Hunt knew all about my Melbourne Cup record, and he asked me to train Rosedale. In America, Rosedale, trained by Charlie Whittingham, had raced mainly as a pacemaker. He loved to bowl along in front. He had excellent breeding, as a son of the Arc de Triomphe winner Vaguely Noble (whom Bunker Hunt had owned), and the bookies were worried enough about him – and me! – to install Rosedale as 4/1 favourite for the 1987 Cup.

During his quarantine Rosedale was trained at a private track north of Cambridge, New Zealand, and I sent Anthony over there to give him some work because while he was waiting for his clearance the horse was getting too fat. As soon as we were able, we flew him into Melbourne, but we had to cut it fine, bringing him in in October, deep into the countdown for the race. Of all the preparations I have made for the Melbourne Cup, Rosedale's was the most unorthodox by a long way.

He ran in the Mackinnon Stakes, finishing a pleasing fourth behind Rubiton after he tore off a shoe. In the Cup itself, we probably erred with our tactics. Rosedale was carrying 56 kilos, and for obvious reasons I wasn't entirely confident in his fitness. I should have instructed John Marshall to let him stride along in the lead if he wanted, as he was used to doing in America. I should have thought of Pat Glennon and Comic Court – no point both of them fighting each other! But I'd seen so many Melbourne Cups lost by jockeys going to the lead too soon, and advised Marshall to hold him a little. Of course, defying my expectations Rosedale came home full of running, fit as a fiddle, to finish third, just half a length behind the winner Kensei. It might be the only Melbourne Cup where I can say that a couple of wrong decisions cost us a win.

THE NEXT AUTUMN WAS ONE OF OUR BEST YET. CAMPAIGN KING won his second George Ryder Stakes at weight-for-age, and followed it up by winning the big Queensland sprint double, the Stradbroke Handicap and the Doomben '10,000'. He would retire with six Group One wins, and is up there with Maybe

Mahal as among the best sprinter-milers that I have trained. With his Ryder win he became my first million-dollar-earner, showing how rapidly things had changed on the prize-money front. In Taj Rossi's three-year-old season, one of the best for our stable, we had won a million dollars in all races across the country over a period of twelve months. Now Campaign King, a three-year-old, had done it on his own.

If Campaign King was good, Beau Zam was better. After tailing off in the spring, he'd spelled well and went on a five-race winning streak in the autumn of 1988. He won the main weight-for-age staying races – the Segenhoe Stakes, the Rawson Stakes and the newly renamed Tancred International Stakes at Rosehill. In the last of those, he started at 6/4-on and beat a field including the Japan Cup winner Le Glorieux by five lengths.

Often when a horse is in the middle of such a hard racing and training campaign, it begins to look tired. Its coat goes dull and its ribs start to show. But I keep feeding them and letting them know they're being cared for, and when Beau Zam turned out for the AJC Derby at Randwick a week and a half after the Tancred everyone was saying how heavy and happy he looked. His coat was gleaming. He won the AJC Derby, over 2400 metres, by five and a half lengths, and the AJC St Leger, over 2800 metres, by a phenomenal ten lengths. I was so excited after the St Leger, I broke with habit and led him into the ring. I was quoted telling reporters that this was my 'greatest moment' in racing. On reflection, perhaps I was caught up in the moment. But Beau Zam, who became my first $2-million stakes-winner in that autumn, was, I believe, the best horse in the world at that time. And coming on top of several fallow years in the Melbourne Cup, I was soaking up the winning feeling.

Beau Zam was a superstar who mixed with royalty. Princess Anne was visiting before the AJC Derby, and asked to ride him in track work. I happily gave her a turn, and she was suitably impressed.

Her mother got to meet him too. As this was the Bicentennial year, Queen Elizabeth was visiting. Of course she wanted to go to the races, and in May the Queen Elizabeth II Stakes was run in her honour in Canberra. Only six horses started, but they included Beau Zam and the 1986 Cox Plate winner, the New Zealand champion Bonecrusher. In all of his wins, Beau Zam hadn't beaten a horse quite of Bonecrusher's quality, and I was nervous about his chances. He'd already had fifteen races that season, and if it hadn't been for that special race I would have sent him to the spelling paddock after the St Leger. But when I put the idea to Jack Eastgate of entering Beau Zam in the race and meeting the Queen, he beamed and said: 'I couldn't agree with you more!'

On her many trips to Australia, the Queen often made time to go to the racetrack, and I was privileged to be someone she remembered from previous visits. A message would come to me: 'Her Majesty would like to talk to you.' And I would dart off to wherever she was, often the jockeys' room or somewhere very close to the action. She does love racehorses. Usually our conversation was just pleasantries, but I think she was most comfortable among genuine racing people.

The day of the Queen Elizabeth II Stakes in Canberra, Her Majesty seemed interested in talking with me about racing, but she was a bit distracted. One of the more memorable episodes of that day was that Bob Hawke, the Prime Minister, had a habit of putting his hand on her elbow or arm or back, and Her Majesty was far from amused. Either he didn't know that you were not meant to touch the Queen, or that was just his way around women and he couldn't help himself. Whichever it was, a big scowl came across the Queen's face as she was trying to talk to someone or watch the races, and you didn't know why she was looking so sour until you looked behind her, or to her side, and there was Hawkie with his hand on her again. There's even a photo of me beside Her Majesty, watching the race, with Valmae and Jack Eastgate behind us, and the Queen looks like she's bitten into a lemon. Why? If you look to the side of the picture, there's a male hand grabbing the Queen's elbow. Guess whose that is!

It was a heck of a race, so maybe her face was just contorted with the tension of it. The field raced as a small pack until the home turn. Just as Bonecrusher started his sprint, Beau Zam accelerated with him – and slipped. Bonecrusher got away from him, taking a commanding lead into the straight. But Beau Zam was cool and determined, and wound up to chase the older horse. In the last few strides he ran Bonecrusher down, winning the race by a head. It was a thrill to see my green-and-gold colours take the race, and very exciting to receive the trophy from Her Majesty in a year that made Australians so very proud. It isn't the done thing to repeat conversations with the Queen, and in any case I doubt I said much at all. I remember her saying what a nice colt he was.

BOB HAWKE, INCIDENTALLY, WAS ONE OF THE FEW POLITICAL LEADERS who was both interested in racing as a sportsman and motivated to help it as a Prime Minister. I've only had glancing encounters with the Prime Ministers of my time, and mostly my object in talking to them was to put forward my case for whatever reform I thought they should undertake. You only get a Prime Minister's ear for a short time, so you might as well make the most of it.

I met John Howard quite a few times, either at sporting functions and ceremonies or at the Christmas cocktail party he hosted each year at Kirribilli House, the prime ministerial residence on Sydney Harbour. He would invite people from all walks of life to get together on the lawn overlooking the Opera House and socialise. When I saw him, I'd have about a minute and a half to lobby him on something or other before I'd get moved on. I can't remember what I said to him in his early years as PM, but in the later years I made sure he knew of my opposition to corporate bookmakers and any plans to license them to operate widely throughout Australia. For a while, he kept them restricted, so I was his supporter in that regard. To his credit, he was the only PM I knew to turn up at the Prime Minister's Cup, a race at the Southport track on the Gold Coast. I bumped into him in the mounting yard, where he was wandering about looking lost. He was the type of fellow who often seemed to have taken a wrong door and found himself in the wrong place. I said, 'Prime Minister, perhaps you should go up to the committee room, it'll be safer for you there.' He was very grateful to me for pointing him the right way.

Another year the Gold Coast meeting provided an opportunity to meet a politician who really had his heart and soul in racing: Queensland's 'minister for everything' under the

Joh Bjelke-Petersen National Party government, Russ Hinze. Hinze, a very large man with a gruff manner and very overt pride in Queensland, was hosting me at the Gold Coast Turf Club, where they held an annual lunch to coincide with their yearling sales and main race meeting.

'So, Mr Cummings,' he said, 'what do you think of our lovely club?'

As always, I was thinking about lobbying, not flattery. 'Not too bad,' I said, 'except you could change the track. It's too small.'

'What?' Hinze puffed up. 'What's wrong with our track? How on earth can we make it any bigger?'

I explained that because the far side of the track was confined by a watercourse, the track itself was elongated, suffering from very tight narrow turns at each end. The start for the main race, the Prime Minister's Cup, was on one of the bends. In my humble opinion, I said, it should be widened and reshaped so that it looked more like the better racecourses around the country, with a broader circular shape and more sweeping turns.

Nothing ventured, nothing gained! The next time I went up there, Russ Hinze had done it – the Southport track was now a first-rate facility, the right shape and everything. I'm not sure if they filled in the creek or built bridges over it, but Hinze had listened to every word I'd said and followed it to a tee. There was now a chute for the start so the barrier wouldn't be on the bend anymore. Then, at a dinner in front of 600 people, he made me stand up and accept the credit as the man who had inspired the modernisation of the track. So much for Queensland parochialism: Hinze's enthusiasm for the sport was so strong that it overrode what you'd expect him to do as a Queenslander, which was to ignore any suggestion that came from south of the border.

Bob Hawke, meanwhile, was also a genuine racing follower. He had succeeded Malcolm Fraser, who was a very reserved fellow from the Victorian western districts and didn't seem to have much time for our sport. Hawke, on the other hand, loved to have a punt and got very excited if he won. Sadly for him, it didn't happen as often as it should have. He befriended Colin Hayes, and got all his tips from him. Hawke thought he had some sort of inside running, but I always felt sorry for him, particularly on Melbourne Cup day, because Colin Hayes's horses didn't win too many. Hawke would have been better off sidling up to me and getting his tips, but he didn't. Anyway, I probably wouldn't have given him too much information. I wouldn't want people to think he was the stable 'leak'. I suspected he wouldn't have been the type who could keep a good tip close to his chest.

But as a Prime Minister, he was all right. He granted tax concessions to investors who wanted to get involved in horse racing and breeding. It did a lot of good for the sport in this country, and Hawke was responsible. Unfortunately – and quite indirectly – the tax concessions for racing fed into a big gathering storm that would, by the end of the 1980s, draw me in and send me to the brink of bankruptcy.

15

Betrayed

THE 1987–88 SEASON HAD BEEN ONE OF THE MOST EXCITING of my career, and my horses had won $5 million in stakes, beating Colin Hayes's Australian record. Some observers said I was training with more determination and urgency, but I think it was all about the horses. They tend to make the trainer look better than he is – and worse than he is! In Campaign King and Beau Zam I had a pair of champions, and it's easier to look more vigorous in your training when you have horses who are capable of winning the big Group One races.

The amount of money the horses were competing for now was just staggering. It was only five years since Kingston Town and Manikato had become the first Australian racehorses to win a million dollars in stakes, and they needed to compete for several years and win as many as thirty races to do so. Now Beau Zam was the record-holder with *two* million dollars, most of it earned in the one season. The money in the sport was going through the roof.

The reasons behind this increase went back to the 1960s, with the introduction of totalisator agency boards, or TABs, in each state. Once the TAB arrived, people could punt on the horses in any state from their own home or from a TAB office. All they needed to do was read the form guide in their newspaper, set up an account and make a phone call. Or they could go to a TAB outlet in their local shopping centre or, later, at the pub. Previously, off-course betting had been the province of illegal SP, or starting price, bookmakers, who had mined the opening between the punters and the racetrack. The advent of TABs did much to put the SP bookies out of business.

As well as striking a blow against criminals, the TABs delivered an immediate benefit for the sport. In 1961, the first year Victoria had a TAB, the four racing clubs in Melbourne shared an extra £250,000, much of which went into increased prize money. The Melbourne Cup, worth £20,000 in 1962, was worth double that by 1969. It doubled again by 1977, doubled in the next three years to $310,000, trebled in the next five years to a million dollars, and by 1990 it was worth $2 million. In the decade of the 1980s, then, its prize money rose from $310,000 to $2,035,000 – far beyond inflation in the same period. And those were the years I didn't win it! But if I was feeling left out, I could take consolation from the fact that prize money was going up commensurately in all of racing throughout the year, and Beau Zam, Campaign King and Sky Chase were proof that horses could become millionaires faster than ever, without going near a Melbourne Cup.

The inflow of TAB money set off a kind of chain reaction in the sport. Through the 1980s, racing clubs started to compete against each other to raise their prize money and claim the status of having the richest races attracting the best horses. Some even invented new races, such as The Australasian in Perth in 1987 and the Gold Nugget and Magic Millions for two-year-olds on the Gold Coast. More established races like the Golden Slipper, meanwhile, kept upping their prize money to retain their prominence. Everyone wanted to have the richest race, and their feverish competition was warmly welcomed by owners, trainers and jockeys.

Sponsors moved in, pouring huge money into clubs and individual races in exchange for naming rights and signage. Carlton and United Breweries gave the VRC $5 million to sponsor the Melbourne Cup for five years from 1985, the year it hit the million-dollar mark in stakes money. While it remained the Melbourne Cup, a lot of our most historic races sold their names completely: the Stradbroke Handicap became the Elders Handicap, the Tancred Stakes became the Mercedes and then the BMW, and so on. The time-honoured Hotham Handicap, one of the key lead-ups to the Melbourne Cup on Victoria Derby day, was run for 110 years as the Hotham before it was called, successively, the Dalgety, the Crown

Quality, the Ten News Stakes, the Lean Cuisine Quality, and now the Saab Quality. This chopping and changing might have detracted from the colour of the sport, but it vastly increased the prize money on offer.

Because the prize money was shooting up, so was the cost of yearlings. Long gone was the day when I could sneak into New Zealand and pick up a Melbourne Cup winner for a couple of thousand dollars. By now, even moderate racehorses were winning one or two hundred thousand dollars in stakes. And where the cost of yearlings was going up, so must the cost of stud fees and stallions.

Here are a few markers of how fast the sale prices were growing. At the Sydney sales in 1978, I became the first person to spend $100,000 for a yearling, a colt by Mount Hagen from Valour. The next year I paid the highest price on the first day, $55,000, for a filly by Baguette from Victory Roll.

Two years later, in 1981, Robert Holmes à Court spent $850,000 on a Luskin Star colt at the Sydney sales.

At the New Zealand sales in 1987, I spent a total of $2.3 million, including $300,000 for a mare called All Grace (who, unlike the aforementioned purchases, was a good investment – she would pay back many times over in the form of her son, Saintly). At the New Zealand sales in 1988, I paid $800,000 for a Sir Tristram colt out of My Tricia, making him a full brother to derby winners Grosvenor and National Gallery.

And at the Sydney Easter sales of 1988, I became the first buyer to spend a million dollars on a yearling. The colt by Kingston Town's sire, Bletchingly, out of the Showdown mare, Verdi, was a half-brother to a useful horse I was training called Rigoletto. I bought the yearling from Sir Tristan Antico's Baramul Stud. Like Holmes à Court's record-setter in 1981, this colt was no good.

Holmes à Court, incidentally, was one of the strangest fellows I ever met through racing. He was a strong Labor man but also a pure capitalist, moving paper and companies around in a clever way to make himself very rich. He was one of those fellows whose brain was so big it seemed to be in several different places at the same time. Speaking with him, it was hard to get the sense that you had his undivided attention. In the early 1980s, when I was on my way to England for a winter trip, he invited me to drop in to Perth and look at his stud, Heytesbury, an hour south of the city. He had irrigated the 500 acres and set up the stud in 1971 with his mother, Ethnee, and his wife, Janet, who were very accomplished women, and they had stood the Melbourne Cup winner Silver Knight as their first main stallion.

I hadn't seen a lot of Perth, so I accepted his invitation. The soil was surprisingly orange in colour and crumbly in texture, almost semi-arid. The weather, of course, was dry and hot. Comparing it with the lushness of New Zealand, Europe and south-eastern Australia, where I was used to visiting studs, I couldn't believe you could successfully breed horses here. But they looked after the horses very well and the facilities were first-rate. He was very well resourced. He took me to his house in Perth, a big place in the west of the city, and I sat there with him in his study while he did countless things simultaneously. He was watching his stock prices, watching televisions, speaking on the phone, speaking to me and playing chess on a chess computer all at once – and he was winning the game!

I felt unnerved, sitting in a room with a man whose mind was so capacious, watching him for two hours saying, 'Yes, yes,' on the phone, talking to me, and playing chess to break the boredom. I thought, 'What an unusual fellow. Is he concentrating on the man on the end of the phone, on me or on the chess?' I still think about it.

In the end, he came a cropper in the 1980s like so many of us, but in his case permanently. His Bell Resources tried to swallow BHP, and bit off more than it could chew. The whole thing unravelled when John Elliott, at Elders, stuffed him up. In the middle of it all, Holmes à Court got on the phone to the trainers of his horses in Sydney and said, 'Put all the horses on the float, send them back quick!' He had to start selling a few assets pronto. By the end of the decade, he wouldn't be the only one.

THROUGH THE 1980S, THE PRICE INFLATION FOR YEARLINGS WAS extreme. Stud fees were going up, land prices were rocketing, everything had entered the stratosphere.

Because the required initial capital to buy good yearlings had risen so fast, it was no longer possible for individuals like me to go to sales and buy the best young horses on spec, expecting to on-sell them to owners. You just had to raise a lot more money to get involved in the first place.

The pioneers in private syndication were locals, like George Ryder, the founder of the Golden Slipper, who had started his ARABS syndicate in 1970. But the ones who popularised it in the 1980s were foreigners. Robert Sangster established a syndicate that bought Luskin Star in the late 1970s, and by 1981, as a stallion, the horse was worth $6 million. Sangster expanded his syndicates into a publicly listed company, spreading the risk and raising more money from investors who never even smelt a horse. Stallion syndicates were springing up everywhere, and these companies would own forty, fifty, even eighty or more horses. This was the only way they thought they could compete with some new foreign owners coming in, who were even bigger than Sangster, such as the Maktoum family from the Middle East, who would spend tens of millions on a single stallion and millions more on yearlings, mares and tried racehorses.

The TAB money was pouring in even faster in the 1980s. In New South Wales, the amount wagered at the TAB rose from $950 million in 1980 to $3.18 billion by 1990. Staggering! The portion of this that was pumped back into the racing clubs rose from $16 million to $60 million in that decade, mostly into prize money but also into improved facilities and administration.

While this was beneficial for the sport, it forced me to reconsider the way I was operating. I had to find a new way to finance my yearling purchases, and the way everyone else was doing it was to aggregate the large amounts of money swimming around in the financial markets, which were being deregulated through the 1980s and yielded large sums that seemed to be looking for a home, particularly if it was tax effective. As it happened, Bob Hawke's changes to the Australian tax code favoured investment in racehorses, another boon for the industry, but one that could become a trap for the unwitting or the unlucky.

I arranged a scheme alongside the big accounting firms, Coopers & Lybrand and Peat Marwick. I thought you couldn't go wrong with such conservative, powerful names behind you. They gave me all the advice and financial nous and we put together what was called the Cups King Syndicate. Of course it was trading on my name and my ability to pick yearlings, but the whole idea was for it to raise enough money to be competitive in an exploding market and spread the risk among those who bought into the syndicate. There were also considerable tax advantages for the investors, so it all seemed like a good idea at the time, it really did, and I supported a tax break for investment in racehorses; except the consequence was that it combined with all those other factors to add still more heat to the hyperinflation in yearling prices. With the government chipping in to help pay for yearlings, everyone thought, 'You beauty, we can spend more!' The tax-minimisation incentive introduced a careless new element, where it was nothing for some uneducated people to pay a million dollars for a yearling. I can say one thing – it was a good time for those lucky enough to be breeders.

In 1989, on the syndicate's behalf, I bought almost ninety yearlings for a total of $22 million from sales in Sydney, New Zealand and the Gold Coast. At the Sydney Easter sales alone I spent $13.6 million on forty-three yearlings, including $1.5 million for a Biscay colt out of Tommasina Fiesco. It sounds extravagant, but you needed to be spending that much to be in the game, and I understood that with such smart accounting houses as my partners, the way it was being packaged up for investors was pretty much foolproof. I didn't have to spend the money upfront. The agents, such as William

Inglis and Sons, would take the purchases on credit until our syndicate sold its units and raised the cash.

Well, in racing timing is everything. We thought that as the economy had survived the 1987 stock market crash reasonably well, selling the units would be plain sailing. But the recession and steepling interest rates really hit hard in 1989, and all of a sudden there was no money anywhere. It seemed like the world turned from flood to drought overnight. We couldn't sell the units in the syndicates. We sold a few packages, and the auction houses extended my deadline so I could sell more, but by the final deadline of 30 June 1989, I still had sixty-four unsold yearlings on my hands.

At first I didn't think it was such a disaster, personally. My understanding was that the risk was spread between myself and the accounting firms, but when it came to the crunch, the accountants said I was on my own. I'd shaken hands with them and made certain agreements, which I believed we all understood together, but when they brought out the fine print on the contracts they argued that when I thought I'd been doing this in a sophisticated risk-spreading way, I was actually doing what I'd been doing all along – putting up my money, taking all the risk myself. Des Rundle, a senior partner at Peat Marwick in Adelaide and my main contact in the whole affair, went on holidays for the five crucial weeks leading up to the settlement date, completely washing his hands of the whole scheme. Rundle was a member of the Australian Cricket Board and fancied himself as a bastion of the Adelaide establishment. A couple of days before the deadline, he rang me from his holiday, wherever he was, and said, all innocently, 'How is the syndicate going?' You could have seen the steam coming from my ears. He was acting as if he was an innocent bystander, watching with amusement as the scheme went down the drain. This was the first inkling I got that the accountants had bolted with the horse, leaving me holding an empty bridle. In my opinion it was an act of treachery such as I have never known.

Financially, it couldn't have been a much greater disaster for me. I was left holding the unsold yearlings when my creditors finally ran out of patience and called in their debts. Of course it was the worst possible time. I had to sell sixty-four yearlings at the bottom of the market at a moment when nobody wanted to go anywhere near racehorses. Not only that, but by this point in the year, the end of winter, I was caught in no-man's-land in terms of the horses' age. It's easiest to sell thoroughbreds when they're fresh yearlings, or when they're proven race performers. The former are unproven, blank slates of hope; the latter come with some kind of guaranteed track record. The ones I was trying to sell were neither one nor the other – too old to be seen as malleable yearlings, but not old enough to have some form under their girth straps. In September 1989, when the horses were turning two, and therefore needing to find owners to race them quick smart, William Inglis and Sons put up the sixty-four yearlings in a fire sale at their Newmarket yard in Sydney. They called it 'The Night of the Stars'. It felt like anything but that to me. I don't think they meant it as a cruel joke.

One thing about hindsight is it brings out the wisdom in people. There were plenty who said I shouldn't have bought so many yearlings on spec, without firm buyers. These were the same people who'd said what a genius I was for buying a horse like Think Big without a buyer in mind. At the sales of 1973, I'd bought a million dollars' worth of yearlings, several of them with only one buyer lined up. Nobody thought it was a bad idea then.

It was a gruesome night. I sat there hunched down in my overcoat with Valmae beside me. One after another, the year-lings came up with 'No reserve' announced. It was the buyers' market to end all buyers' markets. Plenty of pinstriped suits, plenty of champagne, but not too much cash being waved around.

The auctioneers did manage to find buyers for the yearlings, but at what price? The takings were about $9 million for a group of horses for which I'd paid twice as much. The Biscay–Tommasina Fiesco colt sold for $750,000, half of what I'd paid for it. For $75,000 Tommy Smith picked up a Sackford colt I'd bought for $385,000. Painfully, one of the Smith purchases would turn out to be Pharaoh, who won two Doncaster Handicaps for Tommy Smith's daughter Gai, by then a trainer in her own right.

Tommy had got caught the same way I had, with a slight yet significant difference. He had listed Tulloch Lodge as a public company. His own stables didn't belong to him anymore, but he was able to raise much more cash through the stock market to buy yearlings. It was the same idea as the Cups King Syndic-ate, but the public company formalised the spread in liability. I, for my sins, was working on a person-to-person basis with people I believed I could trust. Hit by the same economic storm as my syndicate, Tommy's company ran into its own kind of difficulties: his main partner, a man called Brian Yuill, was found to be a shonk and went into insolvency in April

1989. Tulloch Lodge had bought eighty yearlings for almost as much as I'd spent. Tommy wasn't personally liable, as I was, because it was a public company, but he was facing the loss of his reputation and his stables if he couldn't find a buyer. In the end, he found an American billionaire called John Kluge to bail him out. Kluge paid $7.5 million for the horses and property, and Tommy was able to keep going.

As for me, the future looked dire. I was left owing something like $11 million to three bloodstock agents: Inglis, Dalgety International and Wrightson Bloodstock. I took the accounting firms to the Federal Court, and the case lasted for six weeks, costing me another fortune in legal fees. I argued that the scheme was quite clear: the accounting firms were my partners in the venture. It dragged on for several more months before the judges came to their decision, and we lost. The Federal Court said no joint venture existed, and the debt was mine alone.

So in May 1991 I was left with a five-year repayment plan. My training income was comprised of 10 percent of all the stakes winnings of my horses. In recent years, that had come to about $300,000 to $500,000 annually. Over the next five years, I would have to give up three-quarters of that income – 75 percent! – to my creditors. As well, there were runners that I owned or leased myself. Of all prize money that they won in black type races, I would have to pay half – 50 percent – to my creditors.

To put that into perspective, the total stakes money in an Australian season was then about $160 million. If horses I trained filled all the placings and got all the prize money in all those races, I would have earned $16 million; $12 million of that would have paid off my debt. So that was all I had to do – train all the placegetters in all the stakes races in a season! More realistically, at the very best it might take me up to a decade to pay it all off. We had to sell our house in Vaucluse, where we'd lived since moving up from Adelaide in 1976. The children had spent their late teens and early adulthood there, and it held many happy memories. But – I was seeking any silver lining I could find – the house needed repainting, so at least I didn't have to do that.

More painful, for me, was having to sell Princes Farm. I had only owned it for a year or two since buying it from John Singleton. Fortunately, a buyer emerged in the form of Dato Tan Chin Nam, so at least, thanks to his generosity, I could continue using the property for our horses.

Selling our house and farm and paying back the debt was a terribly onerous obligation to have to meet at my age, but I could only look forward, not back. If I spent my time regretting what had happened or stewing in bitterness at the accounting firms, it would eat me up and I would lose my passion for racing. I was sixty-three years old when the court order came through, and was damned if I was going to let my last years in racing be spoilt by those who had betrayed me.

And there were reasons to be positive. The repayment plan, tough as it was, was a preferable outcome to bankruptcy. And the court, in its mercy and wisdom, had allowed me to pay back the debt by doing what I loved, which was training horses and winning races. It could have been worse, a lot worse. I still had my family and my health and my confidence in the future. I still had racing. All I'd lost was money. And I'd never been in it for the money, I'd been in it for the competition and the joy of racing those horses. None of that was being taken away from me. I could train my way out of this.

In a way, looking back, I can see that it was all meant to be. Perhaps, if the syndicate had gone well, I would have made a lot of money and run this corporate entity and retired early. Instead, the need to keep paying off that debt reinvigorated me, and shoved any thoughts of retirement to the absolute back of my mind. I had no choice! Sometimes that can be the best way to go forward – when there is no way back.

By the end of 1991, I would be inducted into the Sport Australia Hall of Fame, and would also win my eighth and ninth Melbourne Cups. I knew of only one way to silence my critics, overcome my doubters and pay off my creditors: keep on winning.

16
The golden child

WHILE MY FINANCES WERE GRAVELY WOUNDED, THE STABLE, FUNNILY enough, was going from strength to strength. The horses didn't know what was going on in the accounts department. In the 1989–90 season, I won the trainers' premiership in three different states: New South Wales, Victoria and South Australia. It was my first and only New South Wales premiership, and the feat of winning titles in three states the same year hasn't been done before or since. We won forty-three stakes races, including thirteen Group Ones, in the two seasons from August 1988 to August 1990. Beau Zam won the Rawson Stakes for the second time as a four-year-old, but didn't really train on and was retired to stud in Japan, then New Zealand. Sky Chase won the Caulfield Stakes before going to stud in New Zealand. (I would send the mare All Grace to him, with life-changing results.) Tristanagh won two guineas races and the VRC Oaks, Gold Trump won the Newmarket, and Stylish Century won the AJC Spring Champion Stakes. I had a rising young sprinter-miler I was very excited about called Shaftesbury Avenue. If I had to throw myself 100 percent into racing, this was not a bad time to do it. As always, I have the horses to thank. This time, they really did save my skin.

WHEN I'D SPENT THE DISASTROUS $1.5 MILLION ON THE BISCAY–Tommasina Fiesco colt at the 1989 Sydney sales, the vendor had been David Hains's Kingston Park Stud on the Mornington Peninsula.

A few months later, when I was right in the middle of the mess of the 'Night of the Stars', David sent me a horse to train. This was a chestnut colt who had run disastrously at his two starts, and would have been a prime candidate for gelding if he was not the finest-bred horse in Australia. Little did I know it, but in the same month that I lost millions of dollars and my home, I was picking up my next Melbourne Cup winner.

Hains was one of the most astute and ambitious breeders and businessmen in Australia. He'd owned Kingston Town, the champion mare Rose Of Kingston and her half-sister Spirit Of

Kingston. In 1982 Rose Of Kingston was the first filly since Tea Rose in 1944 to win the AJC Derby, and was Australian horse of the year. There was a connection between David and me already, through these racehorses. Both Rose Of Kingston and Spirit Of Kingston were daughters of Kingston Rose, who was a daughter of Sojourner, the mare bred by Dad and my brother Patrick. And Sojourner's grandparents, on her dam's side, were Powerscourt and Cushla. Powerscourt I have talked about; he was the sire who altered the course of our lives. Cushla, winner of the Port Adelaide Guineas and Adelaide Guineas in 1937, was one of Dad's horses that I'd learnt to ride on. Cushla's mother was St Opera, who, you'll remember, was one of Dad's first winners when he started training in Adelaide after the Great War. It's amazing how everything held together through the generations. There was a kind of poetry in it. All in all, I had every reason to take an interest in Rose Of Kingston and Spirit Of Kingston. Now that I think of it, I wonder why David didn't ask me to train them!

Sometimes the most successful businessmen I've come across are also the most idiosyncratic people, and David was no exception. If I thought Robert Holmes à Court was odd, he was nothing on David. David's strangest habit was to tape-record everything you said. He would invite me down there to look at horses and the property, and we could be walking around a stable, or in his office, or on the phone, or taking a stroll on the golf course, and he'd have his tape recorder going. I couldn't believe it. He'd ask me a question about how a horse was going, or what I thought of it, or whether the right methods were being used, and he put everything I said on tape. It wasn't sinister; it was that he was obsessed with learning all the time.

David dedicated himself heart and soul to anything he took on, and was extremely thorough, which was probably the secret to his success. His resources allowed him to give this thoroughness full rein. He built a two-hole golf course at his Mornington property: hole number one going up, hole number two coming straight back. You could keep playing those two holes forever. When David got serious about learning golf, he would fly Norman Von Nida, the former Australian Open champion and our greatest golfer of the period around the Second World War, down to Victoria to stay at the farm for two or three weeks on end and teach David how to play on his two-hole course. Up and back, up and back: it was quite an eye-opener. David would pick Von Nida's brains and put him on tape too. I thought I was single-minded, but David put me in the shade.

I got to know Von Nida there, and enjoyed his company. David might have had his tape on the both of us, I don't know. I wasn't so keen on golf, finding that for every day I played, it took me three days afterwards to catch up on the work I'd missed. They say golf is relaxing, but I must be peculiar – I found that the game wound me up, and I'd need to get back to work to relax properly.

David Hains was as thorough about his racehorse breeding as he was about his golf and everything else. David wanted to breed internationally, especially in America, and he had bought a former tobacco farm in Lexington, Kentucky, near where the Keeneland sales and racing take place. When he had a top-flight mare in Australia, he would send her over to one of the leading American sires. In 1984, he sent Rose Of Kingston over to mate with the best of the lot: Secretariat.

For many racegoers, Secretariat was the greatest horse

they'd ever seen. I was among them. He won sixteen races as a three- and four-year-old in 1976 and 1977, most famously the three-year-old triple crown of Kentucky Derby, Belmont Stakes and Preakness Stakes. He won the Belmont by, wait for it, *thirty-one* lengths. He was the American horse of the year for both of those years.

This was the first time Australian and American horses of the year had bred. The story goes that when Rose Of Kingston gave birth, the property manager wrote in the foaling book, 'Chestnut colt . . . magic!'

But on the track, Kingston Rule, as the colt would be named, was anything but magic. He was sent to France to be tutored by Patrick Biancone, a top trainer who would bring horses out to Australia for the Melbourne Cup, but the chestnut colt didn't like the soft French tracks and only raced once as a two-year-old.

Kingston Rule was even more ignominious on the track when he came to Australia to be trained by Tommy Smith. He made his local debut in a 1400-metre race for three-year-olds at Warwick Farm, attracting close attention because of his pedigree. He ran last, in the rain, by such a long distance that people were saying it was sad to see a son of Secretariat and Rose Of Kingston so humiliated.

One option was to geld him, as Tommy and David had done with Kingston Town after his equally unimpressive start. But whatever Kingston Rule did on the track, he was massively valuable as a potential stallion, so David wouldn't think of gelding him. Instead, he sent Kingston Rule away for a long rest at Kingston Park and asked me if I would like to have a go at training him.

When I referred earlier to horses who were sensitive to their neighbours in a stable, Kingston Rule comes to mind. He arrived at our stables in the spring of 1989 and seemed to fear other horses. He was highly strung, nervous and moody. Someone said of him that he looked like he was expecting a tiger to jump out from behind every tree.

In the warmer weather, with firming tracks, I patiently worked at understanding him and calming him down. He just needed to relax more, enjoy life. We took him to country meetings before Christmas, not to race but just to be stabled around other horses, to get used to them and see that they weren't going to harm him.

We had him ready for racing in the first week of the new year, on 6 January 1990, in a 6-furlong sprint at Caulfield. He struggled to keep up with the fliers in the first part of the race, but roared home from the turn to finish a long neck second. A fortnight later he won a mid-week mile race for three-year-olds at Sandown, then he won again at the same track two weeks later, also over a mile but this time against open company. He was a handsome chestnut with a white blaze, flashing home with his white markings, or 'socks', on his forelegs.

He kept improving in that preparation, so I kept setting him tougher assignments. When a horse continues to improve, you keep going with it, because you don't know where its improvement will stop. In the back of my mind was the Caulfield Cup and possibly the Melbourne Cup later in the year, but he'd had so few starts that he needed to win something substantial in order to get enough weight to be sure of qualifying for the cups. It can be hard to get into those races, and horses who are all promise and no record just don't qualify.

Kingston Rule ran in a handicap at Flemington next and finished unplaced, hurting himself in the running. The injury was superficial and healed quickly, so we stepped him up for a stakes race, the Carlyon Cup at Caulfield. He went very well there, losing in a photo finish to Marwong, who had won the Caulfield Guineas as a three-year-old. I entered Kingston Rule in the Australian Cup at Flemington next, and he wasn't up to the class of a Group One, but he ran on well enough behind the likes of Vo Rogue, Better Loosen Up and Super Impose.

I was happy with his progress to this point, and thankfully for me he was taking my mind off accounting firms, court cases and nasty paperwork. Maybe, just maybe, he could be one of the rare 'super' horses who lived up to their breeding. It happened so seldom that you were surprised when it did. A disproportionate number of the highest-priced yearlings, with the best breeding in the world, are absolute duds. But Kingston Rule was coming along well on the track, and most importantly he seemed to be enjoying life more.

When he came back from his spell, Kingston Rule ran unplaced in the wet at Moonee Valley. It was only then that we learnt from Patrick Biancone that the horse had hated wet tracks from day one. But then again, Think Big hated the wet too and he won a Melbourne Cup in the mud, so you could never be sure.

Kingston Rule ran in the weight-for-age Memsie and Craiglee stakes, coming home rapidly both times without threatening the winners. He still hadn't qualified for the cups though. He'd had nine starts for us, eleven in his whole career, and he'd only won two nondescript mile races at Sandown.

While everyone was excited about him, he still hadn't done much.

Len Maund had been riding him, but when he finished eighth over 2200 metres at Sandown at his next start, David Hains and I talked about calling in Jim Cassidy. An expatriate New Zealander, Cassidy was doing a lot of riding for our stable and had turned into one of the most assertive, positive riders since flashing to fame with his last-to-first win on Kiwi in the 1983 Melbourne Cup. The only problem I've ever had with Cassidy is that there are two of him. If you get Jim Cassidy in the right mood, committed to his job and fully focused, your horses will have a great chance of winning. If you get the other Cassidy, however . . . Let's say that he and I have had our ups and downs over the years. In 2009 he rode my colt Roman Emperor to win the AJC Australian Derby at Randwick, my first Group One win in Sydney for a decade, so I suppose I'm dealing with the good Cassidy again now.

We wanted to run Kingston Rule in the Underwood, then the Turnbull and Caulfield stakes, in the hope of winning enough prize money to qualify for the Caulfield Cup. His parents were both champions at 10 to 12 furlongs, and we considered that this might be his distance. But the Underwood was too close to the Sandown race, and then he didn't qualify for the fields in the Turnbull and the Caulfield stakes. It was exasperating when we knew he was improving so fast. Our last chance was the 10-furlong Coongy Handicap at Caulfield on the Wednesday before the Cup; Kingston Rule ran bravely but failed by a length to achieve the all-important stakes win.

So he didn't get into the Caulfield Cup. Rain produced a soft track, so maybe he wouldn't have done well anyway and it was a blessing in disguise. The Cup was won by Bob Hoysted's Sydeston, a strong stayer who was, with the New Zealander The Phantom, one of the Melbourne Cup favourites.

Speaking of the Melbourne Cup, we still had to find a way of qualifying Kingston Rule. The Moonee Valley Cup, over 2600 metres on Cox Plate day, was a possibility. The historical indicators weren't good: the last horse to win the Melbourne Cup after winning the Moonee Valley Cup was Wodalla in 1953. But Kingston Rule didn't know that, and we weren't in a position to pick and choose. He simply had to run in it – and he had to win.

At this point we made a slight but telling change to his equipment. As I've said, my preference was often to have male horses gelded young, to take the weight off their front legs. To geld Kingston Rule was unthinkable, but the result was that he was very heavy in the shoulder. When he was galloping on fast tracks, he was jarring his legs and almost giving himself a slight concussion. So after the Coongy Handicap we fitted him out with absorbent rubber 'shock tamers' in his shoes to soften the blow. He seemed to like them. He was also still, in my opinion, 20 kilograms overweight. I had to keep working and racing him to get his bulk down.

The Cox Plate went to Better Loosen Up, the weight-for-age champion who would go on to win the Japan Cup. He wouldn't be running in the Melbourne Cup. But, ominously, Sydeston ran a very fine second and The Phantom stormed home for fourth. Those two went to the top of the Melbourne Cup betting, though there were doubts over Sydeston at the distance and he was carrying a hefty 58.5 kilos after his Caulfield Cup win.

If Kingston Rule didn't win the Moonee Valley Cup, we'd be going to the Melbourne Cup as spectators, or possibly to watch a lightweight outsider we had, the mare La Tristia.

Well, Kingston Rule didn't just win the Moonee Valley Cup. He blitzed it. He sprinted from the 800-metre mark and took the lead going into the short straight, then stayed well, running the race right out. The important thing was that he'd won; he'd qualified. And then we looked at the times and were astonished. He'd set a race record, nearly a course record, and ran his last 4 furlongs at a sprinter's speed of 47.1 seconds.

As Cassidy came in and dismounted, I said: 'Ride him in the Cup.'

Amazingly, he demurred. He said he already had a commitment to Just A Dancer, on whom he'd won the Herbert Power Handicap at Caulfield. I couldn't believe it. Here we had a horse with unlimited potential who had just won the Moonee Valley Cup in record time, coming good for the Melbourne Cup, and Cassidy wasn't sure if he wanted to ride him!

David Hains and I weren't waiting around. We invited the very good Victorian jockey Michael Clarke to ride Kingston Rule in track work that week. I offered him the ride in the Cup, and he said no too! He was gambling that Mick Dittman, Sydeston's regular rider, would lose his appeal against a suspension he'd picked up on Cox Plate day. It was all musical chairs with these riders. If Dittman was ruled out, he would have to give up Sydeston, and Clarke could step in. But if Dittman won his appeal and could ride in the Cup, Clarke was risking being left without a mount.

Meanwhile Cassidy was still humming and hawing. He rode an import from Argentina, Savage Toss, to victory in the

Werribee Cup, and everyone thought he was going to switch to that horse until he said the opposition in that race was hopeless and his choice was down to Kingston Rule and Just A Dancer.

On the Thursday before Derby day, both of those horses were doing track work, and Cassidy was riding them. I wasn't too pleased at our horse being auditioned by a jockey, and it wasn't ideal either for David Hains, who had come to Flemington first thing in the morning to see his horse work.

It so happened that the track was wet. Kingston Rule, true to form, galloped uncertainly and showed a pronounced dislike for the going. Just A Dancer worked like a Melbourne Cup winner, and Cassidy said he would stick with Graeme Rogerson's horse. But he was always hedging his bets, Cassidy – he said he would stick with Just A Dancer only until he saw how that horse ran in the Mackinnon on the Saturday.

David Hains and I had a long talk. We were fed up with all the stuffing around by the jockeys. My son Anthony, who was working as my stable foreman, had suggested to me that Darren Beadman, a young Sydney jockey who didn't have a ride in the Cup, might be a good choice for Kingston Rule. Beadman was the premier Sydney jockey, riding the Ingham brothers' horses for Vic Thompson, but was inexperienced in the Melbourne Cup. Yet Anthony said Beadman was a good judge of pace who followed instructions well. He had just ridden five winners in a day in Sydney. A good listener, who wins races – I liked the sound of that.

Beadman, who grew up in a racing family in Canberra (his father John was a good country trainer), had had a celebrated career as an apprentice, winning the 1984 Golden Slipper on

Inspired at the age of eighteen. He was indentured to Theo Green, one of the best teachers, and then, before finishing his apprenticeship, he transferred his indentures to France, riding for John Fellows at Chantilly. John was an Australian, the son of the trainer of Foxzami, who had beaten Dad's Comic Court in the 1949 Melbourne Cup. Now, after a couple of years over there, Darren Beadman was back in Australia as a full-fledged rider, quite seasoned for a twenty-four-year-old. The more I thought about using Beadman on Kingston Rule, the more I liked the idea.

After an extended conference, David and I agreed that we couldn't wait for Cassidy and Clarke to make up their minds, if they would at all, and so we engaged Beadman to ride Kingston Rule in the Mackinnon Stakes.

If he could get a start in the Mackinnon! Yet again, he missed out. I really couldn't believe it. I sincerely thought I had a special horse who, on his day, was capable of beating any Melbourne Cup field. But between the clubs who couldn't find a place for him in these races and the jockeys who wouldn't commit themselves to ride him, I was feeling distinctly unwanted on the horse's behalf.

Perhaps there was something else to it. I hadn't won a Melbourne Cup since Hyperno. Many of these youngsters wouldn't have known who Hyperno was, let alone the likes of Light Fingers and Galilee. It's possible that they saw me as yesterday's man. I have no doubt that if it was 1968 or 1978 and I had Kingston Rule, I would have been beating off jockeys with a stick.

Still, Beadman was keen. Beadman was always keen, a young-looking, fresh-faced Christian boy.

Because he missed out on a Mackinnon start, Kingston Rule was entered in the Hotham Handicap over 2500 metres, then known as the Dalgety. He carried 56 kilos, 3 more than he would have in the Melbourne Cup. I told Beadman that if he had to use the whip, 'hit him about as hard as you'd hit me'. He knew what I meant. Beadman settled the horse nicely and he ran on from well back to finish runner-up to Mount Olympus. Beadman rode him hard hands and heels, and didn't use the whip. Kingston Rule's sectional times were just as impressive as they'd been in the Moonee Valley Cup, and the bookmakers were starting to get a whiff of fear. Over the next two days they changed their minds about Kingston Rule, eventually rating him as 7/1 equal favourite with The Phantom in an open-betting Cup.

Again, though, there were the doubters. Kingston Rule was ridden in track work on Cup eve by my regular Melbourne track rider, Joe Agresta. Joe is terrific: he rides work for me in the mornings and then goes to his job for the Victorian government as a public servant all day. He's done it for years and loves the horses. He galloped Kingston Rule over 10 furlongs in even time, and track watchers were saying that the horse, having gone so slowly, must be unfit.

On Cup day he was radiant, looking every bit the son of Secretariat and Rose Of Kingston. He had come a long, long way from the colt who was scared of his own shadow and hated other horses. Now here he was, parading in his glowing chestnut coat with his flashy white blaze and socks, in front of 92,000 people and twenty-three other starters. Nothing worried him. He looked perfect.

Beadman rode him as if he was driving a sports car. He tucked Kingston Rule in on the rails just behind the leading group and put him to sleep. The famous Hains colours, gold with red striped sleeves and a red cap, were conspicuous on the rail in eighth place. Kingston Rule's position tight on the fence kept him from pulling or wanting to accelerate too early. At the 3-furlong mark, coming through the home turn, the whole field was accelerating and the Argentine horse, Savage Toss, was in the lead. Beadman rode as if he'd been doing Melbourne Cups all his life: he did precisely what I asked of him. He waited, waited, waited, and finally hooked Kingston Rule out off the rail 300 metres from home. I only had one fear as he went into the lead. Kingston Rule, true to his character, absolutely objected to being hit with the whip. Part of me didn't even want Beadman to be carrying one, but those were the rules. If Beadman whipped him, he might take offence and literally stop running.

As they thundered down the last furlong, The Phantom surged along the inside. I watched Beadman through my binoculars. He threw the reins forward and rode with tremendous rhythm under pressure. And he resisted pulling the whip when every instinct must have told him to do so. The Phantom came up to Kingston Rule's flank. Beadman kept urging him on with the reins and his heels, the 100-metre post came up, then the 50-metre post . . . and The Phantom died a little on his run. Kingston Rule, thrusting out his white-socked forelegs, held off the New Zealander by a length. In doing so he had run 3 minutes 16.4 seconds, the fastest Melbourne Cup in its 130 years. Not bad for a horse in his fifteenth start, who couldn't qualify for any of the key lead-up races. Not bad at all!

The time was extraordinary, and someone pointed out that it would have left Comic Court fifteen lengths behind with his then Cup record in 1950. But I don't think this means Kingston Rule was better than Comic Court. For a start, Comic Court also won at 6 furlongs against top-class sprinters, proving himself over several seasons. And more generally, the Cup thoroughbred hasn't improved that much over the years. We feed them better, we find better veterinary methods, we enhance a lot of small things, but ultimately the racehorse is a racehorse, and having trained them for more than fifty years I can say that they are much the same now as they were in 1953.

As Beadman came in on Kingston Rule, with David Hains leading them, I was more emotional than usual. It had been a long time since 1979, and I was enduring the most traumatic year of my training life. I told reporters that I had grown sick of being told I was a 'has-been'. This felt like a fresh start for me – though it was true that I needed to win about fifty more Melbourne Cups to pay off my creditors.

I felt extremely happy for David Hains. When Kingston Town ran in the 1982 Melbourne Cup, David was told his champion had won. From his position in the grandstand, he couldn't see that Gurner's Lane had sneaked up on the inside. If ever there was a horse that deserved a Melbourne Cup to crown his career, it was Kingston Town. David had missed out then, but now, with Kingston Rule, he had a kind of redemption, or at least a consolation.

Kingston Rule's win also offered me a rare satisfaction as a trainer. Like Hyperno, he had come to me with much promise but question marks over his state of mind. He was said to be too pretty, too aristocratic, for the rough-and-tumble of a

Melbourne Cup. Too much breeding, not enough mongrel. It had been my job to understand what was upsetting the horse, make him happy, and unlock his potential. In the case of Hyperno, the horse had done enough before he came to me for us to know how good he could be. With Kingston Rule, he had done nothing. He was a perfectly bred, impossibly handsome mystery. Nobody knew what he could do, but there seemed so much at stake. He had a whole international heritage of great thoroughbred racing in his blood, uniting all sorts of factors from my father's breeding knowledge right down to the genes of the horse of the century, Secretariat. To have brought that all together, against the obstacles put up by racing clubs and jockeys and fortune itself, gave me the most tremendous pleasure, and when you see photos of me at the presentation of that 1990 Melbourne Cup, I am beaming from ear to ear.

17
The freak

LIKE A WILL O' THE WISP, KINGSTON RULE WAS HERE ONE MINUTE, gone the next. I was certain he would develop into a weight-for-age champion like his parents, and he was placed in the St George and Blamey stakes in the autumn in preparation for the 1991 Australian Cup. But he injured his tendons and was put out of racing for a few months. We tried to get him up again for the spring, but he wasn't right. David Hains sent him off to stand as a sire at Euroa. What a career – very short, but very, very sweet.

THE NEXT YEAR, AFTER MANY YEARS OF WORKING FOR ME, ANTHONY went out on his own as a licensed trainer. I wished him luck. It was the best thing he ever did. But as soon as he went out, I saw him not as my protégé but as another competitor. I think that's how it should be. Otherwise he couldn't earn respect in his own right. I would offer him help if he asked for it, but not at the expense of my own horses. As he said after a big race win some years later, 'Dad has taught me everything I know – but not everything he knows!'

Anthony soon had about fifty horses in training in Melbourne and Sydney, and trained a Group One winner in his first season. He was constantly being compared with Gai Waterhouse and the Hayes sons, Peter and David. But unlike them, he didn't inherit a ready-made stable. Anthony had to start on his own two feet. With such a good teacher, he had a good eye for a yearling, and at the 1995 Sydney sales, he spotted a colt who had some irregularities in conformation but good basics. The colt was passed in but then Anthony bought him for $40,000; gelded, the yearling would race as Might And Power.

Anthony on-sold him to Nick Moraitis, but then made a mistake after the horse had had a few races. Anthony offered Moraitis about $80,000 to buy Might And Power outright. The size of the offer made Moraitis suspect the horse was something special. Moraitis took Might And Power away from Anthony, and gave it to Jack Denham to train. The rest is history, with Might And Power being Anthony's big one that got away.

BUT BACK TO 1991. IF AUSTRALIAN BREEDERS AND RACING CLUBS were competing with each other to offer bigger incentives and newer ideas, the New Zealanders weren't leaving the ground untended either. In 1989 the first Trentham Magic Millions sales were held, in tandem with the usual annual yearling sales. I was there, but I didn't manage the best buy.

Roy Fleiter, a businessman from Melbourne, spotted a chestnut filly by Nassipour, a newly imported American stallion who was just starting his stud career. The filly's dam was Sharon Jane, by Battle Waggon. Both Battle Waggon and Nassipour were by sons of Nasrullah, one of the 'winningest' sires in the world. Sharon Jane also had Summertime, one of my old favourites, on her dam's side.

Fleiter bought her for $16,000, planning to race her with his wife Dorothy and their son Tony, who was the general manager of Dalgety Bloodstock's Melbourne operations. When they went looking for a trainer, they didn't have to go far. The top New Zealand trainer Dave O'Sullivan was a fan of the chestnut filly, so he took her into his care at Matamata.

She would race as Let's Elope – a great name, as her father's sire was Blushing Groom, out of Runaway Bride. Dave O'Sullivan didn't race her as a two-year-old. She raced six times over middle distances in New Zealand as a three-year-old, winning twice, but failed when she had to run on wet tracks, which are more common in New Zealand than in Australia.

In April 1991, a Melbourne owner, Dennis Marks, and his wife Margaret made an approach to Tony Fleiter, wanting to buy young but tried race mares whom they could continue racing for a little while before sending them out to breed. Marks didn't have Let's Elope specifically in mind. He was approaching Tony Fleiter in Fleiter's capacity as a bloodstock agent at Dalgety. Nevertheless, Fleiter felt that Let's Elope, whom he part-owned with his parents, was the type of potential broodmare Marks was looking for. The Fleiters had fielded a fair amount of interest in Let's Elope already, and were considering selling her at a handsome profit.

Marks's agent in New Zealand took a look at the filly, and along with his syndicate manager Kevin White, Marks offered $120,000. The Fleiters accepted. They would miss out on the jackpot, but they'd still done pretty well on a $16,000 purchase.

Marks and White weren't expecting the world. When they sent Let's Elope to me, their highest hope was for her to add some black type to her pedigree before her stud career. The payoff, they foresaw, could be in the prices they could get for her offspring, more than whatever prize money she won through racing.

They also sent me one of their other new buys. They had spent $30,000 for a two-year-old Grosvenor filly called Richfield Lass. In Australia she would race as Richfield Lady. Again, as with Let's Elope, they only wanted to race her for a little while, with modest expectations, as a means to increase her value as a broodmare.

I was embroiled in the Federal Court case now, spending far too many hours with lawyers in my attempt to get the accounting firms to accept responsibility for their part in the failed syndicate. But my training methods are so straightforward and

Deep in conversation with Harry White during trackwork in the late 1970s.
He looks like he's trying not to think about my choice of clothing.

Sometimes it was hard to keep up with the owners' domestic arrangements. The delightful Susan had been part of Leilani's connections winning the 1974 Caulfield Cup. By the 1980s, I had to make sure I remembered that her husband was now Sir Frank Renouf, not Andrew Peacock.

A favourite painting of Beau Zam. He had the talent to match his looks.

With Bob Hawke. He loved his racing and was a great ambassador for the industry.

Princess Anne was back in April 1988 to ride Beau Zam in track work at Randwick before the AJC Derby. She'd ridden one of our two-year-olds earlier that week and it threw her off, but she still came back for more.

With Queen Elizabeth II in the stands before the Queen Elizabeth Stakes in Canberra, which Beau Zam won. Valmae's at the back, and Bob Hawke is lurking somewhere near Her Majesty.

Kingston Rule (Darren Beadman), the best-bred horse to win a Melbourne Cup, breaking the race record in 1990.

I've got the Cup, Kingston Rule gets a pat, and David Hains has the grin of a winning owner.

Great camaraderie between trainers at a morning track-work session at Flemington during a spring carnival in the early 1990s. With (from left) David Hayes, Lee Freedman and John Meagher.

She was all over the place on the turn, but when Steven King steadied her down the straight, Let's Elope showed her class.

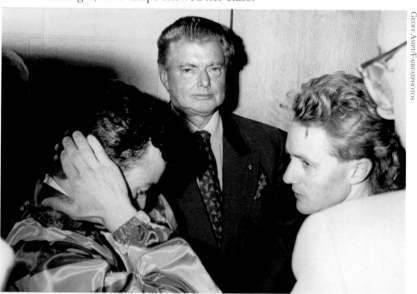

Shane Dye, on Shiva's Revenge, protested Let's Elope's win. King, Dye and I are awaiting the stewards' decision. Asked what I thought about the protest, I said: 'Can't lose!'

I didn't know her for long, but Let's Elope put a smile on my face in tough times.

On the eve of the 1996 Cup, Saintly was happily rolling about at Altona Beach. On race day, he was sound asleep in his stall …

Newspix

... then, relaxed to the end, Saintly gave a galloping exhibition under Darren Beadman.

Newspix/Arthur Edwards

Chin Nam, Beadman and I can't wipe the smiles off our faces ...

… but then the cursed hayfever hit me during the presentation.

With Saintly at his retirement village, Princes Farm, an equine paradise.

Chin Nam liked to spread the enjoyment around and celebrate with friends. Here we are with the connections of Catalan Opening after winning the 1997 Hong Kong Mile.

I was proud of Anthony after his first Group One win with On Air in the AJC Oaks at Randwick in 1998, but now he was a trainer, he was a rival first, a protégé second.

John Marshall waited until the clock tower and then let Rogan Josh loose in the 1999 Cup.

Eleven felt good with Rogan Josh ... but somehow twelve seemed a nicer, rounder number.

In February 1998, I became a living national treasure with a few others. It might have felt like a lap of honour, but I am nowhere near retiring.

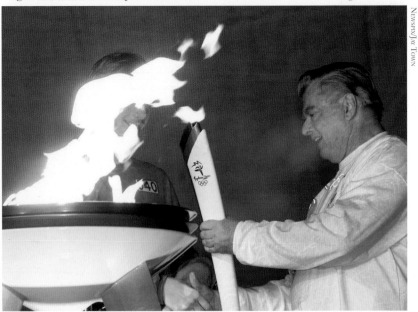

The honours were humbling. Here I am lighting the community cauldron with the Olympic Torch at Flemington in 2000.

John Howard comes to say hello to Valmae and me at an Australian Racing Hall of Fame dinner at Crown Casino in 2001. I thought he did a good job until he let the corporate bookmakers in.

I've been drinking from the fountain of youth! With (from left) George Hanlon, Harry White, Scobie Breasley and Roy Higgins at the official opening of Champions – Australian Racing Museum and Hall of Fame at Federation Square in July 2004.

RIGHT: I've tried to keep my distance from jockeys, and here's why: Glen Boss getting familiar after we won the 2005 Caulfield Guineas with God's Own.

Mark Dadswell/Getty Images

ABOVE: In the office at Leilani Lodge. It hasn't changed much since the 1970s – nor have I!

Newspix/Brett Costello

A horse is a reflection of its trainer. On the eve of Viewed's 2008 Melbourne Cup, I am nothing if not relaxed.

Close as a boarding house scrape of butter – literally! Blake Shinn got Viewed home over Bauer to give us Cup number twelve.

I always thought he was lucky, from that initial two-up game onwards. By 2008, Chin Nam was the most successful owner in Cup history, with four wins.

A dozen Melbourne Cups … now, a baker's dozen has a nice ring to it, doesn't it?

Three generations of Cummings – Anthony (middle), his son James, and me – after Swick won the VRC Classic at Flemington in November 2008. James was soon to start working in my stable and get some good tuition!

driven by commonsense, they can continue to function in my absence. My Melbourne stable foreman, Leon Corstens, just had to follow the written instructions and keep me informed when he observed anything out of the ordinary.

It was only an afterthought to enter Let's Elope in the Caulfield and Melbourne cups. We tended to enter dozens of horses each year, many on the off chance that they might surprise us. That year we entered forty-two horses. Let's Elope was considered to be on the outer limits of even this very liberal policy. At the absolute last minute, the stable called Dennis Marks and asked if he wouldn't mind lodging the $1000 entry fee for her for the Caulfield Cup. (Kevin White, by then, had been bought out of the ownership group.) Dennis thought about it for a minute, and then, just as a safeguard against possible regret, agreed to pay it. Ten minutes later the stable called again, to ask him if he wouldn't mind lodging the $1000 fee for her in the Melbourne Cup, too. He said, 'What the hell, why not?' So now we had forty-three Cup entrants. Let's Elope was the 490th of the Melbourne Cup's 490 nominees.

Dennis had an interesting history. As a student at the prestigious Scotch College in Melbourne he had been a horse-mad boy, going out and hiring ponies to ride on the weekends. When he was sixteen, it all came to an end when he was diagnosed with a lung infection that turned very serious and nearly killed him. He was in hospital for nine months while they worked on him, and when he got out he didn't go back to school, instead going to work with his father, who was a furrier with a factory in Collins Street in the centre of Melbourne. Dennis saw a gap in the market for a middle man, and at the age of twenty-two became a fur retailer, opening a shop in the famous Block

Arcade. In a way, as I learnt his story, he reminded me of myself: leaving school early, following his father, and then, like me, finding it very slow and hard when he went out on his own. Periods of three days went by when he didn't have a single customer. It was a bit like me training for five years before I had my first feature-race winner.

This was where our stories parted ways. Dennis decided to break with the fur business and lease out a property in the city on which people could park their cars. He was so successful he soon had several blocks around the city and 5000 cars a day parked on them. This led to more property development, car washes and petrol stations, car detailing and repairs, and even developing Melbourne's Luna Park down at St Kilda. He got interested in owning racehorses from the mid-1970s, and did it in a fairly low-key way, with some moderately successful horses and then some broodmares whom he put on a property at Shoreham on the Mornington Peninsula. It was while stocking this property that he came across Let's Elope and Richfield Lady, along with three other fillies and mares.

WE PUT BOTH LET'S ELOPE AND RICHFIELD LADY INTO TRAINING for the 1991 spring carnival. My main Melbourne Cup hopes rested with another of Nassipour's progeny, the gelding Shiva's Revenge. He had won the VRC St Leger and South Australian Derby as a three-year-old, and nearly added the Adelaide Cup. As a comparison of the perceived abilities of Shiva's Revenge and Let's Elope, when the weights were issued in mid-1991 the gelding received 53.5 kilos and Let's Elope the feather-weight of 48.5 kilos.

Let's Elope lived right down to that rating with her first barrier trial for us, finishing thirty lengths behind the second-last horse. We knew she hadn't done much for Dave O'Sullivan, but she couldn't be *that* bad. We kept working on her and began to understand that she had a ferocious dislike for wet tracks, reminiscent of Kingston Rule. When she was in the mood, however, she could run. We entered her in the Milady Stakes at Flemington a month before the Caulfield Cup, and she bolted home from last to finish a long neck behind the winner.

The Cummings mystique affected a few punters, and she was prematurely spoken of as a Caulfield Cup contender. She started favourite in her next race, the Royal Show Handicap at Caulfield, and on a slow track she put up the shutters and finished at the rear of the field. We certainly learnt our lesson.

She was far from a mature racehorse, and had a tendency to weave her way across the track while she accelerated. She was as big as a gelding and when she got going she was like a runaway rugby winger, knocking down everything in her path. This was in evidence at her next start, the Turnbull Stakes over 10 furlongs at weight-for-age at Flemington, but so was her incredible talent. Up against the best gallopers of that season, including Lee Freedman's Durbridge, she veered all over the place under the lightweight jockey Steven King but still sprinted away to win by three lengths.

The same day, Richfield Lady steamed home to win the Edward Manifold Stakes for three-year-old fillies. Not a bad result for Dennis and Margaret Marks, and not a bad effort from the stable having only had the two horses in our care for four months.

There were a number of reasons Let's Elope came along so rapidly in such a short period. Foremost was her unbelievable talent. That season, she was as good as Leilani and Light Fingers, the best four-year-old mares I'd trained. Then there was the matter of getting her settled and happy in her new home. Then, importantly, came the drying out of the tracks as Melbourne was blessed with a warm, sunny spring. Finally, we had to tame her waywardness in the running. She was all over the place like a two-year-old, and we had to do something about that.

She had run in blinkers in New Zealand with some success, and in track work we experimented with the gear; she seemed just the kind of rangy, extravagant galloper who benefited from the focus given by blinkers. All of a sudden, able to concentrate on the job at hand, she showed us how she could gallop. On the Tuesday before the Caulfield Cup we trialled her in blinkers before the stewards, as was required of us, and she went well enough to get their stamp of approval.

With her light weight of 48.5 kilograms, she was backed in to 12/1 for the Caulfield Cup. Shiva's Revenge, meanwhile, was struggling with a virus and looked borderline as to whether he would start. There was some good prospective opposition in the favourites Dr Grace, the AJC Derby winner, and Ivory Way, owned by Arab interests and trained by the Hayes stable.

Let's Elope drew an outside barrier but we were confident that the blinkers were the right choice, and we had faith in

King. He was a young lad, only twenty-one years old, and his father Alby had also been a jockey. Steven hadn't been all that keen on taking up his father's profession, but once he got going he was Victoria's top apprentice and by 1991, as a senior, had stepped up into the leading rank. Working to his advantage was his being a very light jockey, able to ride Let's Elope with her low handicaps.

The Caulfield track was as fast as it gets. From her number 18 barrier, Let's Elope was caught fairly wide all the way around the back of the course, and we were feeling that she might have covered too much ground. But she started winding up from 4 furlongs out, and as she straightened up King gave her a tap with the whip. Rarely have I seen such acceleration at the end of a mile and a half. She absolutely flew down the outside and passed Ivory Way in the last stride, going so fast that she beat him by a full head.

After that, the VRC handicapper wasn't going to miss her. It was an amazing finish and she was given almost the maximum penalty, 2.5 kilograms, for the Melbourne Cup. It was worth bearing in mind, though, that only one mare had ever done the double, Rivette way back in 1939. Only ten horses all up had done it, the last being Gurner's Lane in 1982. As excited as we were about Let's Elope, history seemed to be loaded against her.

Also encouragingly, Shiva's Revenge stormed home for sixth in the Caulfield Cup. He was well behind Let's Elope, but considering he'd been ill and had problems with his hooves, we were very happy with his run.

In the lead-up to the race somebody asked me if, after eight Melbourne Cups and six Caulfield Cups, my trophy cabinet at home was a 'huge place'. I said, 'Well, I hope it's still there next month.' As often happens, they rolled around the place as if I was a comedian, but in fact I was serious. The after-effects of the Cups King Syndicate were so painful at this time that I continually felt on the brink of bankruptcy.

On Cox Plate day, Dave O'Sullivan drew some consolation from the fact that he wasn't training Let's Elope. His gelding Surfers Paradise galloped away with the big race at good odds – though I felt that if Let's Elope had been in it, she would have won.

Away from the track, Let's Elope was pleasing me more and more. The harder she raced, the more she ate. She never left an oat. There was no surer sign that a horse was enjoying racing. To give her a last tune-up for the Cup and also to test my theory that she could compete against the best horses at weight-for-age, I entered her in the Mackinnon Stakes on Derby day. There was always a toss-up between whether to run a horse in the Mackinnon or the longer Dalgety, and I just had a feeling that with her zip Let's Elope would be happier in the shorter race. So it turned out. She was up against Surfers Paradise and the Cox Plate runner-up, Super Impose, and King settled her back in the field. I liked his patience as a jockey. There would always be the temptation, with a headstrong mare like Let's Elope, to release the brakes too early. King waited until he was well into the straight, and then she took the two weight-for-age stars in the matter of a stride or two. She had run the 10 furlongs in an Australian record time of 2 minutes flat. There was little doubt in anybody's mind now, seeing what she'd done to Surfers Paradise and Super Impose, that she would have won the Cox Plate. Lee Freedman said, after seeing her run away from his champion, that the Melbourne Cup was as good as over. Freedman has good horse judgment – he's said that I was his model, so I wasn't going to argue with what he was saying about Let's Elope.

Super Impose would be carrying 60 kilos in the Cup, and was running well beyond his preferred distance of a mile to a mile and a quarter. Even though Super Impose had run second to Tawriffic in the Melbourne Cup two years earlier, Freedman knew that he couldn't give Let's Elope 9 kilos and outrace her. I hoped he was right. I felt that only bad luck could beat her. I had a deep instinct that the 2 miles wouldn't bother her at all.

Shiva's Revenge was coming good just in time too, and I was uncustomarily confident. I also had some hopes for the VRC Oaks winner from the previous year, Weekend Delight, though she was starting at 50/1, a long way behind Shiva's Revenge at 10/1 and Let's Elope, who, notwithstanding some rain the day before the Cup, was backed in to 3/1 favourite. Few people could see her losing.

Cup day was Steven King's twenty-second birthday. There wasn't much I could tell him. Happy birthday? Just be patient on her, and let her go at the 4-furlong mark. She had enough natural acceleration to win from there on her own, without too much hard riding. Then he could come in and enjoy some cake with his Melbourne Cup.

She started from barrier 10, and King was able to bring her in near the fence and save ground as they went down the straight and around the corner the first time. As with Galilee in 1966, it was just one of those Melbourne Cups where I really believed, rather than hoped, that my horse would win.

King let her go at the 4 furlongs, and she swept around the outside of the field. She started to move up on the leaders as they rounded the home turn. I can tell you, there are few better feelings in the world than having a sunny spring Tuesday in Melbourne, watching that field spread out and seek position for the last sprint, and seeing the inevitability of your horse moving up. As they came out of the turn, Let's Elope accelerated again. She hung in – the blinkers never really solved her waywardness – but there were others contributing to a big melee in which a few horses, including Shiva's Revenge, had to pause in their sprints, get rebalanced, and go again.

Let's Elope was leaving all that behind her. She bolted away and won easing down by two and a half lengths. Incredibly, Shiva's Revenge kept going after his check and ran into second place. If he hadn't had such a poor preparation, with his injuries and illness, he'd have given her a real shake. I'm not saying he was ever good enough to beat her, but he would have got closer than two and a half lengths.

While I might have been pleased by scoring another quinella in the Cup, my fifth, the connections of the runner-up weren't necessarily sharing in the celebrations. Shane Dye, who'd been aboard Shiva's Revenge, cried out that he was protesting, second against first. I didn't give Dye a lot of mounts, but on his day he was a very good rider and he'd got the best out of Shiva's Revenge this day. The siren went off and instead of patting ourselves on the back we had to file into the stewards' room for a hearing. Apparently I was the only one who was smiling. As I was walking into the room, someone asked me what I thought about the protest.

'Can't lose,' I said.

Dye was in tears as he told the stewards his mount had been interfered with on the home turn. Several horses were involved, but clearly Let's Elope was a key contributor when she hung in. That wasn't in question. What was up for debate was how much it affected the result. There didn't seem much doubt. Let's Elope had not only defeated the other horses easily, she had won a Melbourne Cup with a more dominant display than had been seen in many years. She finished like Comic Court, like Galilee – like a sprinter. Nobody could have beaten her that day. The protest was duly dismissed, though King copped a six-week suspension for careless riding. It was a serious matter. The chief steward, Pat Lalor, had never before imposed a six-week sentence in twelve years in his job. But he didn't lose sight of the most important thing: you only had to look at the way Let's Elope had finished and you knew she would never have lost. Stewards must not only determine that the interference has been caused, but must estimate how it affected the final margins between the horses. If Shiva's Revenge hadn't been hampered on the turn, he may have run a length or a length and a half faster. But my firm conviction, and others', was that if she'd been challenged more, Let's Elope would have just run that much faster. With her relatively light weight, she dominated the field and was the only conceivable winner.

Even more than with Kingston Rule the year before, in training terms this had all happened in the blink of an eye. Earlier in my career, I'd trained Melbourne Cup winners after knowing the horses for four or five years. I'd had Kingston Rule for only one year, and six months before the 1991 Melbourne Cup I'd never even heard of Let's Elope. As I was still stuck in the gloomy aftermath of the Cups King Syndicate, it was instinctive for me to believe that these two wins, in 1990 and 1991, were a sign of grace, a blessing from the racing gods.

To put some icing on the cake, Richfield Lady won the VRC Oaks two days later, capping a terrific spring for us. Barring the Cox Plate, we'd swept the major Group Ones, with Shaftesbury Avenue winning the Caulfield Stakes, his sixth Group One win. Shaftesbury Avenue was the best sprinter-miler in Australia for a couple of years there, winning from 1000 up to 2000 metres, and he could have won a Cox Plate if he'd stayed sound. But I had no call to be greedy. A champion mare had fallen into my lap, and in a twinkling we had won the Caulfield and Melbourne cups. Enough said.

18

My horse from heaven

Dennis and Margaret Marks had got a lot more than they bargained for. By the end of the season Let's Elope, the potential broodmare they had bought to have a little bit of fun with, was the champion racehorse of Australia. Richfield Lady wasn't far behind.

If it had been up to me, Let's Elope would have raced for several more years. Dennis Marks didn't take much persuasion to bring her into training again for the autumn, and she came back as if she'd barely taken a breath after the Melbourne Cup. She won the Orr Stakes and St George Stakes at weight-for-age, with King aboard again. Unfortunately for him, she kept hanging in when she accelerated, and in the St George she bumped another horse quite badly, leaving King suspended for her next start, the Australian Cup.

Let's Elope made it seven wins in a row, all of them Group races, in the Cup. She galloped away by three and a half lengths for my tenth Australian Cup win. She demoralised her rivals, including once again the brave Shiva's Revenge, who must have been sick of the sight of her.

While we were on a good thing, we saw no reason to stop. I was setting her for the rich Sydney autumn races such as the Mercedes Classic, formerly the Tancred Stakes, but she sprained a ligament in her foreleg in a training gallop, and that was it until the spring.

Have I ever trained a better staying horse? For that season, she was unbeatable. She was an easy pick for the horse of the year award, my first since Beau Zam. I doubt I've trained a better mare – Leilani and Light Fingers are the only ones who bear any comparison. In the spring of 1992, Let's Elope battled with injury and I couldn't get her properly fit for the Cox Plate. She did beat the champion Better Loosen Up in the Super Challenge at Caulfield, but wasn't in the all-conquering form of the previous season. She made it to the post in a field studded with stars such as Better Loosen Up, Super Impose and Naturalism, but she wasn't fully fit. It was a rough race, with a number of horses either hampered or falling. She came second over the line to Super Impose, but was later relegated to fifth place on protest for having bumped Better Loosen Up.

I still had her in the 1992 Melbourne Cup, but there was no point pushing her beyond her limits. She'd had too little racing, and then – another sign? – it rained on Cup day, so I scratched her.

We took her to Tokyo, where she finished seventh in the Japan Cup. She came back bleeding from her nostrils, incurring an automatic three-month ban on racing in Australia. She never raced here again. Dennis and Margaret Marks sent her to America for a few races to be trained by Ron McAnally in California, where she won and was placed at Group level without showing quite the form of her 1991–92 season. Like so many of the best horses, she got injured because she didn't know when to stop trying.

At the end of Let's Elope's career, Dennis made some remarks about my 'ruthlessness' and 'single-mindedness' with the horse. It was a fair call. I am obsessive about what races I want to train horses for, and as far as the owners are concerned, it's my way or the highway. Some of them don't like that. Some of them are fine with it – usually those who win. But the ground rules are clear. I listen to the horse before I listen to the owner, and if the owner wants to learn a bit about racing, he'll refrain from imposing his opinions on me. Dennis Marks had his views, and as the owner of the horse he was always within his rights to take her away from me. While he might have disagreed with some of my decisions as the horse's trainer, he had continued to entrust me with her care.

In 1992–93, Dennis Marks finally got Let's Elope to stud, albeit two or three years later than he'd expected! Due to her record, he was able to send her to America's best sire, Danzig. Unlike many top race mares, Let's Elope was a good breeder. Her filly to Danzig, named Yes I Will, ran some good races in France and then some more for me in Australia. Her son Ustinov, by Seeking The Gold, came to me too, and won some stakes races at the turn of the century, also being placed behind the champion Lonhro in the Caulfield Guineas.

A LIFE IN RACING CAN SEEM TO BE NOTHING MORE THAN A succession of horses. They come into the stable; they eat, they work, they race; they succeed or fail or get injured; they go out to the spelling paddock or retire. And as every batch moves out, a new batch moves in. When I look back on my career, it is of course the horses who take the limelight. So they should. It's all about the horses, and when my wife says I get on better with horses than I do with humans, she's not far off the mark. I keep getting up before dawn every morning, putting on some warm clothes and a snug cap and driving to the stables at Randwick – or wherever I am interstate – with more or less the same routine, day after day, week after week, month after month, and what keeps me continuing is the prospect of seeing what those racehorses have to show me this morning.

But there have been many special humans in my life, none more so than Tan Chin Nam.

After his two Melbourne Cup wins with Think Big, Chin Nam had continued owning horses, but on a fairly modest scale. This all changed when I was in such deep financial trouble in the early 1990s. Even though Kingston Rule and Let's Elope won Melbourne Cups, and Shaftesbury Avenue won six Group Ones, I was still digging my way out of a deep,

deep hole. Having sold the house in Vaucluse, Valmae and I moved to a unit in Elizabeth Bay. We were far from the poor house, but the repayment scheme was a gruelling marathon – rather like a Melbourne Cup! – and it was a constant drain on our resources and morale.

When he saw this happening, Chin Nam decided to buy a lot more racehorses and send them to me. I doubt I could have got through without him. In the early 1990s he funded the purchase of thirty-five horses and sent them to our stables, keeping me going with training fees (which I didn't have to give up to my creditors) and whatever prize money we could win (most of which I did have to give up). More important than the income was the faith he showed in us as a stable. Without a steady supply of racehorses, we might as well have given up.

Buying Princes Farm from me, when I needed the cash, was an extraordinary gesture. He didn't do it out of charity, making sure everything was done at market rates, but later, when I was out of the woods, he sold the farm back to me. I will always be immensely grateful to him.

A young English horseman, Duncan Ramage, moved to Australia and worked in some stud jobs before riding track work for me around this time at Randwick. It was obvious to everyone who met him that he was a lot more than a rider, a clever all-round horseman with a strong background in England. Not only could he ride, but he could diagnose a horse's strengths and weaknesses, and his advice very often seemed to be spot-on. He was living with a Norwegian woman, also a track rider, and they were very impressive people. I gave him a full-time job and sponsored his migration into Australia.

He impressed Chin Nam, and in 1991 became racing manager for Chin Nam in Australia.

Chin Nam's influence didn't stop there. As I mentioned earlier, my father was religious, or superstitious, enough to have a priest bless all of his horses. I did the same for many years, inviting Father Dennis Madigan to come to Leilani Lodge to perform the ceremonies. I had known Father Dennis from Adelaide, and he moved to Sydney to be the chaplain at St Vincent's Hospital for many years. Between duties he would pop over to Randwick to say a mass and give a blessing for our horses. And that was just the start of the things he did in and around the stable.

One of my more faithful owners was Cyril Maloney, the well-known and successful Sydney publican who owned a chain of hotels, including the Bondi Hotel. Cyril was quite a character, who you won't see in the honour roll of my Melbourne Cup-winning owners because he never had a horse good enough. This didn't dampen his enthusiasm, as he remained interested in the sport, but it did limit his spirit of adventure. Cyril kept wanting only to buy a one-third share in his horses. I'd tell him, 'You have to speculate to accumulate,' but he wouldn't listen. Consequently, he owned a share in many horses whom I trained, but not many of them had a lot of ability. The best was the black-type winner Nassirich. Otherwise, they were mostly pretty average, which was why I had more reasons to be grateful to him than to those luckier owners whose first horses happened to win Melbourne Cups. Cyril has always loved racing, and that's what has kept him involved. It's always the unlucky owners, who don't have a lot of success yet keep persisting, who are the bread and butter of a good stable.

Anyway, the point of talking about Cyril Maloney was that Father Dennis, as well as blessing our horses and looking after the patients at St Vincent's, also married Cyril and his wife at the St Vincent's chapel at six o'clock one Saturday morning. But some time after that, Father Dennis died, and I stopped having the horses blessed. The AJC's chaplain, Brother Dan, wasn't an ordained priest and so wasn't qualified to bless a racehorse. I could only countenance a Catholic doing the job, not a Protestant, given Dad's Catholic fervour. He'd have said that having a Catholic priest was the only sure way of making direct contact with the good Lord.

So after Father Dennis Madigan died, our horses and stables weren't being blessed. Did that have something to do with my bad luck at the end of the 1980s? Chin Nam believed in luck and the things you can do to bring about a turn for the better. He brought a Tibetan feng shui professor from California to go through Leilani Lodge, which Chin Nam believed may have been carrying unlucky spirits. This fellow wore a gorgeous white gown and had an even more gorgeous assistant with him.

Water is a bad thing in feng shui, because it carries wealth away from you. The first thing this professor saw at our stables was a toilet. He wasn't happy with that. He placed a mirror in front of it so that the grass outside – a good sign – could be reflected on the dunny door, instead of the water being in view. When the professor went to Princes Farm, he saw our wealth being taken downstream from us on the Nepean River. He put in another mirror. It isn't part of my belief system, but who's to say he wasn't right? The proof of the pudding is always in the eating, and my luck did seem to change for the better after these events.

Not that Chin Nam was any kind of holy fool. He doesn't like to part with money, and the price of everything seems to surprise him. He's continually complaining about things being too expensive. I suppose that comes from having been around for a long time. But it got too much one day for another owner, Mac Whitehouse, who owned hotels in Kings Cross. They were both sitting with me in my office and Chin Nam was going on about the cost of this and the cost of that, and Mac said, 'Stop, I've heard enough. How much do you want? Half a million? A million? Name it and I'll give it to you right here, I'll write you a cheque here and now if it'll make you shut up.'

I MENTIONED EARLIER THAT IN THE NEW ZEALAND SALES OF 1987 I had acquired a Sir Tristram filly who would go by the name All Grace. She wasn't any kind of racehorse but her pedigree was good: she was a cousin to my champion colt Taj Rossi and was also related to Dark Eclipse, a Golden Slipper winner. Her bloodlines were close to Storm Queen and Stormy Passage, two of the more special horses in my early career.

Before she could race, All Grace was injured and retired. I sent her to breed and in late 1991 she went to New Zealand to be served by Sky Chase, the top galloper I had bred myself and trained to several wins as a two- and three-year-old in 1987 and 1988. The next spring All Grace threw a lovely chestnut foal at the Turangga Stud at Scone, where I sent a lot of my broodmares. The foal was just a couple of months old when

Let's Elope had her last Australian races for us in the spring of 1992.

When Let's Elope won her Melbourne Cup, the VRC came good on a promise they had made to me back in 1979. In that year, Hyperno had become my seventh Melbourne Cup winner. I made a joke about the tiny size of the replica trophy the trainer was awarded for winning the Cup. It was a fraction of the size of the real thing, which went to the owners. It looked like a toy Melbourne Cup. Valmae said, more seriously, that I should be given a full-sized one. She also noted that the practice of giving the trainer a 'toy' Melbourne Cup had only started recently, in 1973, meaning that I didn't have one for Light Fingers, Galilee or Red Handed. (Valmae had had three miniatures made for our mantlepiece.) The VRC awarded them retrospectively, and as well as those three I was given one on Dad's behalf for Comic Court's win in 1950. As for a big Melbourne Cup, one of the VRC committeemen was Doug Reid, who had owned Maybe Mahal. Back in 1979 he said, 'Bart, if you can win ten, we'll give you a full-sized one for yourself.'

For a decade it hadn't looked as though I'd win eight, let alone ten. But then Kingston Rule made it eight, and Let's Elope gave me number nine. True to their word, the VRC allowed a larger replica to be crafted for me, and put it away in the committee room. It was about three-quarters the size of the real Melbourne Cup. It would wait in that room for five years.

We brought the Sky Chase–All Grace colt that we'd bred along slowly. We spent many hours walking him, maturing him, building his physique and getting him ready for racing. This is what we do with all juvenile horses, but from the beginning he had a lovely tractable way, a strong intelligence, a good girth, a long barrel and that eye-catching chestnut coat with white socks on his hind legs. We gelded him, and he had one start as a two-year-old in 1994, but I had to send him out to the spelling paddock again. He was still growing, very fast, and I had to give his temperament time to catch up with his size and ability.

He won his first race against other three-year-olds over 6 furlongs at Newcastle in 1995, coming from a wide barrier. His owner for his first four starts was Valmae, and in our stable colours of green and gold diagonal stripes he won on his debut, then came second and won again in three-year-olds' races at Randwick. His name was Saintly.

Feeling that I had a horse with a bit of promise on my hands, I invited Chin Nam into the ownership. It was a way of defraying the risk at a time when I had to watch every cent, and also I owed Chin Nam a debt of gratitude for all the help he was giving me. We still haggled over price, in a gentlemanly way, and settled on a total value of $110,000 for the horse.

It was the morning of the Caulfield Cup in 1995 when Chin Nam agreed to buy Saintly. That afternoon, Lee Freedman's Doriemus won the Caulfield Cup. Meanwhile, at Randwick, Saintly won an inconspicuous race for three-year-olds. A top three-year-old trained by Gai Waterhouse, called Nothin' Leica Dane, was racing in the cups against the grown-up horses and doing very well. When he came second to Doriemus in the

1995 Melbourne Cup, he was already being spoken of as a strong favourite for the 1996 Cup. There was also the John Hawkes-trained Octagonal, who had gone on from being a runner-up in the Golden Slipper to mature into the star three-year-old of the spring, winning nothing less than the Cox Plate. Among those headline-stealers, few would have noticed the chestnut three-year-old winning at Randwick.

I didn't have a runner in the 1995 Melbourne Cup, and yet again my obituaries were being written. Since 1965, the only years I hadn't had runners were 1972, 1985 and 1995. So it had happened before, but now that I was closing on seventy years old, a lot of observers were ready to put me out to pasture. I was actually asked when I might win my next Melbourne Cup, and I said, 'In about twelve months.' They thought I was fooling around with them.

Chin Nam, always one to spread the costs around, offered shares in Saintly among his friends in south-east Asia. He gathered a group including his nephew, Tony Tan, and a Singapore plastics manufacturer named Eddie Hong. There was also the chief surgeon of Gleneagles Hospital in Singapore, Dr Lim Chock Peng. Chin Nam sold 75 percent of the horse in this way, and then he offered the last quarter to an Indonesian banker. This man declined, so Chin Nam graciously offered that 25 percent back to me. I took him up on his offer, pleased to retain part-ownership in a horse with such potential, but also grinding my teeth a little that whatever prize money I won as a part-owner would be garnisheed by my creditors.

As soon as the ownership was all sealed, we took Saintly down to Melbourne for the Carbine Club Stakes, a mile race for three-year-olds on Victoria Derby day. Racing in Chin Nam's

chequerboard colours with yellow sleeves and a chequerboard cap, he bolted away to win the race by two and a half
lengths. Of course he attracted little attention, as Nothin'
Leica Dane and Octagonal slugged it out in the feature race,
the Derby.

The colours, by the way, were a design of my own. Chin
Nam is a devout chess player – it says a lot about the way
his brain works, thinking several steps ahead, always strategic
in his outlook. He was president of the International Chess
Federation among his many other interests. His early horses,
such as Think Big, had raced in my stable colours, but when
he came back in the 1990s as such a white knight for me,
I devised racing silks in the black-and-white checked pattern
of a chess board.

When Chin Nam first saw the colours, he wasn't too pleased.
Black and white, he said, were the colours of mourning in his
culture. So I added gold sleeves to the design, and those were
the colours that Saintly and many other horses of Chin Nam's
would make famous.

Saintly ran second as favourite in the Sandown Guineas
at the end of the spring carnival, and immediately I tucked
him away for the autumn. He was still maturing. He went to
Princes Farm, gambolled around in the sun and fed on the rich
grass, then came back in the unsuitable Expressway Stakes
over 6 furlongs at Randwick in the late summer. He showed
his potential by beating one of the best older sprinters around
in Juggler, and then finished second to Juggler in another race
before heading down to Melbourne for the Australian Cup.
I really wanted to see how he'd go over a bit more distance, at
weight-for-age against some classy mature horses. I thought

he was good enough to win and instructed Darren Beadman to ride him wide on the track and keep him clear of trouble. The horse was still immature, with an ungainly galloping style, and I was worried about his reactions under the pressure of racing Group One rivals in a tight pack. Beadman followed my instructions as always, and Saintly exceeded even my most optimistic forecast, dashing away with the race, my eleventh Australian Cup, after racing so wide that he probably covered half a furlong more than any other horse.

Beadman had covered a fair bit of ground himself since he'd won the Melbourne Cup on Kingston Rule. Soon after that race, he moved to Hong Kong to chase success there. But it hadn't gone very well. He suffered a couple of serious falls, and was suspended on a charge of not allowing a horse called Better Choice to run on its merits. He came back to Australia and suffered from depression before remembering what he was good at and returning to top-level riding. When Saintly came along, I was able to convince him that my horse would be a better ride even than Octagonal.

I had no hesitation in pitting Saintly against Octagonal, Nothin' Leica Dane and another star three-year-old, Filante, in the classics of the Sydney autumn. The four of them staged some epic battles, but Octagonal was the champion of the season, winning the Canterbury Guineas, Rosehill Guineas, the Tancred Stakes (then called the Mercedes Classic) and the AJC Derby. Saintly kept trying and kept improving, and ran Octagonal to a long neck in the Derby. They both crossed the line more than two seconds faster than Dulcify's race record. Horses should always be judged by the quality of the opposition they beat, and Octagonal earned his reputation as a champion by virtue of the names of those who finished behind him. But while Octagonal and Nothin' Leica Dane were precocious horses hitting their peaks in their three-year-old year, I had a strong intuition that Saintly was still learning to race and would not be at his best until the next season.

Still, I wasn't absolutely certain that Saintly was a 2-miler. My usual Melbourne Cup program for a horse of such potential would have led through the Caulfield Cup and either the Mackinnon or the Hotham, but that was for dour stayers who needed a lot of mileage in their legs. Every horse is different, and there's no formula to training a Melbourne Cup winner. Saintly had a certain brilliance about him that made me wonder if he wasn't more of a Cox Plate horse. Having won that race only once, with Taj Rossi, missing out with Beau Zam when he was flat after his rugged Caulfield Cup and then not getting a start with Let's Elope in 1991 before she nearly won in 1992, I was keen to set the Cox Plate as a major spring target. But aiming at the Cox Plate and the Melbourne Cup was a difficult training exercise, as evidenced by the scarcity of horses who had won the double. In fact only three horses had won the Melbourne Cup after winning the Cox Plate: Nightmarch in 1929, Phar Lap in 1930 and Rising Fast in 1954. Kingston Town, winning the Cox Plate before being pipped in the Melbourne Cup in 1982, had come the closest since then. Winning that double was probably the ultimate statement of a horse's champion qualities.

I brought Saintly back for the Warwick Stakes over 7 furlongs at Warwick Farm, and he ran second to Filante, who was at his best over a mile up to a mile and a quarter.

A week later the Cup weights came out, and Saintly was

given 55.5 kilograms for the Melbourne Cup. I thought that was a bit much, given that the Australian Cup was the only race he'd won over more than a mile. Doriemus, who had won the Caulfield and Melbourne cups the year before, was being asked to carry only 3 kilograms more than Saintly. Octagonal, a Cox Plate winner and horse of the year whom Saintly had never beaten, would carry only 1 kilogram more than our horse. The top Irish stayer Oscar Schindler had the same weight as Octagonal. The Sydney Cup winner Count Chivas, who had finished between Octagonal and Saintly in the Mercedes Classic, only had a kilo and a half more than Saintly. I didn't think Saintly's record justified his being handicapped up with those horses. My doubts about Saintly over 2 miles only intensified with those weights; perhaps it would be better to save him for a weight-for-age campaign.

He took on Filante again in Sydney, in the Chelmsford Stakes at Randwick over a mile at weight-for-age. The other horse was too good, but Saintly was closing in on him at the line. His next start, the Hill Stakes at Rosehill over 1900 metres, showed that he was developing a taste for more distance. Coming from midfield on the turn, he ran straight past Nothin' Leica Dane to win going away. He seemed to be in top shape now.

Some of his rivals were coming good too. Octagonal, who had been out of sorts in his comeback races in the early spring, won the Underwood Stakes at Caulfield, prompting great excitement among the racing public, who had nicknamed him 'The Big O'. Overseas, Oscar Schindler showed that he might have cheated the VRC handicapper by winning the Irish St Leger, and a couple of weeks later he ran a strong third in the world's most prestigious race, the Prix de l'Arc de Triomphe in Paris. I couldn't see how it was fair that this horse would only carry a kilogram more than Saintly if they ran in the Melbourne Cup, but there was nothing I could do about it now.

I entered Saintly in the Metropolitan, a good test of whether I should aim him for the Melbourne Cup or not. But over the October long weekend, things started to go awry. On the Saturday, I gave him a tune-up in the Craven Plate over 10 furlongs, and at 13/4-on, unbackable odds, he loomed up to win but faltered over the last 100 metres and was beaten by a Waterhouse horse called Adventurous. Maybe he needed the extra ground of the Metrop? I watched him through the weekend and could see nothing amiss. His coat was shining, he seemed content, and he was cleaning out his food bin. But then, on the Monday of the long weekend, he couldn't redeem himself. Again he strode up to the leaders, Hula Flight and Nothin' Leica Dane, but he couldn't finish off the job and came third.

I was a bit perplexed and disappointed; I certainly believed Saintly was better than the horses who had beaten him in both of his races that weekend. I didn't know if he'd gone off the boil, or if my efforts to relax him and train him to stay had been too thorough. It was hard to tell, from his Metropolitan run, if he needed more distance or less. Or had he resented the whip? Beadman had given him a good whack during the Metrop; maybe, as with Kingston Rule, the jockey needed to be told to hit the horse no harder than he would hit me.

Saintly was another riddle waiting for its solution. Aren't horses always like this? I was even more quiet than usual as I went about my business. My staff would wonder if I was angry or brooding, but the truth was that I was running the combinations through my head: how to work him, how to feed him, how to program his races. With Saintly, there was even more at stake than there usually was. I'd bred him myself, I'd raised him, and I part-owned him – not in partnership with any ordinary owner, but with the man who had done so much to help me in my moment of need. My belief in the horse's talent was unshakable, but I was mulling over and over the question of how to help him realise that talent on the racetrack.

In the end, there was nothing for it but to go to Melbourne and see if Saintly could repeat the liking he'd shown for Flemington on his previous two visits. He was unbeaten there, and sometimes horses just like a track and a way of going. Flemington has such a long straight, it was possible that Saintly needed the full length of its 2¼ furlongs to wind up.

Or maybe not. Maybe he had the zip to win a shorter race on a course with very tight turns and a brief finishing straight, such as the Cox Plate. On the face of it, Saintly seemed to be just the kind of horse who was undone by Moonee Valley: big, long-striding and slightly erratic at times. He had never raced there, so I had no evidence to go on. There were two powerful intuitions pulling me in opposite directions: one, that he needed Flemington to stretch out and wind up, and two, that he was more talented than any other horse going around. I was undecided, going this way and then that, entering him for the Caulfield Cup but then withdrawing him. It was won by the mare Arctic Scent, with Doriemus close up behind the placegetters.

As I was searching for answers, I realised that the rubber girth strap Beadman had used to ride Saintly the previous autumn had been stolen, and the saddle he'd been wearing in the Craven Plate and Metropolitan had shifted backwards. It might have been something as simple as that – his girth strap wasn't tight enough. Or maybe a leather strap was uncomfortable for the horse. People scoffed at me for putting this forward as a reason for Saintly's disappointing runs, but we were all searching for answers and sometimes it can be something as mundane as that. Remember that in the mind of the racehorse, an ill-fitting girth strap can be the most distressing thing in the world, particularly when he is under pressure at the end of a hard race.

Speaking of Beadman, he was one person who never lost faith in Saintly. Beadman had ridden Octagonal earlier in his career, but when it came to a choice between Octagonal and Saintly, Beadman opted for our horse. It was a brave decision, particularly when Octagonal beat us in the autumn. But maybe Beadman knew something we didn't. He was a very devout Christian lad, who would later give up racing to become a lay preacher. When he said God had called him to the ministry, I suggested he get a second opinion. He was such a good rider, I saw him as a great loss to our sport.

He said, 'But the good Lord spoke to me.'

I replied: 'Well, I've been going to church for years and He's never spoken to me.'

But Beadman was serious about his spirituality, and with Saintly's name, and his nickname 'the horse from heaven', Beadman kept riding him with a conviction that he had a higher power on his side. My father, and Father Dennis Madigan, would have approved. But I was quite serious about Beadman. As far as his powers of perception and awareness were concerned, he was the best jockey I had known since Roy Higgins. When he gave up racing to start sermonising, Beadman drew about 3000 people to his first service. After a couple of years, his attendance had dropped down to about three. People, that is. The church often talks about a 'calling', and Beadman had missed his. As a preacher, he made a very good race jockey. Fortunately he realised that and came back to the sport.

AFTER HE MISSED THE CAULFIELD CUP, SAINTLY WAS SET FOR the Cox Plate. He galloped at Moonee Valley in the week leading up to the race, at the traditional well-attended and highly publicised 'Breakfast with the Stars' track-work session. With a tighter girth strap and stable saddle he outsprinted all the favourites. Filante, who had just won the Epsom on the same day Saintly was beaten in the Craven Plate, was a top pick, as was Juggler. Octagonal didn't seem to have the pep of his previous campaigns, but he was not to be taken lightly attempting to win the Plate for the second year in a row. There were, as usual, ten other top-class entrants, all with a chance of winning. Every year the Cox Plate attracts the cream of Australian racing, but some years are definitely stronger than others; I have no doubt in saying this was one of the better fields.

It had been twenty-three years since I'd won my only Cox Plate, with Taj Rossi. It was not a part of my usual Melbourne Cup plans, and I never thought the timing of the Cox Plate, just ten days before the Melbourne Cup, was quite right. I wanted to race Cup horses on Derby day, so to run them on Cox Plate day the week before would have thrown their preparation out of whack. The one successful exception was Kingston Rule, who had needed the racing on Cox Plate day to keep his weight down and also to qualify him for the Melbourne Cup. But he had run in the Moonee Valley Cup, which, while longer than the Cox Plate, attracts a lower quality field without so much pace on throughout.

At the same time, I still wasn't 100 percent sure if Saintly was on a Melbourne Cup preparation. The Cox Plate might yet turn out to be his main spring mission. It agitated me, if only because I was taking a route I'd never tried before.

Saintly galloped again on the Thursday, and went very nicely. But I still couldn't get a feel for whether he would finish his races off, or fade under pressure as he had up at Randwick. As they lined up for the Cox Plate, he was still not among the top picks for the punting fraternity. Never having raced on the saucer-shaped Moonee Valley track, he was a victim of the conventional wisdom, which was that the straight, which is a little less than a furlong in length, wouldn't give him enough time to wind up. He had a wild galloping style, with his hind legs tucking right up underneath him and his forelegs stretching a mighty distance out in front. He often looked to be on the brink of catastrophe. Such extravagant movers weren't meant to do well at Moonee Valley. The general expectation was that he might run on well for a minor placing, or finish behind the placegetters, coming home strongly enough to convince me to give him a Melbourne Cup start. In the punters' and bookmakers' minds, I would never set a horse for the Cox Plate – it was only a stepping stone. But they didn't know what was inside my head, and I didn't know what was inside Saintly's!

As it turned out, he didn't really handle Moonee Valley. He raced just behind the leading pack all the way, and when they came around the turn Filante, Juggler and All Our Mob lined up three abreast to fight it out. Octagonal had had enough. Saintly was all over the place, his legs flying everywhere, clearly off-balance. Beadman hit him with the whip twice, and he seemed to resent it again. Beadman tucked his whip away. Once they straightened up, Beadman was able to settle him, get him on all four legs, and unleash a withering final burst at the same time. The three leaders were milers right at the limit of their endurance, and Saintly was just warming up. He showed incredible talent and courage to get going, and even in the last 50 metres it looked like he would come up short behind Filante and All Our Mob, but once he was moving he went past them in the last couple of strides, flashing home by a head.

Beadman stole the show in the mounting yard by throwing a star jump as he got off the horse, but I was quietly letting a few emotions out. The weight-for-age championship did not figure prominently on my record, and while it was gratifying to have won so many Melbourne Cups it was something else again to win the race regarded as the one that decides the best horse in the country. I'd had champions in Let's Elope, Leilani, Beau Zam, Hyperno, Galilee and Light Fingers, but none of them had won a Cox Plate – for the most part because I hadn't entered them. To have done it, and won it, with a horse I'd bred myself, owned and trained, and to have done it while still in the mire of my repayment schedule, after everything that had happened . . . well, the hayfever set in and made my eyes water a little.

That's true, by the way. I'm often accused of shedding a tear after a Melbourne Cup. People don't realise how chronic my hayfever is. The last time I cried at a racetrack was during a dust storm at Balaklava when I was a boy.

Good horses can win what you train them for, and with Saintly it might just have been a matter of him getting enough miles in his legs. It might have been the girth strap. It might have been the anticlockwise Melbourne way of going. It might have been Beadman's judicious use of the whip. Whatever it was, Saintly was fully in tune now, and one of my first thoughts after he came into scale at Moonee Valley was that I was going to run him in the Melbourne Cup.

Would he stay the 2 miles? somebody asked me.

'Yes,' I said.

How did I know?

'Instinct,' I said.

BEFORE THE MELBOURNE CUP, SAINTLY WAS INVITED TO THE Japan Cup, which would be run at the end of November. We accepted, feeling that we had a horse who could achieve what was beyond Bounty Hawk and Shaftesbury Avenue, who had run an unlucky third. At that point I was actually more confident about Saintly winning in Tokyo than I was about his chances in the Melbourne Cup. Two miles might stretch him, but 12 furlongs would be right in the slot.

In spite of his Cox Plate win, he was nowhere near favouritism for the Melbourne Cup. So much for the years when I could enter welter-class stayers in the Melbourne Cup and they would start as favourites! Oscar Schindler was all the rage. I was among the many trainers who believed the handicapper had thrown him into the race. With his recent record, he should have been carrying closer to 60 kilos than the 56.5 he had. His trainer, an Australian based in Europe called Kevin Prendergast, made the wise comment that he'd prefer people to be making all these laudatory comments the morning *after* the Melbourne Cup. He also made the unwise comment that Saintly looked like a 'pipe' after the Cox Plate and wouldn't stay the 2 miles.

I didn't race Saintly in the Mackinnon, wanting him to have a rest after the Cox Plate. People jumped on the unconventionality of this, as my Cup horses nearly always raced on Derby day. But they didn't understand – none of my Cup horses had just put their hearts into winning a Cox Plate. Instead, I gave Saintly his normal morning gallop over 10 furlongs at Flemington, and he came home in 12 seconds, a sprinter's speed, for his last 200 metres.

I told the reporters that when a horse gallops that well on Derby day, he doesn't lose in the Melbourne Cup. I joked that the VRC had better polish up that tenth cup they'd put away for me. But nobody was listening, except for Doriemus's trainer Lee Freedman, who said that when he saw Saintly gallop that day he 'felt sick'. Everyone else was saying Oscar Schindler was a shoo-in. In the Mackinnon, there were good runs from Nothin' Leica Dane, Count Chivas and the Caulfield Cup winner Arctic Scent. As the betting heated up for the

Melbourne Cup, Oscar Schindler was a firm favourite ahead of Doriemus and Nothin' Leica Dane. Saintly was on the next line at 8/1.

Saintly drew barrier number 3, a great advantage because it was so close to the fence. On our way to the track on Cup day, Valmae and I looked in on him at the stables. He was sound asleep! I turned to Valmae and said, 'He's going to win the Cup.' In the race, I instructed Beadman to ride him the way he'd ridden Kingston Rule: take him into the rail, save ground, go quietly, then let him go on the home turn. The key, always, was not to go too early. I knew Saintly was fit enough and talented enough to take a position anywhere in the field, so I didn't have a firm opinion on whether Beadman should race him forward or further back. To me, it didn't really matter. If the horse was as fit as I thought he was, he'd do all the work himself and the jockey just had to be patient and avoid trouble.

I went up to my usual place in the stand and picked up my binoculars. They broke evenly, and Beadman followed Shane Dye on Nothin' Leica Dane, who went onto the rails in the front half of the field. Behind Saintly, Oscar Schindler drifted towards the rear and Damien Oliver followed him on Doriemus. The leader for most of the race was another of the European visitors, Grey Shot.

As they went around the back of the course Saintly looked very relaxed, and Beadman had him on a long, loose rein. Watching, I just felt a wave of calm confidence come over me. Saintly kept up with the accelerating field as they entered the home turn, 600 metres from home, maintaining his balance far better than in the helter-skelter of the Cox Plate. When they hit the straight, with 450 to go, Beadman eased him out off the fence and gave him a shake. No whip was needed. Saintly glided past Grey Shot. Behind him, nothing was able to mount any kind of finishing burst. Saintly turned the straight into an exhibition gallop. He had a stride length like Phar Lap, about 6 metres. I'm certain I've never trained a horse with such a stride. This was one of the stronger Melbourne Cups, and Saintly toyed with them, eating up the ground as if this was the race and distance he'd been waiting for all along. He won by two and a quarter lengths, slowing down; it was such a pleasure to watch. They rarely felt this easy, with everything falling into place on the right day.

I never thought I'd rate one of my gallopers up with Galilee, but Saintly was right there alongside him. I'd trained him, I'd owned him, I'd bred him, I'd raced his father and bred his mother and grandmother. There's not much more you can do. The only thing I hadn't done was ride him.

Sir William Deane, the Governor-General, gave me the replica trophy that the VRC had stashed away. The Flemington crowd gave me three cheers, a very generous gesture considering how many of them would have been tearing up their betting tickets. Ten Melbourne Cups – it's hard to know what to say. The veteran racing man Bob Charley said something very fitting and flattering about me. He said, 'If I was a horse, I'd want to be trained by Bart.' That hit the mark.

As a rising sixty-nine-year-old, I genuinely felt that I was training as energetically and ambitiously as ever. After the disaster of the syndicate and the repayment plan, I was making up for lost time. Like a well-performed stayer, I was racing with a handicap. My winning share from Saintly's Melbourne

Cup should have been $143,000 before tax. Instead, after my creditors got their bite, I earnt $35,750. But I couldn't waste my energy or spoil my pleasure with chagrin. Just as it had been since I'd lost the court case in 1990, I had nowhere to go but forward. I told the reporters I was 'just hitting my straps' in 1996, and they laughed. They didn't know how serious I was.

SAINTLY DID GO TO THE JAPAN CUP, BUT HE CONTRACTED TRAVEL sickness and did not race. There had been a significant change in the travel arrangements for horses going to Japan. In the early days of the Japan Cup, Qantas flew its 747 Combi, specially fitted out for freight and passengers, direct from Sydney to Tokyo. Once that route and conveyance ended, we had to fly via Hong Kong, unload the horse there for six or seven hours, then resume the trip. After the change was made, no Australian or New Zealand horse won the Cup.

Saintly would only start once more in his career. We brought him home for an autumn campaign, and he ran in the traditional lead-up to the Australian Cup, the Orr Stakes over 7 furlongs at weight-for-age at Caufield. He missed the start, looked like a stayer among sprinters, and fell more than five lengths behind the leaders. At the turn he looked to have no chance: he had to go back and around some tiring horses when Beadman hooked him to the outside. But then he unleashed that finishing burst with his huge stride and overwhelmed the opposition. I've never seen a horse, sprinters included, gallop the last 50 metres of any race as fast as Saintly went that day.

It was all looking very good until we galloped him in track

work on the artificial track at Flemington after the Orr Stakes. If I knew then what I know now about artificial surfaces, I would never have let Saintly near it. The Americans use them, and if we copy them in this we'll have the same results as if we copy them in Wall Street. Artificial surfaces are a disaster for racehorses. Saintly pulled up sharply, and when the vets took a look at him they found that he had torn one of his tendons.

It was a heartbreaking moment. I wasn't there at the time, and my stable foreman, Reg Fleming, broke the news to me over the phone. Reg could barely speak, he was crying so hard. Like Kingston Rule, Saintly had damaged the tendon beyond repair. Unlike Kingston Rule, he was a gelding and wouldn't be bundled straight off to stud. We would try, over the next year, to get Saintly ready to race, but whenever any pressure was put on his tendon it was clear that he was in too much pain. He would not race again. In his last three starts, he'd won the Cox Plate, the Melbourne Cup and the Orr Stakes. He was just getting going. He was only four years old and we never saw the best of him. He was a people's favourite too: there have been popularity votes over recent years, and he consistently polls at or near the top, ahead of other champions of the recent era such as Might And Power, Octagonal and Makybe Diva.

But that's that. The lovely chestnut went to Princes Farm, and he lives there in comfortable retirement to this day. In his honour, I named our Flemington stables Saintly Place. I owed him that at the very least. After a very long night, he showed me the brightness of the new dawn.

19
Wonderland

N~O SOONER HAD~ I ~WON MY SECOND~ C~OX~ P~LATE THAN A THIRD~
came along. Racing is funny that way. It follows its own time-
tables, and you just have to be ready for the windfalls when
they come and be stoic when luck turns against you.

Dane Ripper was not like Saintly, a Melbourne Cup
horse who was versatile and talented enough to win over
10 furlongs. Dane Ripper was more like the typical Cox Plate
winner: a sprinter-miler who could extend to the distance.

In fact, before the 1997 Cox Plate she had never raced further than a mile.

She was bred by her owners, Ron and Joy Codner. They had owned the mare Red Express, whom I had trained until around 1990. Ron had been a Spitfire pilot in the Second World War, flying in the Battle of Britain for the Royal Air Force, and had migrated to Sydney where he became a successful hotel broker. When Red Express retired, they were looking for a groom for their bride, and I suggested they send her to Danehill.

I was having a rich run with fillies at the time. I don't know exactly why this was. Maybe the compassion and soft touch I bring to my relations with horses is most appreciated by the weaker sex. Not that they *are* weaker. In fact, with improved breeding and medication, the gap between female and male horses was narrowing, causing periodic debate over whether set-weights races should be adjusted so that females didn't have to carry so much less weight than the males.

The season Saintly won the Melbourne Cup, 1996–97, I had twenty-one stakes winners and nine Group Ones, my best year in nearly a decade. Two three-year-old fillies were the leaders among their age group: Dashing Eagle, who won the Flight Stakes and 1000 Guineas, and Danarani, who won the Storm Queen Stakes and AJC Oaks. Both were daughters of Danehill, the American-bred stallion who was the first of the great shuttle sires.

As I said, Nelson Bunker Hunt was the earliest to my knowledge to come up with the idea of shuttling a sire between breeding seasons in the Northern and Southern hemispheres. But the idea gained its momentum from the success of Danehill. Foaled in 1986, he was a son of Danzig, winning four from nine starts as a racehorse before he went to stud in Ireland. His sons there included Desert King, a two-time classic winner who became very well known to Australians as the sire of Makybe Diva.

Danehill had been raced by his breeder, Khalid Abdullah. On his retirement he was bought by the Australian breeder John Messara, who stood him at his Arrowfield Stud near Scone. Ireland's Coolmore Stud then bought an interest, and the stallion was shuttled between the two studs, serving mares in both the Northern and Southern hemisphere seasons, with amazing results. Danehill sired everything from Golden Slipper winners such as Merlene to classic-winning three-year-olds and 2-milers such as Saintly's great rival Nothin' Leica Dane. His sons included Redoute's Choice and Flying Spur, who on their retirements turned into two of the top sires in Australia in recent years. Danehill died in a freak accident at Coolmore Stud in 2003. Being led by hand through a grazing paddock, he reared up on his hind legs, fell awkwardly and broke his hip. He had to be put down at the age of seventeen.

I was one of the first Australian trainers to get onto the Danehill bandwagon – before it became a bandwagon. I was coming out of the Inglis sales at Newmarket, Randwick, one Easter when I saw a man sitting on a bale of straw looking very depressed.

'What's wrong, mate?' I asked him.

'Oh, the boss is gunna sack me – the horse I brought here got passed in.'

'Which one was it?' I said.

'A Danehill.'

At that point Danehill was not as highly regarded as a sire as he later became, and I said to the man, 'Give me a look at it.'

It was a nice-looking filly that had been passed in at about $60,000. 'Tell your boss I'll take her for $70,000,' I said.

I duly bought her, and she turned out to be Danarani, the AJC Oaks winner two years later.

Dane Ripper came out of Danehill's 1992 visit to Australia when he mated with, among other mares, the Codner family's Red Express. She was a daughter of the Victoria Derby winner and son of Sir Tristram, Sovereign Red. The breeding couldn't have been much better. The sad part of it was that Ron Codner had passed away in 1990, the year they went to Arrowfield to take a look at Danehill for the first time. Apparently Ron grew ill on that trip, and didn't survive, but he was so taken with Danehill that his wife Joy and daughter Gae, who took over the operation, were determined to carry out his wishes and keep sending Red Express to the sire. Danehill and Red Express produced a colt who was no good as a racehorse, but the next year, when Joy and Gae sent Red Express to him again, she produced a strapping filly who would race under the name Dane Ripper.

A heavy-framed bay filly, Dane Ripper needed plenty of racing and this probably explained her tardy development. As a late three-year-old she won the Stradbroke Handicap against the males over 7 furlongs in Brisbane, but it wasn't until her four-year-old year that she showed what she was made of.

Her time at the top was short but notable. For the 1997 Cox Plate, she was grossly underrated, starting at 40/1. She hadn't raced at Moonee Valley and hadn't raced beyond 1600 metres, but I knew she was better than a 40/1 chance.

Yet I wasn't sure about even starting Dane Ripper in the Cox Plate until the last minute. I had entered her in two races that day: the Plate, over 2040 metres, and the feature mile race. In the week leading up, we trotted and cantered her to get her to relax. When I told Roy Higgins I was thinking of starting her in the Cox Plate, he said, 'You're mad.' That only made me more determined!

Damien Oliver had no ride in the Plate, so I engaged him for Dane Ripper. Even then, I hadn't decided on starting her. On the morning of the race, Gae Codner was flying down from Sydney to Melbourne and found herself on the same flight as Geoff and Beryl White, the owners of the Cox Plate favourite, Filante.

'What are you heading down for?' Geoff White asked.

Gae Codner told them about Dane Ripper running at Moonee Valley. 'I think she should have a good chance in the mile race,' she said.

'That's nice,' said Mr White. 'We're just so excited about the day. We have the favourite for the Cox Plate. He ran second last year, but we really hope he's going to win today.'

Kindly, and being in such a buoyant mood, the Whites offered her a lift from the airport to the track and said that they would give her a lift back again at the end of the day. They wished her luck in the mile.

Gae Codner didn't want Dane Ripper to run in the Cox Plate, because she didn't think the mare was good enough. She told me she thought we should scratch her, but by now I had made my decision: Dane Ripper would run in the Plate. Maybe it was Roy Higgins' challenge. Maybe I just had a feeling about her. That morning, after riding her in track work, Joe Agresta simply said, 'Bart, she couldn't be fitter.' As Damien Oliver mounted her, I told him very simply: 'Save her.' She was quite tempestuous, and would have wanted to go too early. As she was unproven at the Cox Plate distance, I didn't want her to test out her stamina by turning the race into a long grind home. When a horse is doubtful at a distance, it suits her best if the race is run slowly at first, so that she can use her acceleration to advantage in a sprint home. Many weight-for-age races pan out in this way, because the weaker horses don't want to turn them into a staying test and often the jockeys of the stronger horses don't want to sit out in front and set themselves up as a target. So weight-for-age races tend to be more tactical in the running than handicaps. This is why the greatest weight-for-age horses, like Kingston Town and Saintly, possess, as well as staying power, the ability to sprint suddenly and decisively.

The Cox Plate, however, is seldom run in this usual weight-for-age way. Because the field is of such high quality and most of the horses have been set for the 10 furlongs of the race, it is usually full-bore from the gate.

The 1997 Plate was typically hard-run and Oliver rode Dane Ripper a treat, holding her and holding her until he saw a gap between runners open up on the home turn. Dane Ripper dived through, and got to the line a length and a half ahead of Filante, who had also finished second behind Saintly the previous year.

I felt a little sorry for the Whites. Their property was next door to ours at Princes Farm, and they owned the great sprinter-turned-sire Marscay. It was unlucky for the same horse to come second in the Cox Plate twice in a row, to different rivals prepared by the same trainer. As for Gae Codner, she was mortified. She had told the Whites Dane Ripper was only running in the mile, they had given her a lift from the airport, and now her mare had come out and dashed their hopes. She was too embarrassed to find them and take up their offer of a return ride to Tullamarine.

Dane Ripper came back in the autumn to win another two big weight-for-age races. She beat the champion Might And Power in the St George Stakes at Caulfield, and then won the Australian Cup at Flemington.

I had a broken ankle at the time, from an incident when a horse had jumped on me at the stables, and was getting about on crutches. Still, I was so excited I jumped up and down on my bung ankle and didn't feel a thing. I thought she was better than Might And Power, who was about to assume the mantle of horse of the year; but unfortunately she didn't have a chance to challenge him seriously. She was injured after winning the Manikato Stakes at Moonee Valley in 1998 and was rushed off to stud with a record of twelve wins from twenty-eight starts.

I was having plenty of luck with the Danehills. In 1998 I sent All Grace to him, and she foaled a very nice-looking colt at Princes Farm. I sold him for a million dollars, the first seven-figure sale of any yearling in Australia since the ill-fated bubble of 1989. This one was a rare case of an expensive yearling turning into a good racehorse. As Aucash, he was bought by Patrick Biancone, who was acting as an agent for the trainer Ivan Allen, and won seven times in Hong Kong, netting a total of $HK6.2 million in his nineteen starts.

Thanks mainly to Saintly and the Danehill fillies, I was once again being noticed by the media and by other trainers and owners. I turned seventy in 1997, but they might have made the mistake of thinking there is a mandatory retirement age for horse trainers. I hadn't had the slightest thought of retiring, but there was an assumption around the place that I was winding down. Well, as Chin Nam says, to assume makes an 'ass' out of 'u' and 'me'. I wasn't going anywhere. In 1997–1999 I had Catalan Opening winning two Group Ones, including the Doncaster, and Allez Suez winning the Epsom. I was still using the same old methods, and to my astonishment there were generations of trainers coming and going without sticking to the basics. Meanwhile I was just plugging away and training winners. I kept turning up to my little timber-clad office at Leilani Lodge and doing my work, the same as always. If my critics or rivals wanted to retire me, they could go ahead. It only made me more determined to keep on going.

IN 1999 I HAD A LOT TO CELEBRATE. FIRST AND FOREMOST, IT WAS the year I finally finished my repayments to the bloodstock agents. What a slog it had been. I'd won three Melbourne Cups in that time, about forty Group Ones in all, and a percentage of everything had gone into paying back a debt I didn't believe I should have been liable for on my own. But I stuck at it, and now I was done. That was my personal Melbourne Cup run.

Free of debt, I was sent a horse from Perth, a refugee from a family dispute. In the early 1990s, farmers Tom and Moya Forrest had bred a colt on their property south of Perth. The colt's sire was Old Spice, a champion producer of winners in

Western Australia, and his dam was Eastern Mystique, whose bloodlines went back to my old favourite Le Filou.

They sold it fifty-fifty to their son Marcus, who was a trainer, and their daughter, Wendy Green. Wendy was a school teacher at Casuarina College in Darwin. In the supermarket one day trying to think up a name for the Old Spice–Eastern Mystique colt, she found herself in the curry section when it came to her. From the parents' names, it was obvious: he had to be called Vindaloo, Tandoori or Rogan Josh. After talking to her brother, she chose the third.

I hadn't heard of Rogan Josh when he was first racing, but the Forrests seem to have been horse people after my own heart: their view on producing the best racehorses was first and foremost based on patience. They gelded Rogan Josh and didn't race him until he was four. Even by my standards, this was a long wait! But it seemed to pay off. He was very big, and took a long time to grow into his height of 17 hands. With horses like that, if you race them before they are fully mature, they will put too much pressure on their joints and bones and either injure themselves or warp their physical development.

Eventually Marcus began training Rogan Josh at Bunbury, on the coast south of Perth, and he won four of his first five starts. Someone came along and offered $20,000 for him, a fair price for a dirt-tracker in Western Australia, and Marcus was keen to accept the offer.

His sister was not. Wendy thought Rogan Josh had more untapped potential, and she'd enjoyed his four wins, so why not keep going? There was a bit of a dispute, which resulted in the gelding going to Perth to be trained by Colin Webster. Wendy wanted to see how just good he was.

In 1997–98 Rogan Josh won several more races in Perth, and a new buyer came along, offering $100,000 for him. His original price, which the children paid to the parents who'd bred him, was $15,000. So the offer represented a healthy profit. Again Marcus and Wendy were divided; Marcus wanted to sell him and Wendy wanted to keep him. Again she prevailed. What would she do with the money? How would she feel if he went on to greater things? She was sentimental about the horse now. Not only had he given her a lot of pleasure with his winning ways, he offered to give her a lot more as he matured. He kept racing for Colin Webster and won the two principal regional races of south-west Western Australia, the Pinjarra and Bunbury cups.

Marcus wanted to send Rogan Josh up to Broome, for the Broome Cup, while Wendy thought the horse was better than that. To give you an idea of the Broome Cup, I went there one year and the race was held up for ten minutes while they cleared the kangaroos off the track!

Now Singaporean interests came along and offered $200,000 for Rogan Josh. This time Marcus wouldn't be put off, and he was determined to pocket the $100,000 share he was due. He was battling hard to train horses, and would have liked to invest the money from selling Rogan Josh into his business.

Wendy couldn't stop him. But she wouldn't let Rogan Josh go to Singapore either. With her husband Bob and her son from an earlier marriage, John-Paul, she scraped together the money to buy out her brother.

Now that was settled, they could get on with racing him. I was over for the Perth Cup at the beginning of 1999, and the first time I saw him Rogan Josh ran second, by a short neck, to King Of Saxony in the big race. He impressed me as a sturdy, strong type who had certainly run out the 2 miles.

He was a rising seven-year-old by now, but had only been racing for two and a half years. When I saw him in the Perth Cup, little did I know what the owners and trainer were cooking up. Colin Webster thought the gelding deserved the opportunity to go to Melbourne for the Cup the next spring. Some racing people are consumed by delusions of their own grandeur, but most, in my experience, are realists. Colin Webster was a realist, and he was humble enough to tell Wendy Green, her husband and her son that if Rogan Josh was good enough to go to Melbourne, he was good enough to undertake a properly thought through and fully planned campaign, rather than a hit-and-run mission from Perth, which was all he could promise.

He persuaded them to give me a ring, and that was how I became involved. I didn't take on every tried horse that people asked me to train, but I remembered Rogan Josh's sterling second place in the Perth Cup and I liked his pedigree. He had in his blood the Le Filou mare Kind Regards, who was the grand-dam of both Sky Chase and the 1998 Melbourne Cup winner Jezabeel. I also liked very much the fact that Rogan Josh had been taken along so patiently early in his life, and consequently had very sound legs for a horse his age. A racehorse is only as old as the amount of racing he's done. Sometimes a three-year-old can have the legs of an eight-year-old, and vice versa. Rogan Josh was a good example of the virtues of waiting.

A FAMILY CONTROVERSY – INVOLVING THE CUMMINGS, NOT THE Forrests – intervened at that point. In July 1999, my son Anthony, who had been steadily improving as a trainer, pleaded guilty to giving forty-five of his horses an implant that contained a banned anabolic steroid called trenbolone. Steroids had been illegal for horses since 1988, and Anthony said he didn't know that the trenbolone was in the implants. He'd been told that the implants contained slow-release herbal remedies and amino acid boosters, all perfectly legal. There was no suggestion the implants had been put in covertly: they were quite visible from the outside, and doing it to forty-five horses suggested that he did it without acting like he had anything to hide. But for his carelessness he was banned from training for eighteen months. It was reduced to fifteen months on appeal, but this was still an enormous punishment, which I, having suffered a twelve-month ban after the Cilldara affair, understood only too well.

Anthony had to lay off his thirty staff, many of whom came to work for me, and disperse the sixty horses he had in training. It was a tough time for him, after losing Might And Power, and I wasn't very pleased at first. He had taken his eye off the ball and been sloppy in his methods, being distracted by a syndication scheme that was coughing up all sorts of problems. While Anthony's attention was diverted, he'd allowed a stud manager rather than a vet to put the implants into the horses, without properly checking what was in them.

It was hard for everybody, and the Cummings name made it harder. I didn't like the association of our name with a drugs scandal. But it's also true that if Anthony's name wasn't Cummings, he probably wouldn't have been punished so harshly.

Anthony was the only one of my children to have shown a strong interest in racing. Sharon worked for me for a short time in Adelaide, but it wasn't easy for girls in racing back then, certainly harder than it is now. For the others, it was probably good to get out of their father's shadow. John went into banking, and moved to the Netherlands. Anne-Marie was the one who showed the most sporting talent, excelling as a swimmer and runner at school. She, Margaret and Sharon all worked for a while before they married and had children, and we now have fifteen grandchildren. But Anthony is the one who has to carry the greatest burden, because people are always trying to compare him with me.

He was a strong individual, however, and would emerge from his suspension in 2001 wiser than before and a better trainer for it.

WHEN I PUT ROGAN JOSH INTO TRAINING, I LIKED HIS ATTITUDE. He was a good eater, a naturally healthy horse with a great constitution. His only problem was that he suffered from ulcers in his stomach. Almost all racehorses suffer from ulcers at some point in their careers. As in humans, it's a natural consequence of the stress they're under. Once a day we treated him with an ulcer paste – it tastes like apples and you paint it on the back of their tongue. He swallowed it down, and it cured his ulcers. In very little time, Rogan Josh was back in tip-top condition.

His heart, conformation and will to win were all in the right place. The big question mark was talent, as the VRC handicapper was telling us. It was all very well to win country cups in Western Australia, but did he have the natural ability to go up against the best handicap and weight-for-age horses locally, from New Zealand and from the Northern Hemisphere? As much as we liked the horse, and admired Wendy Green's optimism, it seemed a bit of a stretch that this dour seven-year-old could match it with all those bluebloods. When the weights came out for the Melbourne Cup, Rogan Josh was given a very modest handicap of 50 kilos, a fair reflection of his record to that point. Most of the topweights were overseas horses, but they were let in very lightly, with none of them getting more than 58.5 kilos. When I think back to how Galilee was given 68.5 kilos in 1967, it breaks my heart. Even Think Big carried more than these European champions. But I couldn't worry about that. History showed that most of the Europeans either didn't turn up or, if they did, they weren't up to the rigours of a Melbourne Cup.

Rogan Josh's first start for us was in August 1999 down the straight 6 at Flemington, and he ran a predictable last. But he looked all right. I wasn't concerned. I had a lot of racing planned for him. Heavy racing was the only way we were going to know if he was good enough for the Cup, and it would have the added by-product of making him rock-hard by November.

He kept racing through September, doing nothing to reduce his Melbourne Cup quote of 250/1. The big local fancies were Tie The Knot and Sky Heights, who were certainly good weight-for-age horses but not in the class of a Saintly or a Let's Elope. So it seemed a lucky year to be mounting an attack with a one-paced stayer.

Rogan Josh first showed a sign that he had more in him than met the eye when he raced in the Herbert Power Handicap, then called the Perrier Stakes, over 12 furlongs at Caulfield a week before the Caulfeld Cup. The Herbert Power is a traditional lead-up for the handicapping stayers who aren't quite up to the class of the Caulfield Stakes, which is 2 furlongs shorter and run at weight-for-age on the same day. Darren Gauci rode Rogan Josh close to the lead and he fought on, winning well, albeit against moderate opposition. But a win is a win, and the Perrier winner got direct entry in the Caulfield Cup – which was a relief, because Rogan Josh was well down in the qualifying order and without that win would not have been able to run in the Cup.

Even so, he was derided. Noting that his best performance was a second place in the Perth Cup, one writer declared that *he* could have run second in the Perth Cup.

It wasn't so funny for the other trainers when Rogan Josh nearly won the Caulfield Cup. I put Chris Munce on him, and he let the gelding stretch out and bowl along with the leaders from barrier 17. Rogan Josh went to the front about 3 furlongs from home and plugged on, holding off the higher-rated horses until the last furlong. Sky Heights won, but nobody could miss the effort of my 'Perth horse'.

He wasn't 250/1 for the Melbourne Cup anymore, that was for sure. He was down to 20/1, kept safe but still a long way from the main fancies Sky Heights and Tie The Knot. Another favourite was the Irish St Leger winner, Kayf Tara, owned by the Godolphin stable and trained by Saeed bin Suroor. The two Australian horses confirmed their favouritism the next week by chasing home the champion Kiwi mare Sunline in the

Cox Plate. Rogan Josh, while pleasing me with his progress, seemed well short of those horses in terms of pure class. But he was strong and a willing worker and I knew he'd get the 2 miles.

A week before the Cup, Kayf Tara, the ruling favourite, injured a ligament and was scratched, putting the cat among the pigeons betting-wise. That was nothing compared with what Rogan Josh did in the Mackinnon Stakes.

I now had John Marshall on him. Marshall, who had spent some time in Hong Kong in mid-career and had polished up his skills, had just won the Epsom for me on Allez Suez, and was riding well. I thought his quiet demeanour was a good match for Rogan Josh. You're always trying to matchmake between horses and jockeys. Often you make the wrong decisions, but that's what lead-up races are for. Marshall was the fourth rider I'd tried on Rogan Josh; I was seeking that blend of quiet will and vigour that I sensed lay beneath the horse's workman-like exterior. Rogan Josh had the air of a quiet achiever; so did John Marshall. Marshall had wanted to ride another of my horses, Ruy Lopez, who had been unlucky not to win the Werribee Cup. Marshall rated him higher than Rogan Josh. As it happened, Ruy Lopez got injured on the training track and so it was a combination of good luck and good management that delivered Marshall the ride – as it so often is.

My instructions to him for the Mackinnon were to keep Rogan Josh from pulling. As a trial for the Melbourne Cup on the same track, the gelding had to learn that he couldn't go too hard too soon. The Mackinnon was a good tutoring experience, and I wanted to see if this jockey could get him to relax. Rogan Josh had raced too close to the lead to win the Caulfield

Cup, and he'd pulled a bit in the Herbert Power too. I knew he was a one-paced stayer, so he had to be raced near the lead, but not to the extent where he would be a sitting duck for the chasers. He wasn't good enough to burn them all off. The key was holding him and letting loose whatever he had in reserve at the end. He wasn't a Saintly; he couldn't accelerate when he wanted and break their hearts. But nor was he a Comic Court; he couldn't go out in front and just keep running away from them. As always with the less talented horses, it was a fine balance getting the tactics and training just right. With a Saintly or a Galilee, there's not much you can do wrong. With a Rogan Josh, you have to do everything just right. So my mind was being well exercised in the lead-up to the Mackinnon.

Marshall kept him relaxed in the Mackinnon, and the 'Perth horse' astounded everyone in the country – except for Wendy Green – by bursting through to win the race. He left all the weight-for-age stars in his wake. Tie The Knot, a multiple Group One winner, failed miserably. Rogan Josh was a weight-for-age winner, no less, at seven years old! It was a surprise to me as much as anyone else, but I didn't mind surprises like this.

He had run 11,600 metres in the campaign, a long distance even by Melbourne Cup standards. We'd left no stone unturned, and if any horse was going to be fit enough when the whips were cracking, it was him. I could have no doubts about his fitness. The question was, was he good enough? And would he be ridden well enough?

When Rogan Josh won the Mackinnon, Wendy Green couldn't be stopped. I'd been calling her 'Wendy in Wonderland' because of her pursuit of a Melbourne Cup dream with a horse that nobody said was anywhere near good enough. A 250/1 chance! That's wonderland. She rang me from Darwin and said she was going to hop into her Holden Commodore with her husband Bob and they were going to drive all the way to Melbourne. She called the car her 'rent-a-dent'. After Rogan Josh's win in the Mackinnon, I said to her, 'You'll be driving back home in a Rolls.'

It was a family affair. Wendy drove down with Bob, her son John-Paul flew in from overseas, her parents who'd bred the horse came from Perth, and so did Colin Webster, the trainer who had so selflessly recommended that they send the horse to me.

On Cup day, Rogan Josh started at 5/1 second favourite behind Sky Heights. That was incredible in itself, given where he'd come from. Three weeks earlier, he'd been 250/1 and an unfancied runner in the Herbert Power. Now he was the Melbourne Cup second favourite. He'd been on the express elevator from the ground floor to the penthouse.

When I was escorting Marshall to the horse, I reaffirmed what I'd told him earlier.

'Don't do anything until you go past the clock,' I said. 'Just wait until the clock.'

The old clock is a landmark on the Flemington straight, about three-quarters of a furlong, or 150 metres, from the finish post. I expected Marshall to have Rogan Josh in third or fourth place on the turn, the point at which it is almost unbearably tempting for jockeys to go for home. It's too far. That straight is all of 450 metres, and it's too much for most horses – even Kingston Town, as 1982 had shown. This was why I'd chosen Marshall as the jockey. I thought he would have the patience and maturity to wait until he passed the clock, and then swoop.

The race was an unruly one, but it didn't affect Rogan Josh. He was in an outside barrier and this time it was an advantage, because he went around the field and took up a forward position, in fourth place one off the rail, while all the jostling took place among the horses on the fence. A number of the favoured starters copped a bump, including Sky Heights, whom Damien Oliver said was lucky to stay on his feet. I've found that when they lose, jockeys tend to make an awful fuss about all the buffeting they undergo. It's never the jockey's fault, is it?

As it turned out, the horses who raced in the front third of the field all finished best. The Italian Derby winner Central Park tried to lead all the way, and very nearly did so. Frankie Dettori rode him well. Marshall only had to follow him . . . and wait until the clock. That he did, just as I had instructed, and Rogan Josh, in Wendy Green's light blue and white hoops, ground Central Park down to win by half a length. Our second-stringer, Zazabelle, came home in a dead heat for third.

For Marshall, it was the crowning achievement of a very good career. Within a couple of years he had retired to the Sunshine Coast, typically without any big announcement or fanfare. He wanted to spend more time on his two great loves, his family and his fishing, before he got too old. All the same, he said that he never really retired – he would always come back if I gave him a call to offer a Melbourne Cup ride.

Eleven Melbourne Cups, and I never got tired of them. Why should I? Training horses is such hard work and you never get to sleep in. You run a great risk and carry the burden of the high expectations of owners, punters and the general public. It's not as if the Melbourne Cup comes along every day. I've lived since 1927, and so far only twelve days of those eighty-two years have included winning a Melbourne Cup. It may seem like a lot of success, but years can pass between them, years of hard work and persistence, and so the savour of victory is just as sweet every time.

For Wendy in Wonderland, a Melbourne Cup happens once in a lifetime, and she got to drive back to Darwin – not in a Rolls, but in her old Commodore – with the owner's Melbourne Cup in her boot. It took her two months, and she and her husband stopped at every pub on the way. That's a lot of pubs. She embodied one of my favourite truths in racing, which is how we're all equal on the turf and under the turf. It doesn't matter if you're the Queen of England, an Arab sheikh or Wendy Green, when you go to the races you have the same hopes and dreams and the horses have the ability to give you the same thrills or disappointments. It doesn't matter who you are.

20
The local product

ROGAN JOSH ONLY RACED TWICE MORE. HE FINISHED MIDFIELD IN the Sandown Classic at 12 furlongs a week and a half after the Cup, and then went to Hong Kong for a mile-and-a-half race at Sha Tin, where he came fifth. The next autumn he broke down in training and retired back to Western Australia. And good luck to him! Like Kingston Rule, he was a horse I only knew briefly, but it was a mutually beneficial relationship.

Although I wasn't slowing down in the first years of the 2000s, it seemed like my horses were. In eight years after Rogan Josh's Melbourne Cup, I only trained seven Group One winners. The best of them, Australian Cup and Mackinnon Stakes winner Sirmione, is a very good middle-distance galloper but I had nothing of the class or potential possessed by my Melbourne Cup winners. You can't run the race for them, and my Cup starters in those years were mostly triers who never looked like winning.

Now that I was well into my seventies, I was receiving accolades and testimonials all over the place. I was inducted into the Australian Racing Hall of Fame, and felt honoured and humbled by that, as I was by other gongs. Nevertheless, these things tend to create an impression that you're doing a victory lap. The opposite was true. I was working as hard as ever, and was just as enthusiastic about the horses, no matter how modest their records. The thing I'd learnt is, you never know which of those humble underperformers is going to be next year's Melbourne Cup or Cox Plate winner. You just never know. And not for one minute in those years did I lose the appetite for winning. It will be obvious by now that I am a highly competitive animal. Yes, I am patient and compassionate with the horses, but that's not because I'm a softie. It's because I believe that's the best way to get them to run faster. What I love most of all is winning races, and the bigger they are, the better. I don't think that has dimmed one iota since I started out. If anything, it's grown stronger.

DUNCAN RAMAGE, THE ENGLISH TRACK JOCKEY I HAD HELPED sponsor to live in Australia, had started working as Tan Chin Nam's racing manager in Australia in 1991. Ramage knew the vet at Turangga Stud at Scone, where Saintly was foaled, a man named Phil Redman. And Redman's best mate, since university, was a hobby breeder called Ian Johnson.

Johnson had worked in the mining industry as a senior executive with CRA (as Rio Tinto used to be called) and Newcrest. After retiring, Johnson bought a little farm near Wisemans Ferry, just north of Princes Farm on the outskirts of Sydney. On his farm, called Finch's Crossing, he had a handful of broodmares he sent to the stallions he could afford. He wasn't a commercial breeder by any means; he was a hobbyist, but he also knew what he was doing.

He owned a mare called Lover's Knot, who could boast some pretty good bloodlines: her grandfathers were Seattle Slew, the American champion, and Sir Tristram. In 2003 Ian Johnson sent her to the Irish stallion Scenic, himself full of royal blood, a son of the Northern Dancer sire Sadlers Wells. Scenic had been standing in Australia for a few years but was not highly sought after at stud. He had bounced between the west and east coasts without any consistent success. His best-known progeny were the three-quarter brothers Universal Prince, who won an AJC Derby, and Blevic, who won a Victoria Derby.

After starting his stud career in Ireland, Scenic was shuttled to several Australian studs between 1990 and 1994. Then he stood at Collingrove Stud in New South Wales for four years, Durham Lodge in Western Australia for six years, and back to Victoria before he died in 2005. You often find that stallions who don't become fashionable move a lot from place to place, as one stud owner after another has a crack at making the horse a success. In 2002 Johnson chose Scenic, basically because the sire's stud fee was economical for such a pedigree. It was a value-for-money decision. There was not a scrap of Australian blood in either sire or dam until the offspring, a colt foaled in 2003, whom Johnson wanted to sell as a yearling in 2004.

Phil Redman, the vet at Turangga, put Ramage in contact with his mate Johnson, and this was how it came about that Ramage was visiting Finch's Crossing in winter 2004. Ostensibly his purpose was to offer general advice on bloodstock. It was a rainy day, but Ramage's eye was caught by one particular yearling colt. It had a good girth, low knees and low hocks – the basic geometry I liked in a staying horse, the rules of thumb I'd passed on to Ramage fifteen years earlier. Ramage asked a few questions about the colt, and it turned out that this was the yearling Ian Johnson had been wanting to sell.

Ramage wasn't there on a buying trip, but the look of the Scenic–Lover's Knot yearling changed his mind. He offered Johnson $50,000, which Johnson accepted the same day. This was how Chin Nam came to be the owner of Viewed, a name Johnson had already registered. The name obviously related to Scenic, but Johnson was a sophisticated man and there was a double meaning: 'Vie' is French for 'life', and 'wed' is the tie of marriage – hence the connection to Lover's Knot.

Nice name, but it didn't mean much the day I saw the horse. When he was brought to me as a juvenile, he was light as a

cork. I can't say I was bowled over. I sent him off to Princes
Farm with one aim in mind: feed him up.

There was no question of racing Viewed as a two-year-old.
But he ate well and grew, and developed his condition to the
point where we could take him to Leilani Lodge in mid-2006
and put him into light work. He followed his program, staying
healthy and gaining maturity around the stables and track. He
had his first race start in August 2006. He took a while to learn
how to race and to win, but eventually he came through in a
7-furlong race against fellow three-year-olds at Warwick Farm.
It was his sixth start.

He won two more races, over middle distances at Rosehill,
as a three-year-old. In the middle of 2007 Chin Nam asked
Ramage for a horse he could send to Hong Kong. Chin Nam's
son was living there, and was interested in racing, and Chin
Nam wanted to give him a horse to have some fun with.
Ramage suggested Viewed. He was an entire horse with some
potential and pretty good breeding, so perhaps he could pick
up some black type in Hong Kong on his way to a career at
stud.

This was the year of the outbreak of equine influenza
(EI) in the eastern states of Australia. EI stopped the spring
carnival from taking place in Sydney, and immobilised horses
throughout the country. All horses stabled in Sydney had to
remain where they were, to stop the virus from spreading.
The outbreak had been a direct result of catastrophic failure
in the quarantine system. It shouldn't have been allowed to
happen, and I was as dismayed – furious, really – as everyone
else involved in racing. Quarantine used to be watertight
when horses were coming into Australia, but with the growth

of the shuttle stallion industry, and red tape being cut to allow European raiders to take on the Melbourne Cup, there were all sorts of people wandering in and out of quarantine – blacksmiths, farriers, vets, you name it. I believe all of these imported horses should have had their own fumigated transport. You can never be too safe with quarantine. But over time, the regulations hadn't been followed, or the authorities had lowered the threshold of what was acceptable, and the result was that we suddenly had an overseas disease threatening our entire racing industry and people who should have known better were running around as if it had caught them unawares. It was a case of shockingly bad management and slack enforcement of regulations.

I had sixty horses bunged up at Randwick, unable to leave. I was frustrated because they were the best team I'd had in several years. The upshot for Viewed was that he was not allowed to travel as far as Rosehill, let alone Hong Kong. But it was a blessing in disguise, for him and us anyway. If not for equine influenza, Viewed would certainly have gone to live in Hong Kong from 2007.

For the other horses in our stable, too, the EI shutdown might have had a silver lining. Some of them were immature and benefited from being given time to feed and grow. It also helped reinforce my philosophy of patience when I was talking to the owners. Now that they didn't have any choice, some of them might have realised that the world wouldn't end if they didn't race their horses every weekend. Anyway, by the end of it, when the horses were let loose again, they were all leaping about like frisky yearlings, kicking their brands off – by which I mean, the horses *and* the owners!

IN HIS FOUR-YEAR-OLD SEASON, 2007–08, VIEWED WON FOUR MORE races, from 1300 metres up to 12 furlongs. In the winter of 2008 he really showed his potential, winning the Brisbane Cup by seven lengths on a muddy track. But the Brisbane Cup was not what it used to be – literally. Once a Group One 2-mile race, like all the cups in the major cities, it had now been downgraded to Group Two and was run at a mile and a half. A step in the wrong direction, I thought. I'm a fan of 2-mile races for the sake of the breed in Australia and to maintain the variety in the sport. Traditions, also, should mean something. Once you downgrade races like the Brisbane Cup, you reduce the incentive for Australians to breed horses with stamina. And once the stamina goes, the breed is on a slippery slope. We're already on that slope. In the last thirty years, only six Australian-bred horses have won the Melbourne Cup: Just A Dash, Black Knight, Subzero, Saintly, Rogan Josh and Viewed. We've done well to produce juveniles, sprinters and sometimes classics winners, but not to produce 2-milers.

Still, I was happy for Viewed to win the Brisbane Cup, of course – a win is a win. The portents were not so good, as the last horse to win the Brisbane and Melbourne cups in the same year was Macdougal in 1959. But as so many of my horses had shown, they don't read history books.

After the Brisbane Cup, Viewed went out for a short spell before returning to race in the spring carnival in Melbourne. He moved into Saintly Place and thrived. Although he was a stallion, he had the tractability of a gelding and was easy to train. Sometimes they really buck the trend; Hyperno, although gelded, was more cantankerous than any stallion, while an entire horse such as Viewed was quite even tempered.

After some renovations to the course the access route onto Flemington racetrack had changed, so what was formerly a ten-minute walk had turned into four times that length, a 3-kilometre trek around to the far side of the course so that we could get in. This was an irritation, but I wouldn't have the horses floated. We'd just walk them all the way around and use it as exercise. It might have annoyed the staff at first, but you can't go wrong if you're doing more walking in your life.

The extra exercise turned out to be vital for Viewed, because he had an interrupted Cup preparation, to say the least. He ran eighth at 1400 metres and seventh in the 1800 metres Underwood Stakes at Caulfield, and then he was due to start in the Turnbull Stakes over 2000 metres at Flemington in early October, but he had an elevated temperature in the lead-up and we had to withdraw him. He came good in the next few days, and we entered him in the Caulfield Stakes. But we had to scratch him after he got himself into a bizarre tangle. His foot became caught in the barrier stalls, he hurt himself trying to yank it free, and he was out of the race.

He was lucky to get a start in the Caulfield Cup, as he was so far down the qualifiers' list that he needed to rely on higher-up horses dropping out. He just squeaked in, but once he was in the race he seemed full of running, steaming home from the back of the field. Unluckily, he had nowhere to go in the last half-furlong and couldn't get into his full stride. He came tenth, which was not a bad run at all if you were watching it closely. Much was later said about his rotten form leading into the Melbourne Cup, but there is a fine line between his tenth in the Caulfield Cup and what could have been a fast-finishing third or fourth. The only difference was luck. If punters don't analyse a horse's run closely enough, and consequently let it drift in the betting, then that's not my fault!

We entered Viewed in the Mackinnon Stakes on Derby day. I bumped into the horse's breeder Ian Johnson on our way through the turnstiles. He asked me how Viewed was going, and all I could say was that whatever he did that day, he'd be better on Tuesday. Would it be enough? Who knew? I certainly didn't. As always with the Melbourne Cup, the race itself is its own fitness test. You don't know a horse is fit enough until the end of those 2 miles.

The Mackinnon gave us no help at all in assessing the horse's readiness. Yet again he was flying through on the inside but was held up and couldn't get a run. He finished eleventh of eleven runners. Again, he was going better than he looked, but if you went by the form sheet it read eighth, seventh, tenth, eleventh.

It was the most frustrating preparation for a Melbourne Cup that I could recall, because I sensed that the horse was fit enough but couldn't get a read on him because we weren't seeing his full potential in those races. His being blocked from finishing off his races meant that we weren't able to draw any conclusions about his stamina, or even about what riding tactics suited him best. Even worse, Chin Nam was potentially missing out on some prize money. How was the horse really shaping up? I couldn't tell. Also, it was an unconventional preparation for me. As Viewed had raced in Brisbane in the winter, I hadn't wanted to put too many miles in his legs during the spring. But had I given him enough?

At least he was relaxed. Observers contrasted the difference at track work between the European horses and mine. The European gallopers, once they'd worked, were followed around by great entourages of trainers, vets, farriers and so on. Not leaving a stone unturned, fussing about. Meanwhile I'd just be hanging around peacefully with my horse and the track jockey, Joe Agresta, with a couple of others, sharing a joke. The horses, I've always found, prefer to mix with people who are having a good time at work.

One boost we had was the services of Blake Shinn, the top Sydney rider, in the Cup. Steven Arnold had ridden Viewed previously, but I was very pleased to engage Shinn. I only wanted Viewed to get a fair opportunity, which he hadn't had in the Caulfield Cup or the Mackinnon. I also had Moatize, a promising four-year-old who won the Hotham Handicap (Saab Quality) on the Saturday, ridden by Clare Lindop. That day she won the Victoria Derby on Rebel Raider, so she was obviously brimming with confidence. But both of our horses started at outsider's odds. Viewed was the less favoured, at 40/1. It's a reflection of how the punters had forgotten about me. Even though Viewed and Moatize hardly had world-beating form, if this had been 1968 or 1978 they would both have started at around 10/1, such was the bookies' fear of the Cummings name. But memories can be short, and on this day it suited us quite well.

For the tactics employed by some riders, the 2008 race was the most extraordinary Melbourne Cup in memory. The Irish trainer Aidan O'Brien had three starters – the second favourite Septimus, Honolulu and Alessandro Volta – all flown in from Europe and given the red carpet treatment by the VRC. My concerns about the VRC's willingness to make things easy for the Europeans had come to a head. In 2008 something like half of the field were Northern Hemisphere horses. It's all very well to introduce a foreign flavour, but this was getting out of hand. I have nothing against the individual European trainers and the horses' connections, but the racing club should not have been setting aside so many places for them. For every one of them that raced, an Australian horse was missing out. And for every Australian horse missing out, that was a potential lost opportunity for our breed to develop the stamina it sorely needs.

The running of the race was a farcical affair, at the front of the field at least. Aidan O'Brien's three jockeys set off as if they were running in the Newmarket. Either they overrated their own horses or underrated the opposition – or both. It was commented later that their approach was arrogant and contemptuous, expecting the rest of the field to fall back and let them have their own way, just like the VRC had. I'm not going to say that myself, but their riding tactics were strange, very strange. The three jockeys were called in by the stewards later, and they had nothing to say except the obvious: they thought their horses were fit enough to go out so fast and blow the field away.

What happened was, Septimus, Honolulu and Alessandro Volta went so fast for the first mile, they began going backwards before they entered the long sweeping home turn. Aside from being bad tactics, the riding was dangerous for the rest of the field. As the front-runners stopped, Blake Shinn had Viewed perfectly positioned. He was midfield and one off the fence. Like all my previous Cup winners, Viewed was relaxed in the running. He could have been nodding off to sleep as he jogged along in the middle of the field, comfortably carted along by the pacemakers out front.

Were they pacemakers for something else? As I watched, I wondered if the Europeans were operating as a team – Septimus and the others making the pace for another one to come home from the rear. But which one?

As they entered the straight, Shinn's main task was to stay clear of any leading horses who were falling back. He hooked Viewed out off the fence and went for home. Had he gone too early? He hadn't waited for the clock, like John Marshall on Rogan Josh. He wasn't sitting on a Ferrari, like Darren Beadman on Saintly or Steven King on Let's Elope. He wasn't able to take a last shot at the leaders, like Harry White on Think Big. I always felt more comfortable having the last shot, but this would turn out to be most reminiscent of Red Handed's duel with Red Crest in 1967.

The dueller, in this case, was Bauer, trained by Luca Cumani. Bauer was another of the northern raiders. But he was owned by a local syndicate headed by the retired Test cricketer Simon O'Donnell and ridden by a local, Corey Brown, and he was ridden well. I don't know if there was a plan to set a fast pace for Bauer's advantage. It's hard to imagine. But as the field sorted itself out down the straight, Bauer was clearly the one. He came up on Viewed's flank as they passed the clock, and I could see Bauer and Brown going past us. But Bauer seemed to die a little on his run – or Viewed kicked again, it's always hard to tell. Both jockeys were giving it everything. Just as with Red Handed and Red Crest, or Hyperno and Salamander, it was down to the bob of the heads in the end and only centimetres were in it. Bauer's tail was ahead of Viewed's as they crossed the line, but Bauer was a small horse – what about their noses? Neither jockey knew who had won.

The developed print needed a magnifying glass to separate Viewed and Bauer. By a nostril, Viewed had won. I had a neat dozen. For the third time, my horses had been in the closest possible Melbourne Cup finish, and for the third time, we'd won by a short half-head.

The cameras had all focused on Bauer after the horses were slowing down, and Simon O'Donnell and his co-owners had to go through the heartbreak of thinking they'd won before discovering that they had not. But he was seeing the bright side. He said: 'We thought we had won the Melbourne Cup and I am really glad we had that experience because we might never have it again. It shows how hard this race is to win. And to think Bart has won twelve of them. Incredible.' Amen to that.

In the mounting yard with Chin Nam, we were all very pleased, and presented a front to suggest that we weren't surprised at all. To be honest, I was neither surprised nor unsurprised – because of his strange preparation, Viewed had remained a mystery until that afternoon. I asked Chin Nam what odds he had got. He was a little disappointed: he had backed Viewed at 30/1, not the 40/1 that was on offer later in the day. But considering the multi-million-dollar prize money, I don't think it mattered very much. And then we were informed that, with four Melbourne Cup wins, Dato Tan Chin Nam was the most successful owner in the history of our race. Not bad for a bloke who got involved in the sport through a game of two-up.

21

An eye for a horse

A BAKER'S DOZEN? I LIKE THE IDEA. AFTER ROGAN JOSH WON HIS
Melbourne Cup in 1999, my eleventh, I used to say how I liked
the idea of twelve Cups; it seemed like a nice number to round
things off. Now I'm not so sure. A baker's dozen has a strong
appeal. By the time you read this, you may know whether or
not I have won the 2009 Melbourne Cup. At time of writing,
our stable has just won the AJC Australian Derby with Roman
Emperor. He looks promising, although it is a rarity for AJC

Derby winners to back up and win the Melbourne Cup in their next campaign. Yet it was a rarity to win the Melbourne Cup after winning the Moonee Valley Cup with Kingston Rule, the Cox Plate with Saintly, and the Brisbane Cup with Viewed, and none of those horses cared about precedent. So we'll see.

Chin Nam has some good horses with me, including the filly Think Money. Will his chequerboard colours get up again? Will my good friend win a fifth? I also have Moatize, who ran home for a very promising sixth in Viewed's 2008 Melbourne Cup, and Dandaad, who won a minor staying race on Melbourne Cup day in 2008. And of course the plan is to get Viewed absolutely right for two in a row. He had a short campaign in the autumn, running some good races up to 12 furlongs, and we didn't take too much out of him.

Perhaps my next Melbourne Cup winner is a horse I haven't heard of yet. That was the case with Rogan Josh and Let's Elope, horses who were never on my radar until they came to me a few months before the Cup. Perhaps it will be a horse I do know about, but is brought to me by owners who want a different approach – like Hyperno or Kingston Rule. Or perhaps, as I am still buying yearlings, it will be a few years away, a horse that follows the hoofprints of Light Fingers, Galilee, Red Handed, Think Big and Gold And Black, a youngster who is still only a year or two old. The beauty of the game is that you just don't know what's around the next corner.

I see clouds on the horizon for the sport. The trend towards using shuttle stallions has a compelling economic logic, but I worry about how it's going to affect the breed. The chemical testing of mares to time to the minute when it is best for a stallion to cover them, knowing precisely when their ovaries are releasing their eggs, allows sires to cover more mares and operate more cost-effectively. But I wonder if this isn't going to wear the stallions out. Nowadays some of them are covering 300 mares a year. Not even Errol Flynn could do that!

While betting revenues continue to increase, attendances at race meetings seem to be in permanent decline. At the Doncaster Mile day in 2009, only 15,000 spectators turned up to Randwick. If that's not the lowest ever, I don't know what is. Administrators have tried to arrest the slide by promoting 'fun fair' kinds of days at the track, but it hasn't done much to arrest the long-term slide. In my view, the most appealing drawcard about a day at the races is . . . the races. To see those horses, with the jockeys in their flashing silks, is a beautiful thing for me after fifty-six years as a trainer. The competition still gets my blood running. I can't see why it shouldn't be the same for anyone else who takes an interest. The strength of the sport is the thrill and colour of a horse race, having a bet or even just watching for fun; people of all ages whose curiosity is sparked by that spectacle will come, and keep coming.

Racing is a sport which has been addressing threats ever since I started training in 1953. The bottom line is now such an overriding concern for the clubs that you wonder if they ever think of the horses' welfare. We see too many inconsistent patchy surfaces, which not only endanger the horses and jockeys but detract from the spectacle, because the worse the condition of the track, the less likely riders are going to want to risk a final charge from the back of the field. Late finishers like Galilee, Storm Queen and Saintly always become crowd favourites; who can forget Kiwi coming from last to first in the 1983 Melbourne Cup? It would be terrible if the variable condition of racing surfaces did us out of this marvellous spectacle.

There are constant stresses and challenges for a trainer in today's world. The administration of some of the racing clubs has left a lot to be desired. There are too many poorly attended midweek city meetings, diluting the strength of fields. More race meetings should be spread into country tracks, where the presence of better horses would increase the sense of occasion. Likewise, such a move could strengthen the Saturday metropolitan meetings. Too much racing can only kill the goose that laid the golden eggs, by weakening race fields and increasing the chances that horses will get injured. Once the horses, rather than the profits, are put first, the flow-on effect will be felt by trainers, owners, riders, breeders and punters; in other words, the entire racing community. It always has to be horse first, people later.

The AJC and the STC, the two Sydney clubs, have been debating whether or not to merge. Their cash flows are under threat and there has been talk about selling off the STC's Canterbury racecourse. I don't know what will happen, but would only like to see one guiding principle, which is that the welfare of the sport – as opposed to those of rival interest groups and camp followers – be paramount.

Another current issue is the use of whips, with the clubs moving to place restrictions on how the jockeys apply the 'persuader'. Animal welfare groups, among others, go so far as to call for whips to be banned. As you will know from this book, I am the last trainer to urge the overuse of whips. With some of my Melbourne Cup winners, such as Kingston Rule and

Saintly, the whip was so counterproductive I almost wished the jockeys didn't carry them. But every horse is different, and some respond very positively to a few strokes of the whip. My point is not that I am particularly pro- or anti-whip. It's horses for courses! My point is that the decision on how to use the whip should be in the hands of individual trainers and jockeys, not of regulating authorities.

A much greater danger to the sport overall is posed by corporate bookmakers who don't return percentages of their turnover to racing. When Sir Chester Manifold set in train what would become the state-owned network of TABs, he gave racing a blessing that kept on giving. The regulation of revenues so that a fixed percentage went back to the racing clubs gave an infusion of blood into the sport. Inflation did get out of hand in the 1980s, but that was due to other factors, not least greed and the involvement of too many people who didn't know enough about horses. The regular injection of TAB money into racing was, and is, absolutely vital. With the privatisation of TABs and the advent of corporate bookmakers, all of that is in danger. The public companies that now own the TABs are not concerned with the welfare of horses, or with the sport of racing. They are concerned with their current-year results and the wishes of their shareholders. Corporate bookmakers are not legally obligated in perpetuity to give back to racing some percentage of what they take out. For many years, based in Darwin, the corporate bookmakers were bleeding the racing system dry. Then they were set loose on the rest of the country, via the Packers' Betfair and the deal it did with the Tasmanian government. Such corporate bookmakers rely on the races for their revenue, but they don't seem to see it as a two-way street. If betting money flows away from racing and doesn't come back, there will be fewer races, weaker competition, and ultimately a depleted betting industry. It is in the corporate bookmakers' own interests to give more back to the sport, but for as long as they aren't compelled to do so, I see them as the greatest threat to racing today, and the Howard federal government made a great mistake in allowing their spread.

It's not money that drives me. All I need is three meals a day. Any more and I'd get indigestion. And you only need one roof over your head. I have been stung by financial reversals, it's true, but the memory, while painful, doesn't motivate me to pile the stuff up. It's not the promise of money that gets me out of bed at three o'clock every morning; it's the promise of the horses.

I still go to work every day at Leilani Lodge, getting up in the morning to check on the horses and clock them in their work. We have some of the most loyal and competent staff a horse trainer could ever hope for. Some of our people, at our head-quarters at Randwick, at Princes Farm and at Saintly Place, have been with us for decades, providing the kind of profes-sional application that I could not have survived without. Bill Charles, my racing manager in Sydney, has been in the industry for forty years and acts like the other half of my brain. He saw Tulloch win at Randwick as a boy and has worked everywhere from Tehran to Macau. He has been with me since 1996 and does most of the programming of the horses. The foremen I have had over the years have included Guy Walter, Leon Corstens, John O'Shea and John Morish, among others who have turned into professional trainers in their own right. As the foreman in my stable they have had to take on a lot of responsibility, representing me at the races and barrier trials, checking the horses' gallops, bandaging their legs, feeding and watering them, and managing staff. It's a big job. As I write, I have appointed a new stable foreman in Sydney. John Thompson, who has held the position for eight years, is going off to train for the mining magnate Nathan Tinkler's Patinack Farm operation. In his place, I am bringing in a young fellow who has been working for Anthony. Having always selected on pedigree, I like this boy's bloodlines. He is my grandson, and will be the fourth James Cummings in five generations to work with horses. Having been with his father, Anthony, for a while now, no doubt James will be looking forward to getting some real expert guidance.

But I remain a hands-on boss. When we have horses racing interstate at the big meetings, I go to supervise. Why, at my age, would I keep toiling so hard? Well, even in a morning canter, I still love to see horses in their work. When you see a good one like Light Fingers, with a rapid, rhythmic, low grass-cutting stride, her head, back and tail all in one perfect line, you have a vision of heaven. Or my version of heaven.

Every Sunday, I am back in Sydney and go with Valmae to spend the end of the weekend at Princes Farm, the most relaxing place in the world. I still fish when I can, and still go to church. I am a creature of habit. I like what I have been lucky enough to do, and still consider that I am applying the rules of training horses that I learnt from my father. I don't feel like I imagined an octogenarian to feel. Within myself, I am the same as ever. Much has changed, but not the basic foundations.

My training methods have always put the horse first. I am a gentle person by nature, and thoroughbreds seem to respond to that. They are not machines, and they do not exist for the purpose of making money out of racing for their owners. Sometimes they have that innate will to win, it's just part of their make-up, the same as with humans; and sometimes it needs some gentle coaxing to bring it out. But there's no point overdoing it – force it and you get the opposite result. Once I saw one of my strappers nagging a horse, and I said, 'You keep growling and you'll be growling out the gate.' If a fellow is going to kick the khyber out of a horse because it treads on his toes, you end up with a horse shrivelling up in a corner. The horse isn't thinking right, which means he is not thinking about winning, he's thinking about what is frightening him. He doesn't sleep well and he doesn't travel well. You can walk in on some of ours when they are lying down in the boxes and they won't even get up, because they know you aren't going to hurt them. Being a horse can be just like going to hospital. A fellow won't go to hospital if he thinks the matron is going to belt him up.

While I am always ambitious for more success, I don't think anyone has accused me of being greedy. I won't drive racehorses until they break down. Often the best ones do end up breaking down, but that is because they try too hard. They don't know any different, and that is what makes them great.

I love horses now as much as ever. I am happy in their company, and they are happy in mine. I have made many acquaintances through racing, and I have many valuable, loyal and skilful employees, but ultimately my closest companion is Valmae. Between her and the horses, I have few other needs for companionship. Valmae says I love the horses more than I love people because the horses don't answer back. But they do answer back, in their own language, and my eyes and ears are open to what they are saying. They are continually sending us messages. The ability to listen – to horses, and to humans – is something I learnt from my father, but also it is something I have refined through my own efforts. I am known as a man of few words because I am much more interested in what I can learn from others than in extolling my own so-called genius. I'm too scared of being wrong. Tommy Smith was a great spruiker, a great talker, but if you look back on it, most of the time his predictions were overconfident. I don't like talking myself up, or my horses. I prefer to listen to others and let my results do the talking for me. As Chin Nam likes to say, 'Great people talk about ideas, average people talk about things, small people talk about other people, and legends never talk.' He said it, not me.

A few years ago, the Melbourne trainer Rick Hore-Lacy expressed great surprise when I asked him about the beach-swimming routine he was using for his champion Redoute's Choice. I've always been a great advocate of swimming horses, and was interested in what he was doing. He couldn't believe that I would be asking questions of him, after all my success on the track. But that success would quickly come to a halt if I stopped learning and stopped asking questions. It doesn't matter who they are, if someone involved with horses is doing something that piques my curiosity, I will go in there and ask questions about it. I have no ego or pride on that issue.

I turn eighty-two this year and have no intention of slowing down or giving up. You're only as old as the horses you train, and mine are as young as two years old. I was made a Member of the Order of Australia back in 1982, at the age of fifty-four, and many probably thought I was on my way out then. Flattering honours have followed – being named one of Australia's Living Treasures by the National Trust in 1997, being inducted into the Sport Australia Hall of Fame in 1991 as well as the Racing Hall of Fame in 2001, and having my face put on a stamp by Australia Post in 2007. The VRC named a race after me and gave me life membership, and in 2008 Racing NSW established a medal for jockeys and trainers in my name. The VRC even put up a statue of me! Well, fools and their money are easily parted. I became a great attraction to the pigeons of Flemington.

All of these symbols of recognition tend to prompt the question of retirement, but it's a question asked by others, not by myself. Training horses is my job. I never set out to be a horse trainer, but now that I have done it for a while, I don't know what I would do without it. I still want to win. Everyone gets rushed out of their jobs before they wear out, and I am determined to wear out first. I'm not going to be like the man who hits his head against a brick wall because he likes the relief he gets when he stops. I'm not going to stop training unless health forces me. I like it while I am doing it. My asthma and allergies continue to bug me, but if they are the worst of it, I have little to complain about. I still think that when Dad and I went to see that specialist, Dr Barlow in Adelaide, and he told me to stay away from the horses, we were throwing away our money.

Half a century ago I studied race results and concluded how many of our staying races were won by horses bred in

New Zealand. It's now common knowledge, and when I go to New Zealand the roads to those horse studs are worn bare by the tracks of Australian trainers and buyers. But just because others are doing it, I haven't stopped, and nor do I have any intention of doing so. Next January, I will be back on the North Island. The competition is stiff, the prices are higher, but not everyone has an eye for a horse. Human nature hasn't changed: people with money in their pockets and big dreams in their heads are always looking for a perfect horse that doesn't exist. This leaves the door open for someone like me, who sees things a little differently. I can't put into words what an 'eye for a horse' means, exactly. But you either have it or you don't. I believe I still have it. And when I go to New Zealand this coming January, I will go there with a firm belief that there will be a yearling colt or filly there, perhaps with a few superficial irregularities that will turn others off, but possessing stout bloodlines and a big girth and low knees and a certain way of moving . . . and maybe, just maybe, it is destined to be a Melbourne Cup winner.

BART CUMMINGS' GROUP ONE
RACE WINS

1958–59 2 stakes races won

1	SAJC SA Derby	Stormy Passage

1959–60 4 stakes races won

2	VATC Underwood Stakes	Trellios
3	VRC L.K.S. Mackinnon Stakes	Trellios

1960–61 4 stakes races won

1961–62 1 stakes race won

1962–63 3 stakes races won

4	AJC Chipping Norton Stakes	The Dip

1963–64 5 stakes races won

5	VATC 1000 Guineas	Anna Rose

1964–65 12 stakes races won

6	SAJC SA Derby	Ziema
7	VRC Oaks	Light Fingers
8	AJC Oaks	Light Fingers

1965–66 17 stakes races won

9	VRC Melbourne Cup	Light Fingers
10	VATC Merson Cooper Stakes	Storm Queen
11	VRC Sires' Produce Stakes	Storm Queen
12	STC Golden Slipper Stakes	Storm Queen
13	AJC Champagne Stakes	Storm Queen

1966–67 24 stakes races won

14	SAJC SA Derby	Peculator
15	VATC Caulfield Guineas	Storm Queen
16	VATC Toorak Handicap	Galilee
17	VATC Caulfield Cup	Galilee
18	VRC Melbourne Cup	Galilee
19	VRC George Adams Handicap	Storm Queen
20	VRC Lightning Stakes	Storm Queen
21	AJC Sydney Cup	Galilee
22	SAJC Adelaide Cup	Fulmen
23	QTC Brisbane Cup	Fulmen

1967–68 16 stakes races won

24	SAJC SA Oaks	My Lady Fair
25	VRC Melbourne Cup	Red Handed
26	VRC Australian Cup	Arctic Coast
27	AJC Oaks	Lowland

1968–69 15 stakes races won

28	VATC Invitation Stakes	Joking
29	VATC Underwood Stakes	Lowland
30	AJC Sydney Cup	Lowland
31	AJC Queen Elizabeth Stakes	Lowland

1969–70 15 stakes races won

32	SAJC SA Derby	Paradigm
33	VATC Caulfield Cup	Big Philou
34	VATC Oakleigh Plate	Arello
35	AJC Oaks	Gay Poss
36	SAJC Adelaide Cup	Tavel

1970–71 16 stakes races won

37	VATC Caulfield Stakes	Gay Poss
38	VRC L.K.S. Mackinnon Stakes	Voleur
39	VRC Oaks	Sanderae
40	VATC Futurity Stakes	Silver Spade
41	SAJC Adelaide Cup	Laelia

1971–72 10 stakes races won

42	VRC Newmarket Handicap	Crown
43	VRC Sires' Produce Stakes	Century

1972–73 20 stakes races won

44	MVRC Freeway (Manikato) Stakes	Century
45	SAJC SA Derby	Dayana
46	VRC Victoria Derby	Dayana
47	WATC WA Derby	Dayana
48	WATC Australian Derby	Dayana
49	WATC Perth Cup	Dayana
50	VRC Newmarket Handicap	Century
51	VRC Australian Cup	Gladman
52	STC Golden Slipper Stakes	Tontonan
53	AJC Sires' Produce Stakes	Tontonan
54	SAJC Goodwood Handicap	Wise Virgin

1973–74 33 stakes races won

55	MVRC W.S. Cox Plate	Taj Rossi
56	VRC Craven 'A' Stakes	Century
57	VRC Victoria Derby	Taj Rossi
58	VRC George Adams Handicap	Taj Rossi
59	WATC WA Derby	Asgard

60	WATC Karrakatta Plate	Vain Prince
61	WATC Australian Derby	Leica Lover
62	VRC Lightning Stakes	Century
63	VATC Oakleigh Plate	Tontonan
64	VRC Sires' Produce Stakes	Skyjack
65	AJC Australasian Champion Stakes	Asgard
66	AJC Doncaster Handicap	Tontonan
67	AJC The Galaxy	Starglow
68	AJC Oaks	Leilani
69	AJC All-Aged Stakes	Tontonan

1974–75 45 stakes races won

70	AJC Flight Stakes	Cap D'Antibes
71	VATC Caulfield Guineas	Kenmark
72	VATC Toorak Handicap	Leilani
73	VATC Caulfield Cup	Leilani
74	VRC L.K.S. Mackinnon Stakes	Leilani
75	VRC Melbourne Cup	Think Big
76	VRC Oaks	Leica Show
77	VRC George Adams Handicap	Skyjack
78	WATC WA Derby	Bottled Sunshine
79	MVRC William Reid Stakes	Leica Show
80	VATC C.F. Orr Stakes	Leilani
81	VRC Lightning Stakes	Cap D'Antibes
82	VATC Futurity Stakes	Martindale
83	VATC Blue Diamond Stakes	Lord Dudley
84	VRC Newmarket Handicap	Cap D'Antibes
85	VRC Sires' Produce Stakes	Lord Dudley
86	VRC Australian Cup	Leilani

87	SAJC Goodwood Handicap	Kenmark
88	QTC Queensland Derby	Bottled Sunshine
89	QTC Brisbane Cup	Herminia

1975–76 31 stakes races won

90	MVRC Freeway (Manikato) Stakes	Lord Dudley
91	VATC Marlboro (Vic Health) Cup	Cap D'Antibes
92	SAJC SA Derby	Vacuum
93	VRC Melbourne Cup	Think Big
94	MVRC William Reid Stakes	Lord Dudley
95	VRC Australian Cup	Lord Dudley
96	STC Golden Slipper Stakes	Vivarchi
97	AJC Champagne Stakes	Vivarchi

1976–77 27 stakes races won

98	AJC Epsom Handicap	La Neige
99	AJC Flight Stakes	Apollua
100	SAJC SA Derby	Vacuum
101	VRC Craven 'A' Stakes	Maybe Mahal
102	VRC L.K.S. Mackinnon Stakes	Gold And Black
103	VRC George Adams Handicap	Maybe Mahal
104	VRC Lightning Stakes	Maybe Mahal
105	VRC Sires' Produce Stakes	Bold Zest
106	VRC Australian Cup	Ngawyni
107	AJC Doncaster Handicap	Just Ideal
108	AJC Queen Elizabeth Stakes	Ngawyni
109	SAJC Goodwood Handicap	Romantic Dream
110	BTC Doomben '10,000'	Maybe Mahal

1977–78 32 stakes races won

111	STC Canterbury Guineas	Belmura Lad
112	AJC Flight Stakes	Sun Sally
113	AJC Derby	Belmura Lad
114	SAJC SA Derby	Stormy Rex
115	VATC Caulfield Cup	Ming Dynasty
116	VRC Victoria Derby	Stormy Rex
117	VRC Melbourne Cup	Gold And Black
118	WATC WA Derby	Stormy Rex
119	WATC Marlboro '50,000'	Stormy Rex
120	VRC Lightning Stakes	Maybe Mahal
121	VRC Newmarket Handicap	Maybe Mahal
122	VRC Australian Cup	Ming Dynasty
123	AJC Doncaster Handicap	Maybe Mahal
124	AJC The Galaxy	Luskin Star
125	AJC Oaks	Invade
126	AJC Queen Elizabeth Stakes	Ming Dynasty

1978–79 18 stakes races won

127	AJC Metropolitan Handicap	Ming Dynasty
128	VATC Caulfield Stakes	Lloyd Boy
129	VRC Newmarket Handicap	Better Beyond
130	STC Golden Slipper Stakes	Century Miss

1979–80 13 stakes races won

131	VRC Melbourne Cup	Hyperno
132	WATC WA Derby	Lloyd's Gold
133	VRC Australian Cup	Ming Dynasty
134	STC Rosemount Classic	Stage Hit

1980–81 15 stakes races won

135	VATC Caulfield Stakes	Hyperno
136	VATC Caulfield Cup	Ming Dynasty
137	VRC L.K.S. Mackinnon Stakes	Belmura Lad
138	VRC Newmarket Handicap	Elounda Bay
139	VRC Australian Cup	Hyperno
140	STC Rawson Stakes	Hyperno
141	STC Rosemount Classic	Cordon Rose

1981–82 22 stakes races won

142	AJC Spring Champion Stakes	Best Western
143	AJC Metropolitan Handicap	Belmura Lad
144	VRC L.K.S. Mackinnon Stakes	Belmura Lad
145	STC Rosemount Classic	Sheraco
146	STC Storm Queen Stakes	Sheraco
147	AJC Oaks	Sheraco

1982–83 16 stakes races won

148	VRC Pure-Pac Stakes	Foregone Conclusion
149	SAJC Australasian Oaks	Royal Regatta
150	STC H.E. Tancred Stakes	Trissaro

1983–84 18 stakes races won

151	VATC Underwood Stakes	Trissaro
152	AJC Epsom Handicap	Cool River
153	VRC Victoria Derby	Bounty Hawk
154	VRC Oaks	Taj Eclipse
155	WATC Western Mail Classic	Bounty Hawk
156	WATC Australian Derby	Bounty Hawk

157	AJC Derby	Prolific
158	AJC Sydney Cup	Trissaro
159	SAJC Goodwood Handicap	Leica Planet

1984–85 9 stakes races won

160	VATC Underwood Stakes	Bounty Hawk
161	VRC L.K.S. Mackinnon Stakes	Bounty Hawk
162	VRC Australian Cup	Noble Peer
163	STC George Ryder Stakes	Hula Drum

1985–86 6 stakes races won

164	VRC Lightning Stakes	Hula Chief
165	AJC Doncaster Handicap	Hula Chief
166	SAJC Adelaide Cup	Mr Lomondy

1986–87 16 stakes races won

167	VRC Gadsden Stakes	Taj Quilo
168	STC George Ryder Stakes	Campaign King
169	AJC All-Aged Stakes	Campaign King
170	AJC Champagne Stakes	Sky Chase
171	SAJC SA Derby	Sharks Fin
172	QTC Queensland Oaks	Round The World
173	BTC Doomben '10,000'	Broad Reach

1987–88 28 stakes races won

174	AJC George Main Stakes	Campaign King
175	AJC Spring Champion Stakes	Beau Zam
176	VRC Victoria Derby	Omnicorp

177	STC Rawson Stakes	Beau Zam
178	STC Rosehill Guineas	Sky Chase
179	STC George Ryder Stakes	Campaign King
180	STC Tancred-International Stakes	Beau Zam
181	AJC Derby	Beau Zam
182	AJC Champagne Stakes	Full And By
183	BTC Doomben '10,000'	Campaign King
184	QTC Stradbroke Handicap	Campaign King

1988–89 23 stakes races won

185	VATC Caulfield Stakes	Sky Chase
186	SAJC Australasian Oaks	Stapleton Lass
187	STC Rawson Stakes	Beau Zam
188	STC Orlando Classic	Red Express
189	AJC Sires' Produce Stakes	Reganza
190	QTC Sires' Produce Stakes	Zamoff
191	QTC Stradbroke Handicap	Robian Steel

1989–90 20 stakes races won

192	AJC Spring Champion Stakes	Stylish Century
193	VATC 1000 Guineas	Tristanagh
194	VRC Oaks	Tristanagh
195	VRC Newmarket Handicap	Gold Trump
196	STC Canterbury Guineas	Interstellar
197	STC Rosehill Guineas	Solar Circle

1990–91 15 stakes races won

198	VATC Show Day Cup	Submariner
199	AJC George Main Stakes	Shaftesbury Avenue
200	VRC Melbourne Cup	Kingston Rule
201	VRC Oaks	Weekend Delight
202	VRC Honda Stakes	Shaftesbury Avenue
203	VRC Lightning Stakes	Shaftesbury Avenue
204	VRC Newmarket Handicap	Shaftesbury Avenue
205	AJC All-Aged Stakes	Shaftesbury Avenue
206	SAJC SA Derby	Shiva's Revenge

1991–92 24 stakes races won

207	VATC Caulfield Stakes	Shaftesbury Avenue
208	VATC 1000 Guineas	Richfield Lady
209	VATC Caulfield Cup	Let's Elope
210	VRC L.K.S. Mackinnon Stakes	Let's Elope
211	VRC Melbourne Cup	Let's Elope
212	VRC Oaks	Richfield Lady
213	WATC WA Oaks	India's Dream
214	VATC C.F. Orr Stakes	Let's Elope
215	VRC Australian Cup	Let's Elope
216	VATC Blue Diamond Stakes	Riva Diva

1992–93 12 stakes races won

217	VRC Gadsden Stakes	Unspoken Word
218	SAJC Australasian Oaks	Our Tristalight
219	SAJC SA Oaks	Our Tristalight
220	QTC Stradbroke Handicap	Never Undercharge

1993–94 15 stakes races won

221	MVRC Manikato Stakes	Never Undercharge
222	SAJC Australasian Oaks	Tristalove

1994–95 9 stakes races won

223	AJC Flight Stakes	Danarani
224	AJC Derby	Ivory's Irish

1995–96 10 stakes races won

225	VRC Australian Cup	Saintly

1996–97 21 stakes races won

226	AJC Flight Stakes	Dashing Eagle
227	VATC Caulfield Guineas	Alfa
228	VATC 1000 Guineas	Dashing Eagle
229	MVRC W.S. Cox Plate	Saintly
230	VRC Melbourne Cup	Saintly
231	VATC C.F. Orr Stakes	Saintly
232	STC Ansett-Storm Queen Stakes	Danendri
233	AJC Oaks	Danendri
234	QTC Stradbroke Handicap	Dane Ripper

1997–98 9 stakes races won

235	MVRC W.S. Cox Plate	Dane Ripper
236	VRC Chrysler Stakes	Catalan Opening
237	VRC Australian Cup	Dane Ripper
238	AJC Doncaster Handicap	Catalan Opening

1998–99 9 stakes races won

239	MVRC Manikato Stakes	Dane Ripper

1999–2000 13 stakes races won

240	AJC Epsom Handicap	Allez Suez
241	VRC L.K.S. Mackinnon Stakes	Rogan Josh
242	VRC Melbourne Cup	Rogan Josh

2000–2001 2 stakes races won

2001–2002 5 stakes races won

243	VATC 1000 Guineas	Magical Miss
244	VRC Oaks	Magical Miss

2002–2003 1 stakes race won

2003–2004 2 stakes races won

2004–2005 5 stakes races won

2005–2006 8 stakes races won

245	MRC Caulfield Guineas	God's Own

2006–2007 11 stakes races won

246	MRC Caulfield Guineas	Wonderful World
247	QTC Queensland Derby	Empires Choice

2007–2008 8 stakes races won

248	VRC L.K.S. Mackinnon Stakes	Sirmione
249	VRC Australian Cup	Sirmione

2008–2009 4 stakes races won

250	VRC Melbourne Cup	Viewed
251	VRC Classic	Swick
252	AJC Derby	Roman Emperor
253	Tatt RC Queensland Winter Stakes	Russeting

BART CUMMINGS' WINNERS OF
THE AUSTRALIAN HORSE OF THE YEAR AWARD

Dayana
1972–73
VRC, SAJC SA, WATC WA and WATC
Australian derbies, WATC Perth Cup

Taj Rossi
1973–74
MVRC W.S. Cox Plate, VRC Derby,
VRC George Adams Handicap

Leilani
1974–75
AJC Oaks, VATC Toorak Handicap, VATC Caulfield Cup,
VATC C.F. Orr Stakes, VRC L.K.S. Mackinnon
Stakes, VRC Australian Cup

Lord Dudley
1975–76
VATC Blue Diamond Stakes, VRC Sires' Produce Stakes,
VRC Australian Cup, MVRC Freeway (Manikato) Stakes,
MVRC William Reid Stakes

Maybe Mahal
1977–78
VRC Craven 'A' Stakes, VRC George Adams Handicap,
VRC Lightning Stakes, VRC Newmarket Handicap,
BTC Doomben '10,000', AJC Doncaster Handicap

Hyperno
1980–81
VRC Australian Cup, VATC Caulfield Stakes,
STC Rawson Stakes

Beau Zam
1987–88
AJC Spring Champion Stakes, STC Rawson Stakes (twice),
STC Tancred-International Stakes, AJC Derby

Let's Elope
1991–92
VATC Caulfield Cup, VATC C.F. Orr Stakes,
VRC L.K.S. Mackinnon Stakes, VRC Melbourne Cup,
VRC Australian Cup

Saintly
1996–97
VRC Australian Cup, VRC Melbourne Cup,
MVRC W.S. Cox Plate, VATC C.F. Orr Stakes

BART CUMMINGS' MELBOURNE CUP
RUNNERS AND THEIR PLACINGS

1958 Asian Court 12th

1959 Trellios 5th

1961 Sometime 6th

1965 **LIGHT FINGERS
      1st**
      Ziema 2nd
      The Dip 18th

1966 **GALILEE 1st**
      Light Fingers 2nd

1967 **RED HANDED 1st**
      Fulmen 9th
      Ziema 12th

1968 Lowland 4th
      Arctic Coast 6th
      Swift General 23rd

1969 Swift General 5th
      General Command
        13th
      The Sharper 20th

1970 Tavel 4th
      Voleur 6th
      Moomba Fox 19th

1971 Pilgarlic 10th
      Tavel 10th

1973 Dayana 12th

1974 **THINK BIG 1st**
      Leilani 2nd

1975 **THINK BIG 1st**
      **Holiday Waggon
      2nd**
      Leica Lover 20th

1976 Gold And Black 2nd

1977 **GOLD AND
      BLACK 1st**
      Ming Dynasty 8th
      Vacuum 20th

1978 Panamint 10th
      Vive Velours 11th
      Belmura Lad 13th
      Stormy Rex 20th

1979 **HYPERNO 1st**
      Safe Harbour 21st

1980 La Zap 6th
      Hyperno 7th
      Ming Dynasty 17th

1981 Hyperno 6th
      Belmura Lad 7th
      No Peer 8th

1982 My Sir Avon 4th

1983 Mr Jazz 3rd
      No Peer 4th

1984 Bounty Hawk 15th

1986 Empire Rose 5th

1987 Rosedale 3rd

1988   Round The World 5th

1990   **KINGSTON RULE 1st**
La Tristia 9th

1991   **LET'S ELOPE 1st**
Shiva's Revenge 2nd
Weekend Delight 22nd

1992   London Bridge 9th

1993   Great Vintage 4th
Frontier Boy 5th
Tennessee Jack 6th
Our Tristalight 24th

1994   Gossips 14th

1996   **SAINTLY 1st**
My Kiwi Gold 21st

1997   Grandmaster 10th
Alfa 19th

1998   Perpetual Check 9th

1999   **ROGAN JOSH 1st**
Zazabelle 3rd
Rebbor 23rd

2002   Miss Meliss 10th

2003   Frightening 11th

2004   Strasbourg 10th

2005   Kamsky 16th
Strasbourg 18th

2007   Sirmione 12th

2008   **VIEWED 1st**
Moatize 6th

Summary

78 runners, 12 winners, 9 placegetters
15% strike rate win
12% strike rate place
27% strike rate win/place
5 quinellas

BART CUMMINGS' MELBOURNE CUP-WINNING FIELDS

1965 Melbourne Cup

Distance: 2 miles

Track condition: fast

Prize: winner 20,650 pounds & 750 pound trophy; second 5900 pounds; third 2950; fourth 500 pounds

Winning time: 3.21.10

	Horse	Weight carried (st lb)	Odds	Jockey	Trainer	Owner	Official margin	Decimal margin
1	Light Fingers	8 st 4 lb	15-1	R Higgins	JB Cummings	WJ Broderick		
2	Ziema	8 st 6 lb	10-1	J Miller	JB Cummings	ML Bailey	Short 1/2 head	0.1
3	Midlander	6 st 9 lb	20-1	N Pyatt	RE Hoysted	AR Creswick	3 1/2 lengths	3.6
4	Yangtze	8 st 12 lb	33-1	H White	R Dini			
5	Prince Grant	7 st 6 lb	20-1	G Podmore	TJ Smith			
6	Prince Camillo	7 st 8 lb	50-1	P Gumbleton	R Fisher			
7	Red William	8 st 6 lb	10-1	R Mallyon	OM Lynch			
8	Tobin Bronze	7 st 6 lb	15-1	J Stocker	HH Heagney			
9	Craftsman	9 st 5 lb	8-1	P Hyland	AR White			
10	Tasman Lad (NZ)	8 st 2 lb	20-1	D Cameron	HH Riley			
11	Mission	6 st 10 lb	100-1	N Eastwood	JF Quigley			
12	Rosicombe	8 st 1 lb	100-1	F Blackburn	GA Alessio			
13	Sir Wynyard	8 st 7 lb	100-1	A Lister	AG Smith			

	Horse	Weight carried (st lb)	Odds	Jockey	Trainer	Owner	Official margin	Decimal margin
14	Pleasanton	7 st 8 lb	15-1	W Smith	GM Hanlon			
15	Jovial Knight	8 st	20-1	N Mifflin	HG Heagney			
16	Strauss	8 st 8 lb	8-1	D Lake	J Green			
17	Sail Away (NZ)	8 st 7 lb	4-1 FAV	W Skelton	SA Brown			
18	The Dip	8 st 4 lb	66-1	F Reys	JB Cummings			
19	Hunting Horn	8 st 8 lb	50-1	A May	LJ Patterson			
20	Dalento	8 st 1 lb	33-1	I Saunders	J Besanko			
21	Zinga Lee	8 st 11 lb	125-1	B Gilders	WJ McNabb			
22	Piper's Son	8 st 12 lb	66-1	G Moore	MF Anderson			
23	Algalon	8 st	25-1	R Selkrig	GM Hanlon			
Fell	Bore Head	9 st 1 lb	14-1	F Clarke	R Dillon			
Fell	Matloch	7 st 13 lb	7-1	R Dawkins	N Prendergast			
Fell	River Seine	8 st 13 lb	66-1	J Johnson	GM Hanlon			

1966 Melbourne Cup

Distance: 2 miles

Track condition: slow

Prize: winner $41,300 & $2,000 trophy; second $11,800; third $5,900; fourth $1,000

Winning time: 3.21.90

	Horse	Weight carried (st lb)	Odds	Jockey	Trainer	Owner	Official margin	Decimal margin
1	Galilee	8 st 13 lb	11-2 FAV	J Miller	JB Cummings	Mr & Mrs ML Bailey		
2	Light Fingers	9 st 1 lb	12-1	R Higgins	JB Cummings	W Broderick	2 lengths	2.0
3	Duo	8 st 1 lb	10-1	G Podmore	RA Dickerson	J North	1/2 head	2.1
4	Aveniam	7 st 13 lb	25-1	B McClune	J Morgan			
5	Gala Crest	8 st 4 lb	7-1	P Gumbleton	RJ Hutchins			
6	Tea Biscuit	8 st 6 lb	7-1	H Cope	PJ Murray			
7	Gatum Gatum	7 st 9 lb	40-1	F Reys	HG Heagney			
8	Royal Coral	8 st	16-1	P Jarman	RH Claarton			
9	Alaska	7 st 12 lb	12-1	P Hyland	VP Bernard			
10	Terrific	6 st 10 lb	25-1	G Hughes	ME Ritchie			
11	Bore Head	8 st 11 lb	16-1	B Gilders	D Judd			

Horse	Weight carried (st lb)	Odds	Jockey	Trainer	Owner	Official margin	Decimal margin
12 Prince Grant	9 st 1 lb	9-1	G Moore	TJ Smith			
13 Dignify	7 st 5 lb	125-1	W Smith	V Maloney			
14 Trevors	8 st 5 lb	25-1	A Mulley	Mrs A Shepherd			
15 Clipjoint	7 st 10 lb	50-1	J Stocker	ME Ritchie			
16 Coppelius	8 st	200-1	M Moore	B Courtney			
17 Beau Royal	7 st 2 lb	200-1	R Durey	ND Hoysted			
18 Tobin Bronze	8 st 11 lb	7-1	J Johnson	HG Heagney			
19 El Gordo	7 st 6 lb	66-1	N Campton	LJ O'Sullivan			
20 Red Brass	7 st 13 lb	50-1	R Selkrig	HG Heagney			
21 Mystic Glen	6 st 13 lb	200-1	K Langby	FG Hood			
22 Winfreux	9 st 2 lb	50-1	A Lister	CA Wilson			

1967 Melbourne Cup

Distance: 2 miles

Track condition: fast

Prize: winner $41,300 & $2,000 trophy; second $11,800; third $5,900; fourth $1,000)

Winning time: 3.20.40

	Horse	Weight carried (st lb)	Odds	Jockey	Trainer	Owner	Official margin	Decimal margin
1	Red Handed	8 st 9 lb	4-1 E FAV	R Higgins	JB Cummings	Messrs FW Clarke, BM Condon & AG Tyson		
2	Red Crest (NZ)	8 st 6 lb	20-1	R Taylor	JW Winder	IA McMullen, Mrs MF Randle	Neck	0.3
3	Floodbird	7 st 7 lb	80-1	J Stocker	LM Armfield	J Giles, J McTaggart, WE & PJ Petrie	Neck	0.6
4	Padtheway	7 st 9 lb	20-1	F Reys	J Smith			
5	Prince Camillo	8 st	10-1	P Gumbleton	R Fisher			
6	General Command	8 st 7 lb	4-1 E FAV	G Lane	W Wilson			
7	Bellition (NZ)	8 st 2 lb	40-1	H White	GM Hanlon			
8	Sunhaven	8 st 1 lb	33-1	L Burgess	B Courtney			

	Horse	Weight carried (st lb)	Odds	Jockey	Trainer	Owner	Official margin	Decimal margin
9	Fulmen	8 st 13 lb	25-1	M Goreham	JB Cummings			
10	Royal Coral	7 st 12 lb	80-1	D Miller	RH Claarton			
11	Taunton	7 st	100-1	P Alderman	EJ Jenkins			
12	Ziema	9 st 1 lb	12-1	J Miller	JB Cummings			
13	Coronation Cadet	6 st 13 lb	80-1	J Wade	N Forbes			
14	Swift Peter	7 st 6 lb	20-1	W Camer	A Beauneville			
15	Midlander	8 st 11 lb	5-1	P Hyland	ND Hoysted			
16	Jay Ay (NZ)	8 st 8 lb	40-1	P Jarman	DS McCormick			
17	Basin Street	7 st 11 lb	250-1	B Gilders	JJ Moloney			
18	Stellar Belle (NZ)	8 st 9 lb	25-1	RJ Skelton	I Tucker			
19	Special Reward	7 st 7 lb	25-1	WA Smith	AE Elkington			
20	Garcon	8 st 6 lb	12-1	D Lake	TJ Smith			
21	Blue Special	7 st 11 lb	250-1	R Durey	R Wallis			
22	Tupaki	7 st 10 lb	25-1	K Langby	HN Wiggins			

Scratched: Del Charro, Avenium

1974 Melbourne Cup

Distance: 3200 metres

Track condition: good

Prize: winner $105,000 & $3,600 trophy; second $27,000; third $12,000; fourth $6,000

Winning time: 3.23.20

	Horse	Weight carried (kg)	Odds	Jockey	Trainer	Owner	Official margin	Decimal margin
1	Think Big	53 kg	12-1	H White	JB Cummings	RJ O'Sullivan & Dato Tan Chin Nam		
2	Leilani	55.5 kg	7-2 FAV	P Cook	JB Cummings	Hon A Peacock & Mr IW Rice	1 length	1
3	Captain Peri (NZ)	52 kg	14-1	M Baker	JE Wood	Messers JET & L Wood	1 length	2
4	Lord Metric	53 kg	20-1	N Harris	ME Ritchie			
5	Piping Lane	53 kg	50-1	J Stocker	GM Hanlon			
6	Turfcutter (NZ)	53 kg	7-1	D Peake	RC Verner			
7	Battle Heights (NZ)	61 kg	11-2	G Willetts	R Douglas			
8	Igloo (NZ)	57.5 kg	33-1	N Voight	TJ Smith			
9	Bellota (NZ)	51 kg	14-1	S Aitken	RA Campbell			

	Horse	Weight carried (kg)	Odds	Jockey	Trainer	Owner	Official margin	Decimal margin
10	Grand Scale	53 kg	20-1	P Trotter	ML Willmott			
11	Herminia	50 kg	8-1	B Gilders	D Judd			
12	Taras Bulba	47 kg	20-1	L Harbridge	GM Hanlon			
13	Gala Supreme	57.5 kg	15-1	F Reys	RJ Hutchins			
14	Corrobo-ree	55.5 kg	80-1	R McCarthy	TR Howe			
15	Passetreul	56.5 kg	40-1	K Langby	TJ Smith			
16	Sequester	50 kg	250-1	R Setches	RJ Winks			
17	Top Order	43.5 kg	200-1	M Johnston	TJ Hughes			
18	Pilfer (NZ)	53 kg	40-1	J Miller	CS Hayes			
19	Gay Master	51 kg	50-1	E Didham	TJ Hughes			
20	Our Pocket	49.5 kg	160-1	J Letts	BJ Boyle			
21	Big Angel	52 kg	33-1	P Hyland	EW Laing			
22	High Sail (NZ)	53 kg	200-1	A Cooper	TJ Huges			

1975 Melbourne Cup

Distance: 3200 metres

Track condition: slow

Prize: winner $105,000 & $5,600 trophy; second $27,000; third $12,000; fourth $6,000

Winning time: 3.29.60

	Horse	Weight carried (kg)	Odds	Jockey	Trainer	Owner	Official margin	Decimal margin
1	Think Big	58.5 kg	33-1	H White	JB Cummings	Messrs RJ O'Sullivan, Dato Tan Chin Nam & Tunku Abdul Rahman		
2	Holiday Waggon	50 kg	7-1	J Duggan	JB Cummings	D Morrison & CJ Speed	3/4 length	0.8
3	Medici (NZ)	46 kg	125-1	M Johnston	MD Hennah	MD Hennah	3 lengths	3.8
4	Sulieman (NZ)	52.5 kg	11-4 FAV	P Trotter	WC Winder			
5	Captain Peri (NZ)	52 kg	10-1	J Letts	JE Wood			
6	Sindicato (NZ)	53 kg	100-1	J Grylls	RB Priscott			
7	Turfcutter (NZ)	52.5 kg	16-1	D Peake	RC Verner			
8	Dark Suit	51 kg	25-1	R Heffernan	GM Hanlon			

	Horse	Weight carried (kg)	Odds	Jockey	Trainer	Owner	Official margin	Decimal margin
9	Four Leaf (NZ)	51 kg	40-1	E Didham	J Didham			
10	Chelsea Tower (NZ)	54 kg	40-1	J Johnson	E Templeton			
11	Calypso	51 kg	125-1	J Stocker	TJ Smith			
12	Guest Star (NZ)	57 kg	16-1	M Baker	I Tucker			
13	Gay Master	53.5 kg	80-1	A Cooper	TJ Hughes			
14	Fury's Order (NZ)	59.5 kg	11-2	B Thomson	W McEwen			
15	Comrade Caviar	47 kg	100-1	A Matthews	LJ Irwin			
16	Goodness Knows	46.5 kg	20-1	S Burridge	DM Bradfield			
17	Taras Bulba	57 kg	15-1	G Willetts	GM Hanlon			
18	Contere	51 kg	25-1	W Moore	EG Boland			
19	Participa-tor	55.5 kg	50-1	K Langby	TJ Smith			
20	Leica Lover	57.5 kg	10-1	R Higgins	JB Cummings			

1977 Melbourne Cup

Distance: 3200 metres

Track condition: fast

Prize: winner $97,500 & $6,700 trophy; second $30,000; third $15,000; fourth $7,500

Winning time: 3.18.40

	Horse	Weight carried (kg)	Odds	Jockey	Trainer	Owner	Official margin	Decimal margin
1	Gold And Black	57 kg	7-2 FAV	J Duggan	JB Cummings	Mr & Mrs J Harris, Mr & Mrs HB Gage		
2	Reckless	56.5 kg	11-2	P Trotter	T Woodcock	Mrs G Godfrey & RA Walker	1 length	1
3	Hyperno	52 kg	66-1	B Andrews	G Murphy	Mr & Mrs TL North, Mr & Mrs GL Herscu, Dr R Lake	2 1/2 lengths	3.5
4	Gold Pulse	51.5 kg	25-1	M Johnston	TJ Smith			
5	Unaware	55.5 kg	12-1	J Stocker	CS Hayes			
6	Massuk	49 kg	50-1	A Trevena	JJ Houlahan			
7	Valadero	54 kg	33-1	E Didham	TJ Hughes			
8	Ming Dynasty	56 kg	20-1	H White	JB Cummings			
9	Trochee (NZ)	51 kg	30-1	WD Skelton	LP McLean			

	Horse	Weight carried (kg)	Odds	Jockey	Trainer	Owner	Official margin	Decimal margin
10	Van Der Hum (NZ)	58 kg	33-1	RJ Skelton	LH Robinson			
11	Royal Cadenza	57 kg	66-1	R Lang	ES Dromgol			
12	Salamander	54.5 kg	7-1	R Higgins	TJ Hughes			
13	Major Till	51 kg	10-1	R Mallyon	CS Hayes			
14	Yashmak	51 kg	20-1	J Letts	ML Robins			
15	Brallos	52.5 kg	12-1	M Baker	PJ Banham			
16	Wave King	52.5 kg	160-1	R McCarthy	JH Hely			
17	Family Of Man	54.5 kg	25-1	B Thomson	GM Hanlon			
18	Happy Union (NZ)	55.5 kg	20-1	P Hyland	WC Winder			
19	Grey Affair	52 kg	125-1	G Palmer	JJ Atkins			
20	Vacuum	53 kg	50-1	W Treloar	JB Cummings			
21	Shaitan (NZ)	55.5 kg	33-1	R Taylor	W Sanders			
22	Sir Serene	53 kg	14-1	P Cook	TJ Smith			
23	Beau's Demand (NZ)	51 kg	200-1	R Heffernan	RN McDonell			
24	Peteken (NZ)	52 kg	200-1	G Willetts	WP Roche			

1979 Melbourne Cup

Distance: 3200 metres

Track condition: fast

Prize: winner $195,500 & $10,000 trophy; second $60,000; third $30,000; fourth $15,000

Winning time: 3.21.80

	Horse	Weight carried (kg)	Odds	Jockey	Trainer	Owner	Official margin	Decimal margin
1	Hyperno	56 kg	7-1	H White	JB Cummings	Mr & Mrs TL North, Mr & Mrs G Herscu, DR Lake		
2	Salamander	55.5 kg	10-1	R Higgins	TJ Hughes	A Goulo-poulos	Short 1/2 head	0.1
3	Red Nose (NZ)	51.5 kg	16-1	E Didham	T Green	PJ & RD Bell	1 3/4 lengths	1.9
4	Hauberk	51 kg	40-1	P Jarman	RE Hoysted			
5	Cubacade (NZ)	52 kg	13-2	J Wakker	DN Couchman			
6	Warri Symbol	52 kg	6-1	P Hyland	JJ Moloney			
7	Karu (NZ)	49 kg	12-1	W Robinson	J Holme			
8	Magistrate	51.5 kg	16-1	RJ Skelton	IF Steffert			
9	Kankama (NZ)	54.5 kg	50-1	J Stocker	MT Sullivan			

	Horse	Weight carried (kg)	Odds	Jockey	Trainer	Owner	Official margin	Decimal margin
10	Earthquake McGoon	51 kg	25-1	G Willetts	G Murphy			
11	Sarfraz (NZ)	50.5 kg	66-1	A Trevena	JJ Moloney			
12	Pigalle (NZ)	47.5 kg	20-1	B Clements	G Murphy			
13	Love Bandit	48.5 kg	40-1	G Palmer	TJ Hughes			
14	Jessephenie	47 kg	200-1	S Burridge	LT Dixon			
15	Somerset Nile	50 kg	50-1	R Selkrig	CJ Honey-church			
16	Over The Ocean (NZ)	51 kg	100-1	W Treloar	TJ Smith			
17	Iko	49.5 kg	33-1	M Johnston	TJ Smith			
18	Gunderman	51.5 kg	80-1	R Heffernan	TR Howe			
19	Licence Fee (NZ)	49.5 kg	160-1	A Williams	TJ Harrison			
20	Rough'n' Tough (NZ)	52 kg	66-1	G Murphy	TJ Millard			
21	Safe Harbour	49.5 kg	100-1	K Langby	JB Cummings			
Failed to finish	Dulcify (NZ)	56 kg	3-1 FAV	B Thomson	CS Hayes			

1990 Melbourne Cup

Distance: 3200 metres

Track condition: fast

Prize: winner $1,300,000 & $35,000 trophy; second $400,000; third $200,000; fourth $100,000

Winning time: 3.16.30

	Horse	Weight carried (kg)	Odds	Jockey	Trainer	Owner	Official margin	Decimal margin
1	Kingston Rule (USA)	53 kg	7-1 E FAV	D Beadman	JB Cummings	Mr and Mrs DH Hains		
2	The Phantom (NZ)	54.5 kg	7-1 E FAV	G Cooksley	MP Baker	GHC Kain	1 length	1
3	Mr Brooker (NZ)	53 kg	14-1	G Childs	PJ Hurdle	CJ Pearce	Neck	1.3
4	Na Botto (NZ)	50.5 kg	33-1	L Cassidy	PG Hollinshead			
5	Mount Olympus	48.5 kg	20-1	M Carson	DA Hayes			
6	Aquidity (NZ)	54.5 kg	40-1	D Walsh	DM Walsh			
7	Savage Toss (ARG)	57 kg	66-1	B Hibberd	L Freedman			
8	Flying Luskin	55 kg	10-1	P Johnson	TJ McKee			
9	La Tristia (NZ)	48.5 kg	33-1	S King	JB Cummings			

	Horse	Weight carried (kg)	Odds	Jockey	Trainer	Owner	Official margin	Decimal margin
10	Our Magic Man (NZ)	49 kg	33-1	K Moses	M Sullivan			
11	Sydeston	58.5 kg	16-1	L Dittman	RE Hoysted			
12	Just A Dancer (NZ)	51 kg	12-1	J Cassidy	GA Rogerson			
13	Chaleyer (NZ)	50.5 kg	14-1	RS Dye	FB Lewis			
14	Ali Boy (NZ)	50.5 kg	11-1	H White	MJ Phillips			
15	Shuzorah (NZ)	53 kg	10-1	L Olsen	EB Skelton			
16	Tawrrific (NZ)	56.5 kg	25-1	D Gauci	L Freedman			
17	Rainbow Myth (NZ)	51.5 kg	33-1	M Clarke	R Manning			
18	Dalraffin	50.5 kg	250-1	K Forrester	EB Murray			
19	Water Boatman (IRE)	55 kg	10-1	P Hutchinson	DA Hayes			
20	Frontier Boy (NZ)	51 kg	25-1	D Oliver	L Freedman			
21	Betoota (NZ)	50 kg	140-1	R Heffernan	WH Walters			
22	Rising Fear	48.5 kg	330-1	C Browell	L Pickering			
23	Selwyn's Mate (NZ)	49 kg	100-1	B Werner	M Moroney			
24	Donegal Mist (NZ)	50.5 kg	50-1	J Marshall	GG Maynes			

1991 Melbourne Cup

Distance: 3200 metres

Track condition: fast

Prize: winner $1,300,000 & $35,000 trophy; second $400,000; third $200,000; fourth $100,000

Winning time: 3.18.90

	Horse	Weight carried (kg)	Odds	Jockey	Trainer	Owner	Official margin	Decimal margin
1	Let's Elope (NZ)	51 kg	3-1 FAV	S King	JB Cummings	Shoreham Park Pty Ltd (Mgr D Marks) & KW White		
2	Shiva's Revenge (NZ)	53.5 kg	10-1	RS Dye	JB Cummings	SM Medcraft, SP Ghaie, AW Hall, AJ de Natris, JM Martin & IJ Lewis	2 1/2 lengths	2.5
3	Magnolia Hall (NZ)	52.5 kg	50-1	B York	Ms H Page	EJ & Mrs RJ Sperling	Head	2.7
4	Super Impose (NZ)	60 kg	20-1	D Beadman	L Freedman			
5	Ivory Way (USA)	49.5 kg	6-1	M Clarke	DA Hayes			
6	Rasheek (USA)	51.5 kg	25-1	P Hutchinson	DA Hayes			
7	Al Maheb (USA)	56.5 kg	16-1	D Gauci	DA Hayes			
8	Just A Dancer (NZ)	56.5 kg	14-1	J Cassidy	GA Rogerson			

	Horse	Weight carried (kg)	Odds	Jockey	Trainer	Owner	Official margin	Decimal margin
9	Castle-town (NZ)	57 kg	8-1	N Harris	PH Bussutin			
10	Grooming	51.5 kg	40-1	D Oliver	L Freedman			
11	Mahara-jah (NZ)	49.5 kg	50-1	M Johnston	TJ Smith			
12	Moods	49.5 kg	80-1	B Compton	AJ Marshall			
13	Lord Revenir (NZ)	54 kg	14-1	G Cooksley	JB Cummings			
14	Sydeston	57.5 kg	33-1	L Dittman	RE Hoysted			
15	Cool Credit	50.5 kg	100-1	K Forrester	GM Hanlon			
16	Alphabel	53 kg	40-1	G Darrington	DA Hayes			
17	Diego (NZ)	52.5 kg	16-1	L O'Sullivan	DJ O'Sullivan			
18	Te Akau Pearl (NZ)	50 kg	14-1	J Collett	RA James			
19	Nayrizi (IRE)	54 kg	33-1	G Hall	P Hyland			
20	Dr Grace (NZ)	56 kg	40-1	K Moses	G Chapman			
21	Pontiac Lass (NZ)	49.5 kg	100-1	T Allan	MP Baker			
22	Weekend Delight (NZ)	50.5 kg	50-1	G Childs	JB Cummings			
23	Rural Prince (NZ)	49.5 kg	125-1	L Cassidy	GK Sanders			
24	Sunshine Sally	48 kg	330-1	P Payne	GM Hanlon			

*Protest: 2nd against 1st – dismissed

1996 Melbourne Cup

Distance: 3200 metres

Track condition: good

Prize: winner $1,430,000 & $32,500 trophy; second $440,000; third $198,000; fourth $88,000; fifth $44,000; sixth to ninth $30,000

Winning time: 3.18.80

	Horse	Weight carried (kg)	Odds	Jockey	Trainer	Owner	Official margin	Decimal margin
1	Saintly	55.5 kg	8-1	D Beadman	JB Cummings	JB Cummings, Dato Tan Chin Nam, Dr CP Lim, EH Hong & T Tan		
2	Count Chivas (NZ)	57 kg	33-1	S King	L Freedman	RD & Mrs IM Wood, NE & Mrs JL Tsalikis	2 1/4 lengths	2.3
3	Skybeau (NZ)	50 kg	50-1	J Holder	L Smith	MM Smith & A Grayling	Neck	2.6
4	Senator (NZ)	53 kg	10-1	L O'Sullivan	JL Tims			
5	Nothin' Leica Dane	55 kg	7-1	R S Dye	Gai Waterhouse			
6	Doriemus (NZ)	58 kg	13-2	D Oliver	L Freedman			
7	Grey Shot (GB)	55 kg	25-1	P Eddery	IA Balding			

	Horse	Weight carried (kg)	Odds	Jockey	Trainer	Owner	Official margin	Decimal margin
8	Sapio (NZ)	54 kg	66-1	J Wakker	Ms S Kay			
9	Alcove	50 kg	66-1	B York	TJ Hughes			
10	Cheviot	50.5 kg	66-1	D Browne	C Brown			
11	The Bandette (NZ)	51 kg	15-1	N Harris	JR Wheeler			
12	Arctic Scent	51.5 kg	14-1	B Stanley	JW Mason			
13	Istidaad (USA)	53.5 kg	15-1	G Hall	PC Hayes			
14	Circles Of Gold	50.5 kg	16-1	B Prebble	BJ Smith			
15	Oscar Schindler (IRE)	56.5 kg	4-1 FAV	M Kinane	K Prendergast			
16	Centico (NZ)	48.5 kg	125-1	A Payne	JD Sadler			
17	The Phantom Chance (NZ)	53.5 kg	125-1	P Payne	JR Wheeler			
18	Super Slew	51.5 kg	50-1	L Dittman	C Connors			
19	Few Are Chosen	50.5 kg	33-1	D Gauci	Gai Waterhouse			
20	Court Of Honour (IRE)	56.5 kg	20-1	S Marshall	P Chapple-Hyam			
21	My Kiwi Gold (NZ)	49.5 kg	33-1	J Marshall	JB Cummings			
22	Beaux Art	52 kg	50-1	J Hutswitt	DA Edwards			

1999 Melbourne Cup

Distance: 3200 metres

Track condition: good

Prize: winner $1,800,000 plus trophies; second $480,000; third $225,000; fourth $115,000; fifth $80,000; sixth to tenth $60,000

Winning time: 3.19.64

	Horse	Weight carried (kg)	Odds	Jockey	Trainer	Owner	Official margin	Decimal margin
1	Rogan Josh	50 kg	5-1	J Marshall	JB Cummings	Mrs WL Green & JP Miller		
2	Central Park (IRE)	57.5 kg	50-1	L Dettori	Saaed bin Suroor	Godolphin	1/2 length	1.5
3 (dead heat)	Lahar	50.5 kg	140-1	C Brown	P Cave	JL Thompson	1/2 neck	1.7
3 (dead heat)	Zazabelle (NZ)	49 kg	50-1	E Wilkinson	JB Cummings			
5	Travel-mate (GB)	52.5 kg	9-1	D Harrison	J Fanshawe			
6	The Warrior (NZ)	49 kg	50-1	G Grylls	R Otto			
7	Second Coming (NZ)	51 kg	60-1	G Childs	M Moroney			
8	The Hind (NZ)	52.5 kg	11-1	L Cassidy	PC Hayes			

	Horse	Weight carried (kg)	Odds	Jockey	Trainer	Owner	Official margin	Decimal margin
9	Bohemiath	50 kg	20-1	J Patton	J Sadler			
10	Brew (NZ)	49 kg	40-1	L O'Sullivan	M Moroney			
11	Zabuan (NZ)	49 kg	250-1	S Hyland	JJ Moloney			
12	Yavana's Pace (IRE)	53.5 kg	30-1	R Hughes	MS Johnston			
13	Streak	51.5 kg	16-1	G Hall	R Smerdon			
14	Tie The Knot	58 kg	7-1	RS Dye	G Walter			
15	Figurehead (NZ)	50.5 kg	160-1	OP Bosson	Kay Lane			
16	Skybeau (NZ)	52 kg	66-1	L Cassidy	L Smith			
17	Sky Heights (NZ)	56.5 kg	7-2 FAV	D Oliver	C Alderson			
18	Lady Elsie	49.5 kg	66-1	L Beasley	C Brown			
19	Laebeel (NZ)	49.5 kg	10-1	S Baster	J Sadler			
20	Maridpour (IRE)	55 kg	66-1	S Arnold	M Moroney			
21	The Message (NZ)	52 kg	200-1	A Spiteri	J Ralph			
22	Arena	54.5 kg	15-1	D Gauci	J Hawkes			
23	Rebbor (NZ)	49 kg	66-1	C Munce	JB Cummings			
Lost rider	Able Master (NZ)	50.5 kg	50-1	G Cooksley	B Wallace			

2008 Melbourne Cup

Distance: 3200 metres

Track condition: good

Prize: winner $3,300,000 plus trophies; second $835,000; third $420,000; fourth $220,000; fifth $150,000; sixth to tenth $115,000

Winning time: 3.20.40

	Horse	Weight carried (kg)	Odds	Jockey	Trainer	Owner	Official margin	Decimal margin
1	Viewed	53 kg	$42	B Shinn	JB Cummings	Dato Tan Chin Nam		
2	Bauer (IRE)	53 kg	$21	C Brown	L Cumani	Aston House Stud, J Higgins, GG Syndicate, Uthmeyer Racing and OTI Cup Syndicate	Nose	0.1
3	C'est La Guerre (NZ)	54 kg	$21	B Prebble	J Sadler	NC Williams, Mr & LJ Williams	2 lengths	2.1
4	Master O'Reilly (NZ)	55 kg	$26	V Duric	D O'Brien			
5	Profound Beauty (IRE)	51.5 kg	$9	G Boss	D Weld			

	Horse	Weight carried (kg)	Odds	Jockey	Trainer	Owner	Official margin	Decimal margin
6	Moatize	50 kg	$31	C Lindop	JB Cummings			
7	Mad Rush (USA)	53.5 kg	$5.50 FAV	D Oliver	L Cumani			
8	Nom du Jeu (NZ)	54 kg	$7.50	J Lloyd	M Baker			
9	Zipping	54 kg	$15	D Nikolic	J Sadler			
10	Newport	53 kg	$61	C Symons	PM Perry			
11	Ice Chariot	53 kg	$51	M Rodd	R Maund			
12	Guyno (NZ)	52 kg	$151	C Newitt	L Luciani			
13	Littorio	52.5 kg	$31	S King	N Blackiston			
14	Varevees (GB)	51.5 kg	$101	C Williams	R Gibson			
15	Boundless (NZ)	52 kg	$81	G Childs	S McKee			
16	Red Lord	51.5 kg	$101	N Hall	A Cummings			
17	Prize Lady (NZ)	51 kg	$61	M Sweeney	G Sanders			
18	Septimus (IRE)	58.5 kg	$7	J Murtagh	A O'Brien			
19	Barbaricus	50.5 kg	$16	S Baster	D O'Brien			
20	Alessandro Volta (GB)	50.5 kg	$41	W Lordan	A O'Brien			
21	Honolulu (IRE)	55.5 kg	$21	C O'Donoghue	A O'Brien			
Failed to finish	Gallopin (NZ)	53 kg	$31	J Winks	D O'Brien			

INDEX